# James Joyce

## A Student's Guide

*by*

Matthew Hodgart

Routledge & Kegan Paul
London, Boston and Henley

First published in 1978
by Routledge & Kegan Paul Ltd
39 Store Street,
London WC1E 7DD,
Broadway House,
Newtown Road,
Henley-on-Thames,
Oxon RG9 1EN and
9 Park Street,
Boston, Mass. 02108, USA
Reprinted in 1979
Set in Bembo 11/12 pt
and printed in Great Britain by
Redwood Burn Ltd
Trowbridge and Esher

British Library Cataloguing in Publication Data

Hodgart, Matthew John Caldwell
James Joyce.
1. Joyce, James, b. 1882 – Criticism and
interpretation
823'.9'12     PR6019.09     78–40129


ISBN 0 7100 8817 5
ISBN 0 7100 8943 0 PBK

# Contents

# Preface and Acknowledgments

In this book I have tried to provide a general guide to the main works of James Joyce for the benefit of university students reading for honours degrees in English literature or the equivalent and for general readers who are interested in Joyce. *Ulysses* and *Finnegans Wake* are very difficult books and everyone who has found it worth while to read them has been grateful for some kind of guide. There are now, of course, quite a large number of books about Joyce, and my excuse for writing another must be that I have tried to offer something a little different from the rest. Some readers may find my treatment of Joyce's life to be too slight and my emphasis on Irish history to be excessive. But there is a great biography, by Richard Ellmann, easily available, and I have found a discussion of the context of Irish history to be one of the most valuable approaches to the understanding of Joyce's works. And indeed Joyce demands a good deal of historical knowledge from his reader. Some of my interpretations are the standard ones, but I can claim some originality for my ideas about the Christian symbolism of *Ulysses* and about the use of opera in *Finnegans Wake*. I should warn the reader that the former are not acceptable to all who have come across them, but I feel confident that the latter are fairly sound. There is no generally accepted interpretation of *Finnegans Wake*, and perhaps there never will be; my remarks are intended to encourage every reader to begin his or her own voyage of exploration.

It is impossible to mention all the people to whom I have been indebted in the writing of this book, but I should like to mention some of those who have been kind enough to mention my name in their writings on Joyce, in particular James Atherton, Adaline Glasheen and Clive Hart. I should like to pay a tribute to the memory of Frank

Budgen, Harriet Weaver, and my former collaborator Mabel Worthington.

Since there are now several different editions of *Ulysses* with different pagination, I have not inserted page numbers with my quotations. But since all editions of *Finnegans Wake* have the same (or virtually the same) pagination, I have given page and line numbers, to help the reader with this difficult text.

The substance of pp. 47–52 ('Ivy Day in the Committee Room') has previously appeared in *James Joyce's Dubliners, Critical Essays*, ed. Clive Hart, London, Faber and Faber, 1969, New York, Viking Press, 1970; that of pp. 86–93 ('Aeolus') in *James Joyce's Ulysses, Critical Essays*, ed. Clive Hart and David Hayman, Berkeley, University of California Press, 1974; and that of pp. 154–63 ('The Mime of Mick, Nick and the Maggies') in *A Conceptual Guide to Finnegans Wake*, ed. Michael H. Begnal and Fritz Senn, Philadelphia, Pennsylvania State University Press, 1974. I am grateful to the Bodley Head and Random House, Inc. for permission to quote from *Ulysses* by James Joyce, and to Faber and Faber, the Society of Authors as the literary representative of the Estate of James Joyce, and the Viking Press Inc. for permission to quote from *Finnegans Wake*.

# I

## Joyce — the Great World

James Joyce, one of the most remarkable talents in twentieth-century literature, belonged to a great world and to a little world. The little world was the Ireland in which he was born and educated, the great world was geographically the continent of Europe where he passed most of his life, and intellectually the *avant-garde* world of the arts, in its last heroic period. This period has only just closed, with the deaths of Joyce's near-contemporaries Stravinsky and Picasso. It was also a heroic age of science, possibly the last age of great individuals in mathematics, physics and astronomy, perhaps even in technology and the applied sciences. Of course, science has multiplied fantastically even since Joyce's death, but now we are in an age of computers and highly-organised teams of researchers, so that the similarity of science and *avant-garde* art, once quite manifest, is no longer easy to discern. In *Finnegans Wake* Joyce drew a parallel between artists like himself and research scientists, both at the frontier of discovery, as he did with the great explorers who in his lifetime reached many of the last untouched parts of the earth.

Joyce was born on 2 February 1882 in Dublin, now the capital of the Irish Republic but then part of Great Britain. From the age of six to eleven he went to a Jesuit boarding school, Clongowes Wood; from the age of eleven to sixteen he went to another Jesuit school, Belvedere College in Dublin; and from the age of sixteen to twenty he studied at the Catholic National University which is now University College, Dublin. In 1902 he graduated BA and made his first trip to Paris, to study medicine, but he soon returned owing to his mother's fatal illness in the following year. In 1904, Bloomsyear, after hanging around Dublin, doing a little teaching and making a name for himself as a formidable wit, he left once more for the Continent, this time with

Nora Barnacle, the young woman who much later became his wife. He never returned to Ireland, except for two very brief visits in 1909.

Joyce lived in Pola, Trieste and Rome, making a poor living mainly from teaching, and he had great trouble over the publication of his first book of fiction, *Dubliners*, which did not appear until 1914. During the First World War he lived in Zürich, and completed *A Portrait of the Artist as a Young Man*, which brought him fame in literary and artistic circles on its publication in 1916. He then embarked on the long process of writing *Ulysses*, bringing the work to a close in Trieste after the war and finally completing it in Paris where he lived from 1920. After the publication of *Ulysses* in 1922 (when he was forty years old) he achieved a considerable reputation in both Europe and America, and was freed from financial worry by the generous support of a rich English lady, Miss Harriet Weaver.

Joyce remained in Paris until the early years of the Second World War, working on *Finnegans Wake*, which was published early in 1939. The fall of France in 1940 forced him to leave Paris, eventually to return to Zürich, where he died of a perforated stomach ulcer in January 1941, when not yet sixty. His life had been almost entirely a domestic one, and his later years were clouded by his daughter's schizophrenic illness and his own alcoholism and deteriorating eyesight.

For a detailed account of Joyce's life, the reader should refer to Richard Ellmann's exhaustive literary biography. At this point, however, it is more instructive to note the qualities of Joyce's mind that made him receptive to the great world. In the first place, he was immensely learned, with a truly extraordinary memory: there are well-founded reports of his ability to quote whole pages of his favourite prose writers such as Cardinal Newman. He also had a great gift for languages, speaking and reading fluently in Italian (the Joyce family used the Triestine dialect as their domestic language), French and German, and having a working knowledge of Dano-Norwegian (which he learned in order to read Ibsen) and Latin (both classical and ecclesiastical). Although he had to rely on translations of Greek, his knowledge of classical and modern literature was exceptionally wide, and he read very fast. Like T. S. Eliot and Thomas Mann, he was a true polymath. His knowledge did not stop short at literature, for he had a gift for accumulating innumerable details of popular science and general knowledge; this is the Bloomian side of his mind which he satirises mildly in *Ulysses*. Both *Ulysses* and *Finnegans Wake* are vast encyclopaedic compendia, which is one of the reasons why they are not to every reader's taste.

Of the subjects most germane to literature, psychology was perhaps the one he took most seriously. He seems to have remained sceptical about the therapeutic value of Freudian or Jungian psychoanalysis, and probably even about the descriptive value of Freudian or Jungian theories, but he certainly found that Freud's books offered myths no truer or falser than the myths of Christianity or other religions, myths which could be used as striking frameworks for his novels. It seems probable that *A Portrait* is not constructed on Freudian lines, but Joyce undoubtedly read a good deal of Freud before beginning *Ulysses*, where the new Viennese school is mentioned as a clue: Stephen's relationship to his dead mother is treated in broadly Freudian terms. *Finnegans Wake* is, of course, Freudian from start to finish, the two main works employed being *The Interpretation of Dreams* (1900) and, for the killing of the Ur-Father, *Totem and Taboo* (1913).

Joyce's mind and literary procedure are always mythological, and it is doubtful whether *Finnegans Wake* could have been written at all without the great compendium of magic and religion, Sir James George Frazer's *The Golden Bough* (12 volumes, 1911–15; abridged edition in one volume 1922, the year of *Ulysses*). Frazer's methods and conclusions are nowadays often discredited among anthropologists, as Freud's are by psychologists, but he remains, as Freud does, a master of the twentieth century.

The closest relationships of a writer are often those with the generation before his own. By the time he has reached artistic maturity and formed his style, it is usually too late for him to be greatly influenced by his contemporaries. Joyce was most influenced by Flaubert and Ibsen. He imitated the naturalistic techniques of Flaubert's *Madame Bovary* and *Trois Contes*, but had a special affection for the learned fantasy of the *Tentation de Saint Antoine*, which he uses in the 'Circe' episode of *Ulysses*, and for *Bouvard et Pécuchet*. Typically he admired the least-read of Flaubert's work and the one most packed with miscellaneous learning and popular science, like the mind of Leopold Bloom. Joyce was even more influenced by the other great exponent of naturalism, Henrik Ibsen. In this case his admiration was not only for Ibsen's mastery of realistic description and characterisation but also for his myth of the artist as a tragic hero — a myth which was to form a basic theme in the *Portrait* and *Ulysses*. A good acquaintance with Ibsen's mature plays from *A Doll's House* to *When We Dead*

*Awaken*, especially when studied in relation to Joyce's bleak play *Exiles*, will clear up many difficulties in the interpretation of the novels. *When We Dead Awaken* came out in 1900, when Joyce was still at university. He published an essay on it — a rare distinction for an eighteen-year-old boy — and Ibsen himself commended the insights it showed.

In *A Portrait* Joyce admits to admiring Gerhart Hauptmann, the German dramatist who was only twenty years his senior, though resemblances between his work and Hauptmann's are not readily apparent. On the other hand, Joyce never seems to have mentioned Chekhov, yet the effect of Chekhov's short stories is manifest in *Dubliners*, even more obviously than that of Flaubert's *Trois Contes*.

There are no other stories before Joyce's which rely not on the structured anecdote and narrative climax but on the precise and delicate evocation of mood by recounting apparently insignificant details — the Joycean 'epiphany'. What Joyce seems to have admired most in Flaubert, Ibsen, Chekhov (and possibly Hauptmann) was their combination of refinement and strength.

Joyce was not a 'social realist' or an admirer of Zola. Of the next generation of writers, he was closest to the *symboliste* poets, especially to Mallarmé, who makes several appearances in *Finnegans Wake* as the author of *Un coup de dès jamais n'abolira le hasard*, possibly the most difficult work before Joyce's.

Joyce affected to know little about music except song, and by song he tended to mean almost exclusively the more conventional masters of French and Italian opera, who provided the means for the great tenors and sopranos of his age to show their virtuosity: Meyerbeer (*Les Huguenots*), Rossini (*Guillaume Tell*), Massenet (*Manon*), Saint-Saëns (*Samson et Dalila*), Gounod, Puccini, and so on. To this list of the commonest operas played in the international houses only two great names need be added, Mozart and Verdi.

Joyce also pretended indifference to Wagner, but one can be sure that this was a pose. Of course, it was extremely difficult to know much about Wagner before the era of the LP record, unless you were rich enough to go to Bayreuth — even enthusiasts like Mallarmé had to be content with concerts of excerpts. It can be shown, however, that Joyce had a very good knowledge of the libretto and score of *Tristan* and *The Ring* and probably of other Wagnerian 'music-drama'. He had also read some of Wagner's polemical works, which he quotes in *Finnegans Wake* (I. vii). Undoubtedly he drew his use of the literary *leitmotif* — a phrase associated with a character or idea, repeated throughout the whole work, used in *Finnegans Wake* much more intensively than in *Ulysses* — and the new concept of giving an extended narrative a symphonic structure, from Wagner's practice. At the end of *A Portrait* Stephen goes forth to 'forge . . . the uncreated conscience of my race': he is here a type of the young Siegfried liberator-hero, who will re-forge his father's sword 'Nothung', and in *Ulysses* he gives that name to his ash-plant. There are a few other Wagnerian quotations in *Ulysses*, and dozens of them in *Finnegans Wake*. Wagner's was such a comprehensive genius that few men of sensibility in the late nineteenth and early twentieth century escaped his influence: he was possibly a greater force in literature than any single writer of the period, as Mallarmé's 'Tombeau' sonnet to 'le dieu, Richard Wagner' implies. The subject of Wagner in Joyce's works is, however, too vast to be given more than a mention here.

Joyce's relationship to the music of the post-Wagnerian period is less certain. Late Verdi was dear to him, and he enjoyed Puccini as much as opera-goers have done throughout this century. *Madame Butterfly* came out in Bloomsyear, 1904, when he ran away with Nora and a letter shows that he identified her with the heroine; but Puccini is hardly part of the 'modern' movement, for which we must look further east.

Schoenberg occupied a position at the head of the *avant-garde* analogous to Joyce's; their names are often mentioned together, sometimes as men of enormous talent each of whom helped to destroy his own art, as Kingsley Amis has said. But their relationship was largely a parallel or coincidental one, mainly because of the difficulty of hearing Schoenberg's music outside Vienna or America in Joyce's lifetime, not to speak of the difficulty of understanding it. Even today Schoenberg is more praised for his vast intellectual power than enjoyed. He is always described as the inventor of 'twelve-tone' or 'serial' music but in fact much of his work, including *Pierrot Lunaire*, was written before he invented this compositional technique. To describe Schoenberg's work in terms of his techniques is as foolish as to describe Joyce's in terms of the 'stream of consciousness' or 'interior monologue', as often used to be done. As becomes apparent if one follows the works in order of composition from *Verklärte Nacht* (1899), Schoenberg's earlier idiom is that of post-Wagnerian romanticism, using dissonance to express violent and usually painful emotions. Hence his music and that of his Viennese disciples is rightly associated with the movement in the arts and literature called 'Expressionism'. All this is partly foreign to Joyce, who felt more sympathy with the irony of Flaubert and Ibsen than with the ecstatic outpourings of expressionism. It is possible to draw a better comparison between Joyce's art and Schoenberg's later serial music, at least in one respect: in neither is it possible to discern the underlying principle of construction without a long and careful analysis.

*Ulysses* has an elaborate hidden structure, which no reader however attentive could possibly work out during his first reading, and *Finnegans Wake* is structurally even more complicated. The same is true of Schoenberg's most gifted pupils, Webern and Berg, the first of whom has been more highly esteemed by composers than Schoenberg himself, while the second has reached a much wider public. Take the case of *Wozzek*, Berg's more famous opera: the second act has a complete symphony underlying it, with movements in sonata form and so on. But if no one can hear this in the opera-house why did Berg write in this way? The answer seems to be that Berg did not feel free to create unless he set extremely heavy restrictions on himself. He did not ask his audience to understand what he was doing: he wanted them only to follow the drama on the stage and to respond emotionally to the music; and in fact *Wozzek* is a very moving work to many listeners. A handful of musicians will get a special pleasure from studying the score and listening to the records over and over again. The same is true of *Ulysses*, which is a richly comic and touching book to many who care nothing for the Homeric correspondences or thematic construction. Evidently Joyce had to make everything as difficult as possible for himself before he could write freely and spontaneously; and paradoxically enough *Ulysses* is not written in laboured prose but has a wonderfully natural flow. It is possible, however, that *Finnegans Wake* has shared the fate of Webern's later work; it is simply too difficult for all but a devoted few.

There is no equivalent to the structural complexity of the 'Second Viennese' school (Schoenberg, Webern, Berg) in the rest of the 'modern' music of Joyce's lifetime. There is plenty of advanced dissonance and elaborate rhythm in the music of Stravinsky and Bartók, but nothing completely hidden from the audience. It is difficult to explain the similarity of Joyce and the Viennese masters, except by postulating that both were influenced by the progress of the natural sciences. By the turn of this century science had shown that the universe at all levels was vastly more complicated than had been suspected;

Joyce and Schoenberg may have wanted to fabricate an artistic universe as complicated as the physical one, governed by laws like the laws of physics and chemistry. Even the apparently very slight pieces of Webern turn out to be based on elaborate mathematical patterns. Certainly in both Joyce and Webern there is the quest for greater and greater formal refinement.

The modern movement in music and the arts had another aspect, which was centred in Paris rather than in Vienna. This was undoubtedly better known to Joyce, since he moved from Zürich to Paris soon after the end of the First World War and remained there until he had finished *Finnegans Wake*. The father of the Western modern movement was Debussy, whose inspiration was partly literary and partly pictorial, and was associated with the symbolist poets and impressionist painters. The most striking example of the connection between literature and music, after Wagner, was Debussy's *Pelléas et Mélisande* (1902), a very faithful adaptation of the most famous symbolist play of the epoch, written by Maeterlinck, and a key text for many composers, including Schoenberg. A more important link between literature and Debussy's music was his tone-poem inspired by Mallarmé's 'L'après-midi d'un faune', which Joyce certainly must have known, and his wonderful settings of Verlaine's lyrics. If Debussy learned something essential to his art from Moussorgsky, his greatest disciple was another Russian, Igor Stravinsky, a near-contemporary of Joyce's, whose ballet *The Firebird* appeared in 1910. This was a key date in the heroic age of the modern movement, so much of which is centred on ballet, especially that of the great impresario Diaghilev. Diaghilev drew on the outstanding talents of the *avant-garde* in every relevant field, using Picasso as well as Stravinsky. In a sense literature joined in the confluence of the arts, since Mallarmé's *Faune* received its most eloquent interpretation in Nijinsky's choreography and dancing, to Debussy's music, in 1912. Stravinsky's second ballet was *Petrouchka* (1911) and his third *The Rite of Spring*, which caused a near-riot at its first performance in 1913. (Such scenes were also quite common at first performances of works by Schoenberg and his pupils.)

Thus the modern movement began *before* the First World War, when Joyce's contemporaries Stravinsky and Picasso had reached their full maturity. The war itself made comparatively little difference to the arts in Paris; it was perhaps more significant for them that Debussy should have died at fifty-six after years of illness, leaving his great career incomplete. The Ballets Russes continued, with works by Stravinsky, da Falla, Ravel and others, and when Joyce came to live in Paris it was still a major centre of creativity, although perhaps it did not equal the golden age of the 1910s. Diaghilev, up to his death in 1929, was also responsible for bringing much unknown Russian opera to Paris, London and Monte Carlo, and for producing Stravinsky's concert operas *Mavra* and *Oedipus Rex*. He also encouraged the younger French musicians Poulenc and Milhaud, and their older hero Eric Satie. All this is not claiming that Joyce was an assiduous follower of *avant-garde* ballet and music; but it is likely that he was stimulated by the creative ferment of Paris and the urge towards continuous experimentation.

Paris was also the centre of a true modern movement which comprehended painting and sculpture as well as literature. Surrealism had committed members who signed manifestos and took part in public activities, and it had a theoretical programme. It grew out of the 'Dada' movement, or group, which was formed in 1916 in Zürich; Joyce was living there at the time, although it appears that he had no relations with any of the Dadaists.

The leading figures were the Romanian poet Tristan Tzara and the German painter Hans Arp. They were joined by the French painters Picabia and Duchamp in 1918, and moved to Paris in the following year, where the movement became more literary by the addition of the poets Breton, Éluard, Aragon and Soupault. Dada was the first of the anti-art movements to occur in the West, and was based on elegant hooliganism and dandyish subversion. By the violent destruction of all canons of contemporary good taste and indeed of logic the Dadaists hoped to show their contempt of bourgeois society and to bring about its downfall.

Gradually the practical joking and clowning died down, and the group became more serious about aesthetic theory and politics. In 1924 André Breton transformed the group into the surrealist movement, by issuing his *Manifeste du Surréalisme*, to which the Dadaist writers and other young poets subscribed. Breton began by listing the literary ancestors of surrealism, who included Swift, de Sade, Lewis Carroll, Rimbaud, Picasso, and, bizarrely, the dull eighteenth-century poet Edward Young, whose *Night Thoughts* were known in France through a romantic translation. What each of the long list of authors and painters had in common was something irrational or dreamlike or nonsensical. These 'ancestors' included several favourites of Joyce: in particular, Swift and Lewis Carroll are prominent in the plot and Carroll is credited with inventing the punning technique of *Finnegans Wake*. Breton laid down a fundamental creed of the movement, when he stated that what they admired most in art were flashes of beauty produced by the workings of the unconscious mind, without conscious intervention. He naturally invoked the theories of Dr Freud, and emphasised the importance of dreams and automatic writing. Freud was not impressed by the obvious element of charlatanism in the surrealist movement: he said that when he studied an orthodox work of art he always looked for the unconscious content, but when he looked at a surrealist work he always saw the conscious content.

All this must have been of some interest to Joyce, who had been studying Freud rather earlier; he anticipated some surrealist practices in the fantasies of the 'Circe' chapter in *Ulysses*. There is of course a major difference between Joyce and the surrealists: he did not believe in or practise automatic writing, and the vast bulk of his writing is highly, perhaps even excessively, controlled by his consciousness. But he enjoyed mystification and puzzles, and gave a surrealist appearance of randomness and irrationality to the rational and logical jokes of *Finnegans Wake*. He also quite deliberately exploited the Freudian interpretation of dreams and their symbolism; and in *Finnegans Wake* the narrative is disguised by processes akin to Freud's 'censor'.

Although the surrealists used Freud in a dilettante manner, as they did Marx, the movement was successful in attracting much of the outstanding talent of Paris. Even at its worst the movement kept a certain elegance and stylishness. Paul Éluard became the greatest lyric poet of his generation in France and René Char and René Crevel are still much admired. The movement was even more attractive to painters and some of the outstanding men of talent joined the movement (Max Ernst, Chirico and the exhibitionist Dali), or gave their sympathy, as did Picasso, Miró, and the Belgians Magritte and Delvaux. Picasso, one of the greatest painters of this century, even produced some surrealist prose-poetry.

The experimental movies of the 1930s, such as those of Jean Cocteau, were influenced by surrealism. Even music was loosely associated. Poulenc set a great deal of Éluard's poetry, one of the cycles of which is about Picasso and other modern painters. The movement also exported itself to other European countries, with much greater success in the visual arts than in literature. However, very little English surrealist poetry of the 1930s has survived, the best being Dylan Thomas's visionary prose-poems.

9

The first journalist to explain the movement to the American public, by his own account, was Eugene Jolas, who later moved to Paris and founded with another American, Elliot Paul, the review *transition*, 1927–38. Jolas was not only a translator of the surrealists but an intense admirer of Joyce, although he seems to have been a largely uncomprehending admirer. He was at the head of a coterie of Joyce-worshippers in Paris: his flattery did Joyce no harm, and his kindness and helpfulness were invaluable. Jolas published in *transition* a mass of largely worthless experimental writing, much of it by expatriate Americans, but he did discover some real talent, as when he published one of Dylan Thomas's stories. He also produced a quasi-surrealist and windy manifesto of a new movement called 'The Revolution of the Word'. But his greatest service was to print a great deal of *Finnegans Wake* in an early form. Joyce had begun to write *Finnegans Wake* in 1923, but had had difficulty in finding journals that would accept early drafts of chapters. From 1927 until the eve of its publication in book form Jolas took chapter after chapter, having the patience and apparently the finance to cope with Joyce's maddeningly complicated proof reading. He also published explicatory articles on this 'Work in Progress' as Joyce called it (he kept the title secret until it came out as a book).

# 2

# Joyce and Ireland

The little world to which Joyce belonged physically until 1904 and imaginatively all his life was that of Dublin. It was a small but complete city of singular charm, a true national capital rather than a provincial city. Its population in Bloomsyear was about a quarter of a million, fifty years later only about half a million. It remains a city of great architectural beauty, with many fine eighteenth-century houses. It was and is a city of administrators, distributors and consumers, rather than producers; the latter consisted mainly of the great Guinness brewery, Jacobs biscuits and a few distilleries. The economy was sustained by the agriculture of the surrounding land, and through Dublin agricultural produce, mainly the cattle that are prominent in *Ulysses*, was exported to England. In return it received from England coal and manufactured goods and luxuries, for which it was the shopping centre of Ireland. The picture we get from *Ulysses* is of a city of consumers, of eaters and drinkers, shoppers and window-shoppers like Mr Bloom. Despite the nationalist propaganda about exploitation by England, Dublin in the second half of the nineteenth century enjoyed a modest degree of prosperity and commercial expansion. It was the centre for office work, in banking, insurance and the like, and consequently there were a large number of clerks or 'white-collar' workers, who are the backbone of the Joycean world. It was the administrative centre of Ireland, which was a quasi-colony of England, with the Viceroy, bureaucrats, and large numbers of troops and police. It was a social centre, where débutantes came to be presented to the Viceroy in the 'season' and the Protestant landlords of the 'Ascendancy' had their town houses and clubs. Joyce knew very little about this class; the county ladies like Mrs Yelverton Barry remain figures of sexual fantasy for Bloom.

Finally, Dublin was a centre for the higher 'services' of civilisation, education, medicine and religion. It had its two universities, Trinity College for the Protestants, and the National University, to which Joyce went, for the Catholics. School education was also divided on religious lines. The better-off Protestant boys were sent mostly to English boarding schools, the better-off Catholics to the Jesuit-run schools, Clongowes Wood in the country and Belvedere College in Dublin, both of which Joyce attended. There have always been a large number of hospitals in the city and many medical students, among whom in 1904 was Oliver St John Gogarty, the original of Malachi Mulligan and later a famous surgeon. Most of the Irish clergy were educated at the seminary of Maynooth, a few miles out the city. The Roman Catholic Church made its presence felt everywhere, both by the density of churches and the high proportion of townspeople going to them regularly.

In a discussion with the German critic Alfred Kerr in 1936 (Ellmann, 1959, p. 701) Joyce developed a comparison between himself and Ibsen: 'I described the people and the conditions in my country: I reproduced certain city types of a certain social level. They didn't forgive me for it.' This certain social level is basically the Catholic middle class, taken at its widest definition. Of this class the most affluent member in *Ulysses* is Mulligan, who is also unusual in belonging to the literary set. Most of the literary men who take part in the debate on Shakespeare in the National Library are upper-middle-class Protestants, like the absent but often-mentioned W. B. Yeats. None of the Catholics except Mulligan seem to possess much money: even the editor of the newspaper described in 'Aeolus' is temporarily strapped, and the hangers-on who gather in his office are much worse, especially the parasite Lenehan. Simon Dedalus, like Joyce's father, has slid down into grinding poverty, but he is still a gentleman, and can afford to smoke and drink whisky while his daughters have only soup to eat. Bloom has a small private income, and with his irregular earnings as a canvasser for advertisements he is about average in the book in economic if not in social standing. Martin Cunningham is a minor clerk in the British Administration (the Castle), but is kept poor by his wife's drinking. The lowest level are the customers in Barney Kiernan's pub, including the anonymous narrator of the 'Cyclops' chapter; but they are still middle-class, and there is a huge gap between them and the real working class of Dublin, the navvies, carters and tramwaymen whose lives are described in Sean O'Casey's plays and *Autobiographies*. The curious thing is that everyone in *Ulysses* seems to know a great many of the others personally and to know about nearly everyone else. There seems to be a strong unity among this middle class, bound together by religion and politics. Although they are capable of snobbery they do not regard temporary poverty (and all poverty can be regarded as temporary) as a social disgrace. They have the spirit though not the organisation of a Freemasonry (the real Freemasons of Ireland, to which Bloom belongs, were at this time exclusively Protestant and Jewish). To be a member of a subject people and of a once-persecuted religion is in itself a bond; and the bond was further cemented by an almost universal interest in music, drink and horse-racing. Verbal wit, the greatest master of which is Simon Dedalus, and malicious gossip are staples of the community. *Ulysses* itself is a vast and inspired piece of gossip, among other things; and Joyce's knowledge of this community is total.

Behind Joyce's back, as he stood looking eastwards over the sea, from Howth or from the Martello Tower at Sandycove towards England and Europe, were his enemies: the unknown Irish. For a few miles Dublin ran inland until it vanished on the slopes of the Wicklow Mountains and in the flat fields of the north and west. Within his Pale, Joyce knew geographical and social reality as well as anyone — beyond, almost everything vanished into a myopic twilight. He knew the school at Clongowes Wood, a little of Cork from a trip with his father (described in *A Portrait*), and later Galway City where his wife Nora came from. He had never seen much of the Ireland that the tourist remembers with affection: Bantry Bay, Glengarriff, Killarney, the Dingle Peninsula, the Blaskets and Aran, the limestone Burren, Coole Park and Ballylee, Gogarty's Renvyle in Connemara, the great tombs of the Boyne: these places, which speak so powerfully to the imagination, are reduced to a ludicrous catalogue of icons on the Cyclops handkerchief, symbols of chauvinism. Socially his ignorance was just as invincible: 'Joyce had the same contempt for both the ignorant peasantry and the snobbish aristocracy that Yeats idealised' (Ellmann, 1959, p. 104). He could hardly ever have spoken to one of the country gentlemen whose sporting lives are so well described by Somerville and Ross. As for the peasantry, fishermen of Aran or tinkers of Wicklow, they might have been inhabitants of another planet:

*April* 14. John Alphonsus Mulrennan has just returned from the west of Ireland. (European and Asiatic papers please copy.) He

told us he met an old man there in a mountain cabin. Old man
had red eyes and short pipe. Old man spoke Irish. Mulrennan
spoke Irish. Then old man and Mulrennan spoke English.
Mulrennan spoke to him about universe and stars. Old man
sat, listened, smoked, spat. Then said: Ah, there must be terrible
queer creatures at the latter end of the world. I fear him. I fear
his-red rimmed eyes. It is with him I must struggle all through
this night till day come, till he or I lie dead, gripping him by
the sinewy throat till... Till what? Till he yield to me? No.
I mean him no harm. (*A Portrait*)

The history of Ireland is a nightmare, tempered by good humour. It
is first of all the history of a population problem, offering one of the
first examples of a catastrophic population explosion. At the beginning
of the eighteenth century the population was about 2½ million, and
by 1780 it had risen to 4 million, in 1821 to about 6,800,000 and in
1845 it reached an amazing peak of about 8½ million. This was caused
by the success of the potato crop; a countryman could occupy a small
patch of mountain land, get married young and grow enough potatoes
to feed a large family. Then came the Famine of 1845–8 when the crop
failed and no other food was available. Millions died of hunger and of
diseases caused by hunger, and millions more emigrated. The population fell rapidly to 6½ million in 1851 and 4½ million in 1904; and it
has remained about the same ever since. Now, of course, the Irish
countrymen are very well-fed (and are said to eat as much protein as
any people in Europe) but the memory remains. The Famine and the
depopulation is the main fact of recent Irish history. Emigration has
always been important: by 1861 there were 2 million Irish in the
USA and Canada, and 800,000 in Great Britain. The existence of this
huge overseas Ireland, today wealthy and still nationalistic, is a major
factor in the Irish economic and political scene; it is comparable to the
support of Israel by world-wide Jewry. In *Finnegans Wake* the good
brother Shaun is a successful Boston Irishman; his bad brother Shem
is one of the smaller number transported to Australia for political
crime.

The other set of relevant statistics about Ireland concerns religion,
which still remains the biggest single issue in politics. In 1871 Ireland
was 76.6 per cent Catholic; in the twenty-six counties of the south the
Protestants were 10.87 per cent, in the six counties of the north 66 per
cent. (These percentages are about the same today except that in the

south the Protestant figure is halved.) The Protestants are then a minority in the island as a whole, but have a majority in the north, and this has been a cause of division for over a century. The Protestants of the north are the descendants of British colonists of the seventeenth century, the majority of whom were Scots Presbyterians; they have always refused to join an independent Ireland, and have traditionally stood for union with the British Crown. Since the Dark Ages, religion has permeated every side of Irish life; the Irish have always been a truly devout people, probably the most devout in Europe. They have supplied the Church with many monks, friars, nuns, members of teaching orders and so on, who have done the hardest and most unselfish tasks of the Church all over the world. When the Reformation came and the ruling English became Protestant, it was natural for the Irish to remain attached to the unreformed Church; and their adherence to the old cause became a symbol of political revolt. Just as naturally the ruling power proscribed the Roman Catholic Church as politically seditious; and in the Penal days, extending to the end of the eighteenth century, the Church suffered many limitations on its freedom; persecution only increased the natives' loyalty to their priests and bishops.

The Roman Catholic Church has been a militant force in Irish nationalist politics, even when the hierarchy condemned political nationalism, as it has done at various times. But it has been a stabilising, conservative, and even reactionary force in social and intellectual life. One of the reasons for this was the founding of the seminary at Maynooth in the mid-nineteenth century. Before that many Irish priests received their education on the Continent, in Rome and Spain, and consequently some were men of cultivation and knowledge of the world. But once they came to be educated entirely in Ireland their careers were forced into a narrow cycle. The typical Irish priest was a peasant boy — to become a priest was in fact the only way of escaping from peasant life — and he took with him to the seminary a set of peasant values. His fellow students and most of his instructors were men of similarly narrow horizons; and when he became ordained he took back to his parish a peasant view of life with little change. Consequently the Catholic Church imposed on the Irish people a constricted and puritanical way of life, and an impoverishment of the old folk culture. Since the Catholic Church has the monopoly of the education of its flock, the same narrow views were imposed on the schoolchildren. As a result the Irish have remained educationally relatively backward, and as Conor Cruise O'Brien has said, they have been trained to become hewers of wood and drawers of water. The Protestant ethos, on the other hand, imposed a more acquisitive and dynamic attitude to life on members of the Anglican and Presbyterian Churches. Hence the much greater success of the Irish Protestants in business and intellectual life. There is little doubt that Joyce believed that the Catholic Church imposed a stupid and stunted provincial way of life on Ireland. The *Portrait* is a careful documentation of this Catholic educational process; but *Ulysses* is full of satire against the Catholic Church and its civic and educational role. This is perhaps a naïve view, but it is common sense. On the other hand, Joyce deeply loved the intellectual system of the Church, the Scholastic philosophers (as far as he knew them), the medieval principles of allegory, the ritual and symbolism of 2000 years of Roman Christianity. He was also deeply grateful for the literary education he got from the Jesuits; and there was nothing in the traditions of Protestantism that attracted him at all.

The Irish language is immensely important to many Irishmen, but did not matter much to Joyce. The oddity of Irish nationalism is that, unlike Zionism, or French Canadian or Welsh nationalism, it is not really sustained by a language. In the Middle Ages all Ireland was Gaelic-speaking, except for a relatively small English colony around Dublin. The ancient Celtic culture began to break up after the Battle of the Boyne (1690) and there was a catastrophic decline in the Gaelic language during the eighteenth century; by 1800 it is estimated that only half the population could speak it. Nothing could halt the decline; fifty years later the proportion was down to 25 per cent, in another fifty years only half of that again. Today it is probable that the number of native Irish speakers who use the language every day is as small as 64,000. This is despite immense efforts, first by a voluntary association, The Gaelic League, and after independence by the Irish government, to preserve the language. Everyone holding an official position in the Irish Republic, whether in education or in the Civil Service, must pass an examination in Gaelic, which is one of the official languages of the Dáil or Irish Parliament. But the number of people in Dublin who speak Gaelic every day is minute, and the amount of new litera-ture written in the language is also inconsiderable. Joyce, foreseeing the decline of Gaelic and not fired by nationalism, refused to have anything to do with the revival — a self-portrait as Gabriel Conroy in 'The Dead' shows him being snubbed by an ardent Irish nationalist for being a 'West Briton'. The Gaelic League is mocked in the 'Cyclops' chapter of *Ulysses*. Joyce never learned to read the Old or Middle Irish classics, but in later life he did learn a number of Gaelic words, which he inserted into *Finnegans Wake* (see Brendan O'Hehir, *A Gaelic Lexicon for Finnegans Wake*, 1967). But since he did this with a number of other European and Asiatic languages, it cannot be said that his attitude to Gaelic was especially favourable.

The Celts who brought their language to Ireland were not the first invaders. People of the European megalithic culture arrived from Spain and Brittany perhaps as early as 4000 BC (the dates are currently under revision). The finest prehistoric monuments are those of the River Boyne, especially Newgrange, which is comparable in importance to Stonehenge. The megaliths provide the background to the first chapter of *Finnegans Wake*, which goes on to describe a series of invasions. The tall, blond Gaels came in about the fifth century BC, conquering a small, dark pre-Indo-European people, who left their mark on the curious syntax of Gaelic. The Celts had a primitive warrior aristocracy, much like that described in Homer, and an epic literature describing this aristocracy and its heroes. The Ulster Cycle, in which the principal hero is Cuchullin, is thought to reflect the Iron Age culture of the second century BC. The other main cycle is the Fenian Cycle. Finn MacCool (Fionn MacCumhail) is the leader of a band of warriors called the Fenians; he is the father of Oisin (or Ossian) and the husband of Gráinne who betrays him with his kinsman Diarmuid. These stories, which probably have no historical truth, were the basis for James Macpherson's fake epic of the eighteenth century, usually known as *Ossian*, which Joyce often quotes; and of course Finn is the principal hero of *Finnegans Wake*.

The Celtic kings of Ireland emerge from legend into history in the early centuries AD but they still remain shadowy figures. The Church was more important than the civil power during the Dark Ages. The conversion of Ireland to Christianity in the fifth century AD brought a 'Golden Age' of monastic learning and ecclesiastical fine arts. The most famous extant object from this period is the Book of Kells, an illuminated manuscript of the Gospels now in the Library of Trinity College, Dublin. The description of this by Sir Edward Sullivan ('The Book of Kells', *The Studio*, 1920) begins:

Its weird and commanding beauty; its subdued and goldless
colouring; the baffling intricacy of its fearless designs; the clean,
unwavering sweep of rounded spiral; the creeping undulations of

serpentine forms, that writhe in artistic profusion throughout the mazes of its decorations; the strong and legible minuscule of its text; the quaintness of its striking portraiture; the unwearied reverence and patient labour that brought it into being. . . .

Joyce parodies this sentence in the fifth chapter of *Finnegans Wake*, and he said that he had made the Book of Kells the model for the intricacies of his book. One must not take this too literally, but I think it helps the understanding of Joyce if one looks at this and other examples of Celtic Christian art. The Irish monks took Christianity to Scotland, and went as missionaries to many parts of the Continent.

A very poor and primitive peasantry must have given a high proportion of their produce to allow the monks to produce their many treasures of gold and silver. In search of this treasure the Norwegian and Danish Vikings raided Scotland and Ireland from the eighth century onwards. They carried away Irish slaves to Scandinavia and later to Iceland and they founded Dublin as a trading port. Joyce used to say that Dublin was basically a Scandinavian city, and that this explained his sympathy with Ibsen. That is probably fanciful, since all traces of the Norsemen disappeared in the Middle Ages. The Norsemen did not conquer all Ireland, but held only coastal areas. The native princes tried to drive them out, and finally succeeded in 1013, when Brian Boru won the Battle of Clontarf.

The next invasion came in the twelfth century. Dermod MacMurrough, the king of Leinster (1135–71), was deposed in 1167 and fled to England, and asked for the help of King Henry II. A number of Norman knights, led by Strongbow, Earl of Pembroke, entered the country and gradually subdued it. (MacMurrough and his elopement with Devorgilla, wife of O'Rourke, Prince of Breffny, are mentioned in the 'Nestor' chapter of *Ulysses* and again in *Finnegans Wake*, in parallel with Helen of Troy and Parnell's Kitty O'Shea, as examples of the fatal influence of women in politics.) The Norman conquerors soon became Celticised: that is, they turned into Irish chieftains themselves. That has been the fate of all subsequent invaders of Ireland: as they try to replace the old ruling classes, they become partly absorbed by them. Many attempts at colonisation were made over the next few centuries, but none were very successful outside the 'Pale', which was the predominantly English district round Dublin. The 'Old English' of the Middle Ages became assimilated to the Catholic Irish and resisted the Reformation together with them. Since Protestantism was the religion of the foreign power, the Catholic religion became permanently associated with Irish nationalism, and the association grew stronger with every persecution. In the early seventeenth century the first wholly successful colonisation began, mainly by Presbyterian Scots in Ulster. This left the permanently irreconcilable minority in the north, which has made the union of the island impossible.

At the beginning of the seventeenth century the Catholic aristocracy, composed of Norman, English and Celtic landed proprietors, was still mainly intact, and the literary culture of Gaelic-speaking Ireland was still flourishing. Both were destroyed by stages, the first being the confiscation of the Ulster estates to make room for the colonists. This led to the Rebellion of 1641, and then to Cromwell's expedition of 1649 and subsequent massacres. The 'Cromwellian Settlement' included the confiscation of Irish lands in 1654, and the replacement of the traditional landowners by English 'Adventurers'. The old aristocracy made a last effort in support of James II of England after the Revolution of 1688; but his defeat by the Williamites at the Battle of the Boyne (1 July 1690) was followed by further confiscations, and penal laws against Catholics. There was a further parcelling out of land among new English landlords; this was the final stage in the rise of the Protestant 'Ascendancy', and the complete subjugation of Ireland to England.

So far I have been giving a potted version of the naïve account of history found in popular Irish books. It is none the less a living view of history, still taught in schools; the myths that have accrued to it have been potent political forces, and men have lived and died by them. It is perhaps difficult for professional historians to give a detailed and accurate assessment of Irish life before 1700, since there is a shortage of documents. (The Record Office was burned down during the Civil War of 1922 — a superb symbolic gesture, ensuring that early history would remain mythical for ever.) The naïve or mythical view of Irish history is important for readers of Joyce, since he uses it throughout *Ulysses* and *Finnegans Wake*. The fact that it is endlessly interesting to most Irishmen and infinitely tedious to most Englishmen can be a serious obstacle to the understanding of Joyce's major works.

After the seventeenth century Irish history is more comprehensible and better studied. The eighteenth century was a great age for Dublin and for the country gentry. Despite the poverty of the peasantry and the population explosion, many great country houses were built and most of the best buildings of Dublin. This was the age of Swift and of the great orators of the Irish Parliament, independent until the Union of 1801. W. B. Yeats greatly admired eighteenth-century Ireland and its writers — Swift, Berkeley, Goldsmith and Burke — but Irish nationalists do not. Many of the monuments of this age, the great country houses, have been allowed to decay or were burned down by the IRA, but Dublin still presents a wonderfully Georgian appearance. Joyce admired the grace of the eighteenth-century city, and showed a special affinity to at least two of the Anglo-Irish writers of the age, Swift and Sterne, who both appear frequently in *Finnegans Wake*, as does Bishop Berkeley. He was also interested in the skill of the eighteenth-century Anglo-Irish orators like Grattan, as the 'Aeolus' chapter of *Ulysses* shows.

The first great nationalist movement of revolt took place at the end of the eighteenth century. The United Irishmen, led by Wolfe Tone, were Republican revolutionaries, inspired by the French Revolution. The Rising of 1798 was almost entirely confined to the area of Wexford, and was suppressed quickly and brutally, but it became a symbol for the whole country, and led to a fine crop of political broadside ballads; it is also celebrated in later patriotic songs, like 'The Croppy Boy' which is sung in the 'Sirens' chapter of *Ulysses*. Fears of further risings helped to bring about the Union of the Irish and English Parliaments in 1801; this did not in fact mean a major shift of power, since the real administration of Ireland was always in the hands of the British government in Westminster; but it meant a loss of prestige and independence for some of the Anglo-Irish gentry.

In the early nineteenth century the revolutionary movement died down, and the principal theatre of action was the peaceable campaign for Catholic Emancipation, led by Daniel O'Connell, the 'Liberator'. By 1829 this campaign achieved more or less complete success and the Catholic Church could then enjoy its great power openly. Before long the central seminary for training priests at Maynooth was set up, and the control of the Church over the peasantry was greatly increased.

The early nineteenth century was also the period of the population explosion, and the Famine, of which I have mentioned some of the disastrous consequences, came in 1845. Since it became impossible to collect any rents at all in many areas, the wealth and power of the landed gentry was seriously weakened for the first time. The great increase in emigration had an immediate political result: there was now a considerable 'Ireland overseas' which soon possessed many more resources than the native peasantry. It was not long before some of the Irish in the USA and Canada became affluent, and after the middle of the century they sent a great deal of money back to Ireland, both as charitable doles to their relatives and as funds for political and terrorist organisations. This support continues to the present day: the IRA would have collapsed and disappeared long ago but for the flow of American-Irish money and arms. Ireland has long been a 'remittance' country, and the overseas Irish have often been more intransigent than the natives. 'We have our greater Ireland beyond the seas', says the Citizen-Cyclops in *Ulysses*.

The Cyclops also says that

'they were driven out of house and home in the black 47. Their mudcabins and their shielings by the roadside were laid low by the batteringram and *The Times* rubbed its hands and told the whitelivered Saxons there would soon be as few Irish in Ireland as redskins in America.'

For once the Cyclops is right. As J. C. Beckett writes of the post-famine period in *The Making of Modern Ireland*:

There was a widespread expectation that British purchasers would flock into the country, bringing new capital to invest in their estates, and peopling them with highly-skilled English and Scottish farmers. 'In a few years more', *The Times* prophesied, 'a Celtic Irishman will be as rare in Connemara as is the Red Indian on the shores of Manhattan'. Things turned out very differently.

In fact there were very few new purchasers from England or Scotland. Despite the decrease of population, the agricultural situation remained very poor for most of the nineteenth century and there was a continuous background of agrarian discontent and disorder, which took the classic peasant form of guerrilla attacks on landlords and their animals and property.

This movement found a more organised political expression in the Land League, led by Michael Davitt, which campaigned for legal agricultural reform. At the time of Joyce's birth the countryside was unsettled and violent; but by the beginning of the century and certainly by 1916 most of the problems had disappeared. Many of the great estates were divided up, a nation of poor tenants was converted to one of modest proprietors, and the standard of living gradually rose in the east and centre, although the problem of the very poor crofters of the Gaelic west has hardly been solved to this day.

Joyce showed very little interest in the Irish peasantry, and knew little about the west. But he was deeply concerned with two developments of the later nineteenth century, the terrorist movement and the Parliamentary movement led by Parnell. In its modern form, the first dates from the 1850s, when the Irish Republican Brotherhood was formed in 1858. This was a secret organisation whose members were pledged to the setting up of an Irish Republic by force: the president of the IRB, or Fenians, as they came to be known, was automatically the first president of the Republic.

The Fenians also aimed at setting up paramilitary units armed with rifles. In 1866 a group of Fenians who had been training on American soil actually invaded Canada, but were soon repelled. In the late nineteenth century the Fenians were active in setting up or penetrating legal organisations which could be useful to them. One such was the Gaelic League founded by Douglas Hyde and Eoin MacNeill in 1893, ostensibly to keep the Irish language alive; in ten years it had vastly increased its membership and influence, and had become a useful vehicle for intransigent nationalism. It is significant that the Easter 1916 Rebellion was led by Gaelic Leaguers and literary men who were also members of the IRB. Another organisation heavily penetrated by the IRB and very useful to it was the Gaelic Athletic Association (GAA), as we shall see in the 'Cyclops' chapter of *Ulysses*, where the protagonist is the founder, the Fenian Michael Cusack. The object of the GAA was to promote purely Irish games: the ancient sport of hurling, and a fabricated modern sport called Gaelic football. Its members were not allowed to take part in any non-Irish games, such as soccer, Rugby football, tennis or cricket, games which have since their invention been popular in Ireland. The split has continued to the present day, with serious nationalists playing only the recognised Gaelic games; this must have irritated Joyce, a fairly serious cricket fan, as much as the Gaelic League's insistence on the Irish language; and this helps to explain the virulence of his satire in 'Cyclops'. The GAA not only provided yet another vehicle for nationalist propaganda but it also formed the nuclei of revolutionary fighting units. Each local hurling team could and often did transform itself into the local platoon or company of riflemen.

Early in the twentieth century the IRB found yet another instrument in the Sinn Fein movement, founded by Arthur Griffith, who is mentioned in *Ulysses*: someone even alleges that Leopold Bloom gave some of the ideas for Sinn Fein to Griffith, an unlikely story.

Today the political, semi-legal wing of the IRA is called 'Sinn Fein', a slogan that means 'Ourselves alone', i.e. boycott everything British; the full importance of this movement did not emerge until after Easter 1916.

The IRB, though its membership was always small, was fairly popular with the Irish lower classes, as the IRA is today. Even the breakaway group, the 'Invincibles', who committed the Phoenix Park Murders had some popularity with a public that had never been averse to extreme violence. In 1882, the year of Joyce's birth, Gladstone made peace with the Parliamentary and land reform leadership, and Lord Frederick Cavendish was sent to Dublin as Chief Secretary to inaugurate a new and happier era. On the day that he arrived, 7 May, he and the Under-Secretary, Mr R. H. Burke, were stabbed to death in the Phoenix Park not far from the Viceroy's residence. The gang made a successful getaway but were later caught, thanks to an informer, one Carey, who was himself later assassinated. I have given space to this sordid incident, which except for the eminence of the victims has been paralleled hundreds of times in Ireland, because it haunted Joyce. Some reference to the murders appears in almost every chapter of *Ulysses*, and it is typical of the violence from which Joyce recoiled and from which Bloom is meant to offer some kind of deliverance.

Joyce's serious interest in Irish politics began and ended with the Parliamentary movement, and that in fact meant Parnell to him. The history of the legal movement to obtain a measure of Irish independence is part of the history of England. In a sense that is true of all Irish political history — but the 'Home Rule' movement is most intimately connected with the successive Conservative and Liberal ministries from 1870 to 1921. There is no need to go into details in a study of Joyce, except where Parnell is concerned. The Home Rule movement was launched by Isaac Butt in 1870 and in the General Election of 1874 fifty-nine professing Home Rulers were returned, all representing southern Irish constituencies. Charles Stewart Parnell, a Protestant landlord, was not returned to Parliament until 1875 but two years later he succeeded Isaac Butt as President of the Home Rule Confederation. He was a master of Parliamentary strategy, who perfected the technique of holding up all business at Westminster. He was quite fearless and incorruptible; Joyce admired him partly because he was the antithesis of the backslapping, sentimental, oratorical Irish type of politician. The full extent of Joyce's admiration can be seen in 'Ivy Day in the Committee Room' and the Christmas

Dinner scene of *A Portrait*; Parnell's coolness ('indifferent, paring his fingernails') gave Joyce his own life-style. Parnell worked closely with the extra-Parliamentary Land League, which he helped to found, but kept clear of the IRB, as far as is known. In 1881 he was arrested and the Land League was proclaimed an unlawful association; a few months later Gladstone had him released, and tried to set up a new agreement; but this, as we have seen, was the time of the Phoenix Park Murders. Gladstone was converted to Home Rule, and introduced his first Home Rule Bill (which would have given Ireland something like the kind of Dominion status then enjoyed by Canada, not complete independence) in 1886; the bill was defeated. In 1887 a series of articles titled 'Parnellism and Crime' was published in the London *Times*; these alleged that Parnell was in touch with the IRB. In the following year a special commission was set up to investigate these charges; the report of this commission, at which dozens of Irish of all kinds spoke, makes wonderfully comic reading, and was naturally used extensively by Joyce in *Finnegans Wake*. At the end of the sittings the forgeries of one Pigott, who had tried to incriminate Parnell, were exposed; Pigott committed suicide and Parnell came away in triumph.

This was the summit of Parnell's career; and it looked as though he might carry all before him. But later in 1889 Captain O'Shea, who had hitherto been a *mari complaisant*, took him to the divorce court: in 1890 the verdict went against Parnell and Mrs O'Shea, after evidence that was widely reported. The episode of Parnell escaping down a fire escape, for example, was used by every music-hall comedian in England. The Catholic Church proved surprisingly tolerant about the divorce; but the Welsh non-conformists, and other Liberal supporters of Gladstone were outraged and made the Prime Minister break with Parnell. There was a famous debate on the Irish Parliamentary Party in Committee Room No. 15 on Parnell's leadership; the majority went against him, and the party was split. Probably coincidentally, for it had always been doubtful, Parnell's health broke down; and he died of pneumonia in Brighton on 6 October 1891. Joyce was then nine; and at this time Stephen at Clongowes Wood School had his vision of the dead Parnell. Everything in Parnell's life turns up somewhere in Joyce's work, and he urged his readers to get hold of any of the short biographies of his hero. From then on, in Joyce's view, Irish politics were absurd and led by charlatans or idiots, with a very few exceptions.

The Parliamentary movement certainly declined very fast after

Parnell, even though it went on automatically winning all the Catholic seats, and had the English Liberal Party on its side. The absolute hopelessness of Irish politics became apparent after Parnell's death, although it could have been perceived much earlier. The crucial point was the refusal of the Protestants of the north to agree to a Home Rule, or any other form of independence, which would give majority rule to the Catholic south. This position has not changed in the slightest since then, and it would be a fair guess that it never will change. A united and independent Ireland can only be achieved by means of the physical extermination of several million Protestants, a prospect which some diehard Catholics perhaps view with equanimity, just as diehard Protestants would not object to the physical extermination of the Catholic minority in Ulster.

Bloomsyear, 1904, was a time of relative stagnation and calm, as far as the Ulster question was concerned; the old issues, however, as discussed by Stephen and Mr Deasy the Ulsterman, were still smouldering; and it is in this connection that Stephen talks of the nightmare of history. Thereafter the nightmare grew worse.

In the ten years before the outbreak of the First World War, there was the steady situation of the Liberal Party pledged to granting Home Rule, the Conservatives and their Ulster Unionist allies determined to resist it. The Liberals won the General Election of 1906, and in the two elections of 1910 the Irish Party held the balance. It was obvious that the Ulster Protestants were going to resist Home Rule by force, even before the 'Solemn League and Covenant' was subscribed in 1912. In the next year a paramilitary Ulster Volunteer Force was formed, and a provisional government of Ulster was set up, backed by this Volunteer Force. Then the British Liberal Government took a fatal step, out of fairness or impotence or negligence: they allowed a similar Catholic Nationalist paramilitary force to be set up, called the Irish Volunteers, and this soon recruited many thousands. To obtain more rifles both sides engaged in gun-running in 1914. Just before the war tension mounted to a height and almost led to a serious officers' mutiny in the British Army. It is not often realised just how many of the officers, and especially of the successful officers of the British Army, have been Northern Irish Protestants. The officers at the Curragh depot in March 1914 stated that they would refuse to take action against Ulster Volunteers if the latter were to resist the introduction of Home Rule by force. These officers had Ulster friends in high places, including General Henry Wilson, later

Chief of the Imperial General Staff (he was assassinated by Irish gunmen in 1922); and it would not have been easy to resolve the problem if the First World War had not broken out in August of that year. Immediately the Home Rule proposals were shelved for the duration, and the Ulster Volunteers were allowed to join the British Army as complete units.

The war was, curiously enough, fairly popular with the Irish nationalists at first. They were on the side of Catholic Belgium; and many thousands of Irish Catholics joined the British Army and fought, for most of the time with enthusiasm. The increased supply of agricultural products to Britain kept the farmers happy. The only major grievance of the Nationalists seemed to be that the Irish Volunteers were not allowed to join the British Army in a body as the Ulster Volunteers had been; but no one except themselves took the Volunteers very seriously.

However a small group of activists soon decided to make a sacrifice which would transform the whole nationalist movement. The chief of these was Padraig Pearse, who made a notable speech in 1915 at the funeral of the Fenian O'Donovan Rossa, whose body had been returned from America. This did not seem important to the authorities, who were perhaps unaware that many important events in Ireland have been triggered off by graveside orations. Pearse and the other leaders of a breakaway group of the Irish Volunteers were members of the IRB, and they planned a full-scale insurrection that would proclaim the Republic. They may or may not have imagined that they could be successful militarily; certainly their tactics of seizing public buildings in Dublin was the least likely to succeed against a large British army; but they probably did not care. They felt that their example in risking everything would lead to an upsurge of revolutionary nationalism and to eventual victory, and their belief turned out to be justified. The leadership of the Irish Volunteers was against any such direct action, but Pearse and his friends in Dublin decided to act alone, with a small contingent, joined by the very small left-wing Irish Citizens' Army of the trade-unionist leader James Connolly. The Easter Rising began on 24 April with the seizure of the General Post Office, where Pearse called on the shade of Cuchullin for support. The British Army, who were not expecting any trouble, were taken by surprise, but took only five days to defeat the rebels. Pearse and thirteen other leaders were court martialled summarily and shot, while the rank and file were sent to prison camps in England.

The Rising was not at the time popular with the Dublin mob, who hissed some of the survivors; but in a matter of months a heroic mythology grew up around the bloodbath, which was just what the leaders had hoped for. Now the revolutionaries adopted the name and part of the programme of Griffith's small party 'Sinn Fein', and began to win by-elections. The old Irish Parliamentary Party withered away, and after the end of the war in 1918 Sinn Fein had a complete victory in the General Election. In 1919 the Sinn Fein members met in Dublin as the Dáil Éireann, which has ever since been the name of the Irish Parliament; it was declared an illegal body by the British government, and in that year the Anglo-Irish war began. The rebels did not make the mistakes of Easter 1916; they fought an intelligent guerrilla war of ambushes and raids in the countryside, where the large British Army was at a disadvantage. In Dublin they had a brilliant intelligence and counter-intelligence organisation led by Michael Collins, which paralysed most of the British defence. Many atrocities were committed by both sides; but the British government began to see that they could not win. Since there had been no change in Ulster, they had to settle for partition, and two separate Parliaments in Ireland. The Northern Irish Parliament was acceptable to the Ulster Protestants and it was opened by King George V in 1921; Northern Ireland remained under the same system of government until the Stormont parliament was prorogued in 1972. The British government was unwilling to let the southern rebels have the Republic they wanted, and proposed a Treaty which would give the south something like Dominion status, their country to be called the 'Irish Free State'. Both sides were weary after two years of guerrilla warfare, and there were many Sinn Feiners who wanted peace. Michael Collins, Arthur Griffith and Eamonn de Valera negotiated with the British and recommended to the Dáil that the Treaty be accepted; in January 1922 the Dáil approved it by a small majority; an Irish General Election in June 1922 showed that a majority were pro-Treaty. At this point the Civil War began, between Republicans and pro-Treaty Free-Staters. Before long Michael Collins was killed in an ambush; Griffith died a natural death. On the Republican side Erskine Childers, the novelist, who had previously done a great deal for the liberation of Ireland, was executed without trial and Rory O'Connor, a leading officer, was killed in the siege of the Four Courts. He was a close friend of the leading Free Stater Kevin O'Higgins, who was himself assassinated by Republican gunmen a few years later. There were more casualties and atrocities committed during the Civil War than during the Anglo-Irish war of 1919–21, and there was a great deal of destruction of historic buildings in Dublin, including the Record Office containing most of the sources of Irish history.

Joyce was of course out of Ireland throughout this period, but it would be a mistake to think that he was not deeply interested in contemporary politics. At the time of the troubles he was writing *Ulysses* about an earlier period, and it was published just about the time that the Civil War finished. But he began *Finnegans Wake* a year later with a sketch that partly describes Rory O'Connor's death, and most of the leading figures from 1916–23 appear as characters in the book: Erskine Childers, for example, becomes 'Haveth Childers Everywhere', one of the titles of H. C. Earwicker. Griffith, Collins, O'Higgins and other Treaty and Civil War figures are often mentioned, and de Valera is given a satirical treatment in the 'Shaun' chapters and elsewhere. This despite the fact that there is perhaps only one reference to the Civil War in Joyce's biography: Nora took the children to Galway in 1922 (she may have been thinking of leaving James at that time) and during the journey across Ireland her train was fired on, by one side or the other; Joyce typically took this as a personal insult. In a letter (on the subject of publishers) he refers to the most powerful empire in the world being defeated by a gang of naked savages, armed only with crucifixes (and concludes that the only answer is the boot). But as always in Joyce lack of sympathy does not mean lack of interest. He probably found the Civil War particularly appealing as a subject because it was so intimate: the people on each side knew each other very well, even though they were ready to kill each other.

The history of Ireland from 1923 to the end of Joyce's writing life is not of any great interest. Ireland very soon settled down to a placid bourgeois existence, which in the south has not yet been seriously disturbed. Eamonn de Valera was leader of the Fianna Fáil party and Prime Minister from 1932 to 1948. Ireland was neutral during the Second World War. The IRA grew out of the defeated Republican forces of the Civil War; its campaigns waxed and waned, with serious bombing attacks in England in 1939. The hotting-up of politics in Northern Ireland since 1969 is a return to the old days, after a relatively peaceful interval; but Joyce would not have been surprised.

# 3

# Irish Literary History

Ireland has two literary histories, the first that of the Celtic language, and the second that of the English language. The first began with the literature of Old Irish preserved by oral tradition in the last centuries BC and written down in the early centuries of Christianity; the second began with the coming of the English language in the Middle Ages and reached its first peak with the Anglo-Irish writers of the eighteenth century. Joyce knew very little about the first from direct contact with the language. Old Irish is a very difficult language, still known only to a handful of scholars. Modern Irish is more accessible and has a large body of literature, composed up to the end of the seventeenth century and even later; but this too was virtually unknown to Joyce. Gaelic literature of the twentieth century is minimal, although there are a few enthusiasts who continue to write in the language. Anglo-Irish literature is still extremely vigorous and indeed Joyce is one of the greatest exponents. He was also highly conscious of his predecessors and makes frequent references to them in his works, particularly in *Finnegans Wake*.

Joyce in later life learned a little Gaelic, enough to scatter dozens of words and phrases throughout *Finnegans Wake*. But, like all Irish intellectuals, he also read the standard translations of the Old Irish epics and was familiar with Celtic mythology and legend. He was thus perfectly familiar with the stories of Cuchullin and the other heroes of the Ulster Cycle, and with the other main cycle, concerning Fionn MacCumhail (Finn MacCool) and his followers, which he used for the title and basic narrative of his last book. Some of this literature is alluded to in *Ulysses*, especially in the 'Cyclops' episode, but it appears throughout the *Wake*. It is worth noting that Old Irish epic is not wistful and melancholic as James Macpherson made it in his *Ossian*, or as the Anglo-Irish of the nineteenth-century 'Celtic twilight' took it to be. On the contrary, it is violent, grotesque, full of marvels and giants, even Rabelaisian in the strict sense of the word, and therefore a good model for the burlesque marvels of *Finnegans Wake*.

It is less essential to a Joycean to read much later Gaelic literature or the folklore of Gaelic or even the folklore of English-speaking Ireland, for that matter; these remained outside Joyce's ken. This was perhaps a pity, since Ireland is peculiarly rich in folktale. W. B. Yeats was greatly interested in this fascinating material, but he was himself a complete dilettante in folklore, as Joyce must have suspected. After the Irish Free State came into being the Irish Folklore Commission got to work in a thorough and professional manner, collecting hundreds of stories in Gaelic and English, some of the versions of the folktales being of the highest imaginative order. But this was unfortunately too late for Joyce.

The literary history of Ireland that seriously concerned Joyce was the Anglo-Irish one; that is, the tradition of Irish-born writers in English who had something especially Irish about their talent. For Joyce's purposes this tradition began with Jonathan Swift, Dean of St Patrick's Cathedral, Dublin. Many English critics have failed to mention the peculiar Irishness of Swift, and have preferred to mention him as the greatest satirist in the English language and one of the greatest masters of English prose style. But Swift was Irish by birth and for most of his life by residence. In politics he identified himself closely with the Anglo-Irish ascendancy, the ruling group, which did not always see eye to eye with the English government. In the case of the *Drapier's Letters* Swift was in open revolt against the government, and risked heavy penalties for his courage. But it was not the political side of Swift's Irishness that interested Joyce, nor his pre-eminence as a moral satirist. He admired most the 'Prince of Triflers', the master of verbal clowning, the successor to Rabelais. It was Swift's verbal sophistication, his delight in words, rhetoric and absurd logic that presumably Joyce found especially Irish. The essential work for him was probably not *Gulliver's Travels*, but *A Tale of a Tub*, with its allegorical story of the three brothers (representing the Catholic, Anglican and Dissenting churches), told in a powerful low style, with wonderfully absurd digressions. The 'Oxen of the Sun' section of *Ulysses*, in which Joyce imitates Swift, is very much in the style of the *Tale*: Joyce tells a cock-and-bull story about a Papal and an Irish Bull. Joyce also made use of Swift's 'Polite and Ingenious Conversation', the first collection of the clichés of ordinary talk. Swift's personality and biography also fascinated Joyce, especially the theme of madness; and there are countless references to Stella and Vanessa, the 'little language' of the *Journal to Stella* and even more minute details of Swift's life in *Finnegans Wake*.

In that work Swift is always paralleled to Laurence Sterne, who can just qualify as Anglo-Irish, since he was born in Ireland, of an Irish mother; however, since his father was English and he left Ireland in infancy, his nationality is doubtful. Whether Sterne's love of verbal play and tricks with language derive in any way from an Irish tradition is even less certain than in the case of Swift; it is just possible that he learned something from his mother's or the servants' way of talking. This does not really matter much, since Sterne is very like Swift in his Rabelaisian techniques. He is, of course, a much greater writer of fiction than Swift, and is one of the most subtle technicians of the English novel, still unsurpassed. Sterne's narrative devices are remarkable for the liberties taken with time sequence, and for his elaborate and lengthy digressions; but as R. B. Brissenden has pointed out in *Virtue in Distress*, he is wholly naturalistic as regards his characters:

> [his whimsy] can never result in an alteration in the lives of the
> characters in his book, or an alteration in the nature of the events
> in which they are involved — it can result only in an alteration
> in the manner in which these lives and these events are presented
> . . . Within the confines of the novel Sterne (or Sterne/Tristram)
> never suggests that his characters are fictitious.

He may say absurdly that Walter and Uncle Toby have fallen asleep and he has now a spare moment to write his preface; but he has to wait until they fall asleep of their own accord. He thus solved the problem of making his characters convincing, and I believe that Joyce learned from them. *Ulysses*, especially in the 'Circe' and 'Ithaca' chapters, has a fantastic and digressive structure, but the characters continue to live in solid space and real time, moving at a measurable speed about the streets of Dublin, no matter how wild their thoughts. There is no indication that the characters are not real Dubliners in an historical situation (as some of them were). *Ulysses*, like *Tristram Shandy*, combines satire with sentimentalism: in the midst of an unpleasant or ridiculous world, about which the sharpest comments are passed, Bloom remains a 'man of feeling' in the eighteenth-century tradition, kind to animals, having a kind word for nearly everyone, and carrying on mild flirtations in the spirit of Sterne's *Sentimental Journey*. In Sterne sentimentalism goes with eroticism, and these are both conspicuously missing from Swift, the other great satirical master, but *Ulysses* is a great erotic novel.

Sterne's work is firmly grounded in oratory and the drama, both spheres in which the Irish have always excelled. (*Tristram Shandy* contains notable sermons, like Corporal Trim's Discourse on Mortality, and detailed descriptions of bodily action, closely related to stage acting.) From the eighteenth century onwards many of the best orators in the English language have been Irish, as is pointed out in the notes on 'Aeolus', and it is hard to find any first-rate dramatist since Farquhar who has not been Irish: the line begins with Goldsmith and Sheridan (also an orator), and continues to Shaw, Wilde and O'Casey. The Irish theatrical tradition began its great revival in Joyce's early lifetime. Shaw's first published collections, *Plays Pleasant and Unpleasant*, came out in 1898 when Joyce was sixteen; the pleasant plays including *Arms and the Man*, the unpleasant including *Mrs Warren's Profession*. Shaw raised the level of intelligent discussion in popular drama, and was a clever craftsman; but Joyce did not show any enthusiasm for him as an original artist. Shaw's importance for Joyce was that he introduced him to Ibsen, whom he considered an infinitely greater writer, and even on a level with Shakespeare as a dramatist (if not as a poet). Shaw's little critical work *The Quintessence of Ibsenism* (1891) was possibly more important to Joyce than even Shaw's major plays such as *Man and Superman* (1905). Shaw's most Irish play is *John Bull's Other Island* (1904, Bloomsyear) which was written at the request of Yeats for the Irish Literary Theatre. It is an extremely amusing extravaganza on the theme of the educated Englishman's total inability to understand the Irish; the sensitive Irishman Larry Doyle is shown in conflict with the practical Englishman Tom Broadbent. This play, like Shaw's others, has a witty preface, in this case political, but Joyce does not seem to have been impressed by Shaw's ideas and journalism. He parodies the prefaces in *Finnegans Wake* I.vi, conflating them with the polemical works of Wagner and Wyndham Lewis, which he evidently considered to be equally windy.

Oscar Wilde was only two years older than Shaw but his career was almost over before Joyce's began. Most of Joyce's references to Wilde seem to be polite and even friendly, unlike his comments on Shaw. Homosexuality is quite a large theme in *Ulysses* and *Finnegans*

*Wake* and naturally Wilde appears as the exemplar; Joyce was nervous on this subject but not overtly hostile. Wilde could hardly have been a serious influence on Joyce, except in the writing of epigrams.

In Anglo-Irish literary history the outstanding event of the late nineteenth century is the founding of the Irish Literary Theatre Society in 1901, out of which came the famous Abbey Theatre Company. The leading figure in the theatrical revival was W. B. Yeats, who as well as being a playwright was an energetic organiser and propagandist for the new theatre; slightly less important in the light of history were Lady Gregory, George Moore, Edward Martyn, and the actors William and Frank Fay. Lady Isabella Augusta Gregory (1852–1932) has hardly survived as a playwright, her best-known plays being one-act fillers for the Abbey such as *Spreading the News* (1904, Bloomsyear) and the *Rising of the Moon* (1907). More important at the time were her translations and collections of ancient Celtic legend and folklore, which helped to make Cuchullin and Finn familiar figures of literature. Yeats, for example, drew much of his Celtic material from Lady Gregory, who was both his friend and his patroness. Her country house at Coole Park was a centre for literary men and intellectuals, but not of Joyce's kind. Stephen's attitude to her when talking to Mulligan is irreverent.

The first real work of genius to emerge from the Irish theatre was J. M. Synge's *The Playboy of the Western World* (1907), which caused riots in the Abbey, on the grounds that the play was licentious and 'an insult to Irish womanhood'. Before Bloomsyear Synge had written only *In the Shadow of the Glen* (1903), but he is mentioned in *Ulysses* as an established literary figure, perhaps anachronistically; his magnificent one-act tragedy *Riders to the Sea* came out in 1904, while *Deirdre of the Sorrows* was a posthumous work of 1910. The *Playboy* remains irresistible, perfect in construction and in language.

The second writer of great talent in the Dublin Theatre was Sean O'Casey (1884–1964) who was nearly Joyce's contemporary. He too was a master of language; but instead of drawing his verbal inventions from the speech of the peasantry, as Synge did, he listened to the voices of the Dublin slum-dwellers, among whom he was born. His great work *Juno and the Paycock*, presented by the Abbey Theatre in 1924, is a realistic tragicomedy with a fine flow of low and poetic language. A further notable set of riots in the Dublin theatre was provoked by O'Casey's next play *The Plough and the Stars* (1926), which was felt

33

to offer an unacceptably unheroic view of the Easter 1916 Rising; in fact, O'Casey's account is firmly founded on history.

Both Synge and O'Casey were masters of prose: Synge's sober and careful accounts of poverty in the west of Ireland are extremely moving; O'Casey's autobiography is an over-written, over-ripe rhapsody, which manages to convey a fine sense of what working-class life in Dublin in the early twentieth century was really like.

The only other lasting results of the earlier years of the Irish Literary and Abbey Theatres were the plays of W. B. Yeats, and they have survived as great poetry rather than as actable drama. The first of these was *The Countess Cathleen* (1891), about a lady who sold her soul to the Devil in order to help the starving Irish peasantry; the part was written for Yeats's friend Maud Gonne. As so often in the history of the Irish theatre the literary-critical issue in this play became sidetracked: there was a riot at the first performance caused by pious Catholics, who were scandalised by the playwright's heresy of allowing his heroine's soul to be saved at the end. Later plays by Yeats are *The Land of Heart's Desire* (1894), *Cathleen Ni Houlihan* (a one-acter produced in Bloomsyear) and *Deirdre* (1907); still later symbolist plays were written in imitation of the Japanese Noh plays, beginning with *At the Hawk's Well* (1917). Every single play contains poetry or poetic prose of great beauty, which Joyce must have loved and admired; but it is doubtful if he ever thought of imitating them as plays, since his youthful eyes were so firmly fixed on Ibsen, who was at the opposite pole to the new Irish theatre. The nearest that Joyce approaches to the Yeatsian drama is the 'Circe' chapter of *Ulysses*, which is a kind of symbolic play, but this probably owes much more to Strindberg than to any English or Irish writer.

With the exception of Yeats, the history of Irish poetry is a depressing one. The Irish, despite or perhaps because of their great gifts as orators and dramatists, are not a great nation of poets. Joyce who mocked Thomas Darcy McGee and other once popular poets in *Finnegans Wake* would probably have agreed with that sweeping statement, but he would have made one great exception: he greatly admired the work of James Clarence Mangan (1803-49); although he has written with feeling about this minor poet, his admiration still seems rather mysterious. Most of Mangan's best-known lyrics are given as 'from the Irish' and they are some of the most vigorous versions of Gaelic poetry in the English language, but there is little else to be said for them. Thomas Moore has an honourable place in literary history and wrote beautiful words for music, which Joyce probably greatly valued, but the roll-call of the others is mediocrity itself: Joyce is himself a much better poet than many of his seniors and contemporaries, although he did not claim to be a great poet.

Many of the Irish poets, nevertheless, have been people of interesting personalities or have played significant parts in their country's history. Douglas Hyde, for example, was the founder of the Gaelic League and the first president of the Irish Free State. George Russell (AE) did much for Irish agriculture; Thomas MacDonagh was one of several poets who lost their lives in the Easter 1916 Rising (a highly poetic rebellion); Oliver St John Gogarty, the Buck Mulligan of *Ulysses*, was eminent as surgeon, statesman, wit and autobiographer, and wrote some lively verses; James Stephens, Joyce's contemporary, was an admirable literary man, essayist and fantasist, and Joyce admired his real talent for prose.

Although in the twentieth century, among Joyce's juniors, the general standard has been slightly better, it must be said that the main role of the Irish poets has been to contribute to the great body of nationalist myth which the Irish find necessary for their political existence. Their lyrics and satires are an adjunct to the wonderful folk verse and song in which the Irish popular muse has commented on the political and social situation since the eighteenth century. Some of the best of this literature is to be found in the broadside ballads, especially those composed about the events of 1798. Joyce knew these ballads and other folk and popular verse extremely well, and he quotes from them at length in *Ulysses* and *Finnegans Wake* (see Mabel Worthington and M. J. C. Hodgart, *Song in the Work of James Joyce*, 1959). He valued this material not as a minor contribution to serious literature but as the natural expression of the Irish people — I think that he admired a sentimental patriotic song like 'The Croppy Boy' more than most of the poems of Katherine Tynan or Arthur O'Shaughnessy, and he took the title and main theme of his last book from a nineteenth-century music-hall song called 'Finnegan's Wake'. Both *Ulysses* and *Finnegans Wake* are collections of popular culture, and in the latter Joyce even wrote a parody of a folk song called 'The Ballad of Persse O'Reilly'.

The true greatness of Irish verse begins with William Butler Yeats. Joyce's admiration for Yeats as a complete literary man was almost unbounded, with the exception of probable reservations about his skill as a dramatist. We have to be reminded that the Yeats Joyce knew and admired was not exactly the Yeats of modern literary criticism. Today we think first of all of the late poems, beginning with *The Tower* (1928) and *The Winding Stair* (1929), 'Byzantium' and the 'Crazy Jane' series; but I think that to the end of his life Joyce thought of Yeats primarily as the author of the simple and direct lyrics of *The Wind Among the Reeds* and *In the Seven Woods* (1899 and 1903 respectively). He praised some of these lyrics to Budgen, but never mentioned the later poetry. Joyce believed that poetry should be lucid and musical, and thought that Yeats had one of the finest ears of any poet in the English language, living or dead. For complex structures of meaning and texture prose was the better medium, and Joyce knew that he himself could write that sort of thing better than anyone; but he knew that he could not equal the magical power of Yeats or of Verlaine, another great lyric poet. He apparently knew many poems of the younger Yeats and of Verlaine by heart. Yeats was a subject of pride, for with him a small country suddenly showed that it had a literary culture of the highest class, just as Norway had a few years earlier. Joyce parodies Yeats in *Ulysses* and Stephen and Mulligan make rude comments about Yeats's mannerisms of speech and affected critical opinions; but this mockery is wholly affectionate. Joyce was deeply attached to Yeats as the father of modern Irish literature, and not only as the great poet. He almost certainly admired Yeats's qualities as a prose writer, as shown in his essays *Ideas of Good and Evil* (1903).

It is usual among modern critics to deplore Yeats's occultist ideas, and especially the bizarre philosophical-historical-religious system of *A Vision* (1926), which was supposed to have been dictated to Mrs Yeats from the spirit world by means of automatic handwriting; if this is read at all, it is only for the light that it may throw on the later poems. But Joyce, on the contrary, loved *A Vision*, and quotes it extensively in Book II, Chapter ii of *Finnegans Wake*: he was not at all put out by the lack of science or the quaintness of Yeats's system, since he found it fitted in well with the quasi-occultist, Renaissance speculations in which he had also spent much time — but whether he took it seriously as truth is another matter.

Joyce's ancestors in the field of the novel were not Irish, and not all even English; and I do not think he found much to interest him in Irish fiction, which has an undistinguished history. An exception, which is like that of Mangan in poetry, is his fondness for the works of Joseph Sheridan Le Fanu, whose mystery novel *Uncle Silas* (1864) and supernatural story *The Old House by the Churchyard* (1863) he mentions in the *Wake* in several places. I do not believe that Joyce thought much of George Moore; he mentions him only ironically in *Ulysses*. Moore did, however, import some of the techniques of advanced French fiction into the English language somewhat before Joyce: *Esther Waters* (1894) is the first English 'naturalist' novel, vaguely in the school of Zola, and showing the slight influence of Flaubert, the novelist whom Joyce admired most of all.

In my opinion, the best of Moore is *Muslin*, a story without distinction as fiction but an excellent documentary of the Land League troubles of the 1880s, and which gives an accurate record of the wretched beleaguered existence of the landed gentry. Another excellent documentary study of the whole social spectrum in the late nineteenth century is *The Real Charlotte* by 'Somerville and Ross', the pseudonyms of two county and fox-hunting ladies whose *Experiences of an Irish R.M.* is a set of incomparably funny and convincing sketches of country life in the period.

There is no point in listing the indifferent Irish fiction of the first three decades of this century, which Joyce despised or ignored; but two outstanding works that came out in 1939, just before the outbreak of the Second World War, deserve a mention, because they were the last new works that Joyce is known to have liked. One was Samuel Beckett's *Murphy*, some pages of which Joyce quoted to its author. Joyce's memory was prodigious, but he only used it to the full on authors whom he liked, such as Cardinal Newman. This was therefore a considerable compliment to the young Beckett. (Beckett was never Joyce's secretary, as has sometimes been asserted; but they were very close for several years. Joyce said that he loved him like a son; they would sit together in silence for hours, Beckett grieving over the sorrows of the world, Joyce over his own.) The other new work admired by Joyce was Flann O'Brien's *At Swim-two-birds*, an indescribable work somewhat in the tradition of *Tristram Shandy* and *A Tale of a Tub*. Joyce allowed himself to be quoted in a blurb for this book, saying that it was a truly funny work.

# 4

## Joyce's World

The smallest of the worlds that Joyce inhabited was that of his own body. He was very much interested in this world, to the extent of making *Ulysses* an epic of the body, with a different organ for most of the chapters. He had probably not carried his medical studies very far, but he kept up his interest in physiology, as the 'Oxen of the Sun' chapter shows. Since he was a materialist, he probably did not think of the mind as separate from the body, and according to Budgen he believed that physical appearances and actions provided endless clues to the riddle of human personality. Indeed, *Ulysses* could hardly have been written in the way that it was, with its mass of physical data, unless he held some kind of belief in the interaction of body and mind. It seems appropriate, therefore, to say something about Joyce's physique and health, even at the risk of being speculative.

In the first place, Joyce was an alcoholic. That is a hard word to define: Dylan Thomas once said that an alcoholic was someone you didn't like who drank as much as you did. At least Joyce was a very heavy drinker, and especially of white wine. This had one probable physical consequence that has perhaps never been pointed out. White wine often contains sulphur dioxide as a preservative, a chemical that is an irritant to the stomach; it is often forbidden to people suffering from stomach ulcers. His favourite drink may have hastened on the stomach ulcer that finally killed him. But the mental consequences of alcoholism are more dramatic. One of the odder aspects of Joyce's character is his compulsive jealousy. This is well documented, and is a constant theme in his early letters to Nora; it is also the basis of *Exiles* and a major obsession in *Ulysses*: the plot of Bloom's cuckoldry and the elaborate fantasies of 'Circe' are an attempt to exorcise the demon jealousy. To my surprise, I discovered in a standard work on alcoholism that violent sexual jealousy is a very common symptom.

I do not think anyone knows why this should be so, but there is no doubt about its frequent occurrence. I doubt if Joyce knew the reason for his jealousy, although he knew it to be quite unjustified.

Another and better known symptom of alcoholism is depression, from which Joyce certainly suffered. In his youth he showed great resilience and power of recuperation from his excesses, but in his forties his gloom was prolonged and intense. The writing of *Finnegans Wake* was seriously held up by this depression. Joyce had one objective reason for his mental state, namely his daughter's mental illness, which was a very serious worry. He also suffered great pain from his eyes, and had to undergo many operations in the effort to avoid almost total blindness. But his gloom seems to have gone further than can be explained by these external reasons and to have been highly self-centred. He himself remarked on the gaiety of *Finnegans Wake* in contrast to his personal misery. Although he was perfectly familiar with 'boozer's gloom' and uses that expression, he does not seem to have realised just how much of his misery was probably caused by the poisoning of his system by alcohol.

A third symptom is more recondite. A not uncommon effect of prolonged heavy drinking is verbal hallucination: the patient begins to hear voices that speak intelligibly to him. This has been amusingly and convincingly documented by Evelyn Waugh in *The Ordeal of Gilbert Pinfold*. It is possible that the disembodied voices of *Finnegans Wake* have something to do with this condition. It is not an exaggeration to say that *Finnegans Wake* consists only of voices which confess, plead, lecture, threaten, and partake somewhat of the nature of an hallucination. The same is perhaps true of a more popular work for disembodied voices, Dylan Thomas's *Under Milk Wood*. Thomas, of course, used *Finnegans Wake* to some extent as the technical basis of his radio play; but I think that he also found the form congenial to his alcoholic condition. (Thomas, incidentally, also showed signs of severe depression and sexual jealousy in his letters and poems.) Joyce wrote much of *Finnegans Wake* at night, when he was at least partially drunk. There is nothing unique about that, since Byron claimed that he wrote *Don Juan* on gin. Joyce must be near the head of the list of alcoholic writers, who have been commoner in this century than in Byron's: one thinks of Faulkner, Hemingway and Scott Fitzgerald besides the English writers cited, and many other living writers could be mentioned. There is no evidence, however, of the brain damage suffered by some of the others after many years of drinking: apparently

Joyce's memory, which was one of the most extraordinary ever noted in a writer, remained as good as ever at the end of his life.

Alcoholism is believed to be hereditary to some degree: or at least the sons of alcoholics are more likely to become alcoholics than the sons of moderate drinkers. Joyce's father, although he lived to a ripe age, was certainly a very heavy drinker who did his family great financial harm by his drinking. Extravagance and consequent poverty are probably the worst products of alcoholism: Joyce was saved from the latter by the very generous provision of his patron, Miss Harriet Weaver. Alcoholism also forms part of a cultural pattern: Jews, for example, are little given to it as a community, possibly because as a ghetto people they had to be continually wary and on their guard. Joyce is quite correct in making Bloom a sober man. The Celts, and especially the Irish, are among the most alcoholic of peoples: the pub drinking that goes on in *Ulysses* is not exaggerated. The drinking is heavy in 'Cyclops', at the end of which the drunken Citizen-Cyclops attempts violence; and Stephen gets drunk by the end of the 'Oxen of the Sun' and remains very drunk until the end of 'Circe'.

Joyce sometimes wondered if he were mad; and since he knew he was the author of one of the most eccentric books ever written, this was a reasonable question. He was obviously eccentric in many ways, irresponsible about money, extremely withdrawn from the world. But madness is a legal, not a medical expression; a person is only judged to be mad if he can no longer look after himself or if he insists on inflicting damage on himself or others. There is absolutely no evidence that Joyce was mad in this sense; he always remained perfectly clear-headed and capable of looking after himself. He did not suffer from hallucinations, apart from the possible hearing of voices that I have discussed; and although his depression was sometimes acute, it was apparently not bad enough to warrant his being hospitalised. His daughter did have to be hospitalised, after developing schizophrenia in her early twenties. Her violent and confused behaviour caused her parents great distress; and in addition Joyce must have wondered whether her illness had been inherited from himself, or aggravated by his relationship with her. It was not known in those days that schizophrenia, a fairly common disease of young people, is often caused by a disturbance of the bodily chemistry and can sometimes be cured or the symptoms alleviated by drugs. Miss Lucia Joyce is reported happily cured today, and she could possibly have been cured in a few months of such treatment if it had existed in the 1930s. Many authorities believe that schizophrenia has a physical origin and a physical cure; and is not *caused* by tensions in family relationships. It can, of course, be *aggravated* by family relationships, but so can any other disease or even toothache. There is perhaps no reason to believe that Joyce was in any way responsible for his daughter's condition, although his desperate worrying and fussing may have done something to aggravate it. Joyce lived before the days of Laing; but he would have inferred from what he knew of Freud's teachings that the parent was in some way to blame for his child's psychic state; and like most parents of mentally ill children he felt a huge and quite unjustified guilt. This guilt and misery permeated *Finnegans Wake*: it soon becomes clear to any persistent reader that the book explores his relationship with his daughter, in an attempt to confess and expiate the guilt which he need not have felt. The late Edmund Wilson noted in a review of *Finnegans Wake* when it came out in 1939 that the deepest level of meaning concerns the dreamer's relationship with his daughter — a review which Joyce thought only too sharp-sighted.

Joyce writes extensively about sexual practices, including some that have been classed as 'perversions'; the most striking passages are those which dramatise Bloom's bizarre fantasies, in the 'Circe' chapter of *Ulysses*. It would not be justifiable to identify Bloom with his creator in this respect, although some of Joyce's letters to his wife do show some similarities, with their rich and Rabelaisian elaborations. Joyce was certainly not given to *all* the strange perversions mentioned in the 'Circe' chapter, since it has been shown that many of these were lifted directly from Krafft-Ebing's *Psychopathia Sexualis*. But he is known from the evidence of Budgen and other acquaintances to have been a mild fetishist, preferring women's underclothes to their bodies — a view which is amusingly developed in the fifth chapter of *Finnegans Wake*. This deviation he gives to Bloom, adding, though it is not certain if this corresponded to his own tastes, a certain amount of shoe-fetishism in 'Circe' and 'Nausicaa'. Joyce's letters to his wife show him to have been somewhat masochistic in his fantasies, and this trait Bloom certainly shares with him. Von Sacher-Masoch's novel *Venus in Furs* (which, as the title promises, also describes clothes-fetishism) is quoted extensively in 'Circe' and is also mentioned in *Finnegans Wake*. Bloom's fantasies about submission and humiliation, together with his extreme passivity, are obviously masochistic, but they are presented with such comic genius that they must be read as art and not as documents of an obsession. As for the other sexual themes that appear in 'Circe' and elsewhere in *Ulysses*, such as transvestism, Bloom as the 'new womanly man' and even hints of homosexuality in the lives of Stephen and Buck Mulligan, there is not yet enough evidence to make clear connections between biography and fiction.

We are, however, given some data about Bloom's sexual problems, which may bear on Joyce's. In the first place, he no longer has complete sexual intercourse with his wife Molly; and, which must surely be a related fact, he masturbates on the beach at the sight of Gerty MacDowell's petticoat. He is also carrying on a clandestine correspondence with one Martha Clifford, a typist whom he has never met, and does not intend to meet, but from whose letters he seems to get a kind of onanistic pleasure. Some of this we know to have been based on the mild flirtations the married Joyce carried on in Trieste and Zürich, which are fully recorded by Ellmann. A great deal of *Ulysses* is a half-fictional exploration of the Joyces' married life when they were in their thirties. When Joyce ran away with Nora in 1904 they were passionately and physically in love for several years, as their letters show. But at some time after the birth of their second child the physical side of the marriage (which did not become legal until 1932 but was nevertheless a true marriage) went into eclipse, perhaps temporarily but perhaps for ever. He seems to have lapsed into a vaguely fetishistic, voyeurish, onanistic state of sexual being, which is reproduced in the meandering thoughts and dramatised fantasies of Bloom. *Ulysses* may not be a pornographic book but it is certainly a book *about* pornography, a subject in which Bloom, collector of dirty postcards and reader of sexy novels like *The Sweets of Sin* is deeply interested. The point of pornography is not only that it provides a substitute for sex, but that it may provide an experience that goes beyond ordinary physical sex; a hallucinatory, visionary experience, a voyage into the realms of the forbidden and demonic, analogous to the visions of the 'Circe' chapter. Pornography is therefore mind-blowing, like alcohol and other drugs, and although it may not be absolutely a social evil, there are perhaps good reasons for keeping it under control. *Ulysses* is a valuable textbook on the modes and effects of pornography; but it would be hypocritical to pretend that it does not contain a good deal of straight writing on the pleasures of sex, especially in the last chapter. Molly Bloom is not closely modelled on Joyce's Nora, although he took some turns of speech and vagueness of punctuation from her. She is much more of a sexual symbol than a real person that Joyce knew, although her 'feminine psychology' has been justly praised for its accuracy. Nor is she a projection of Joyce's sexual and marital problems, and to that extent she is outside the orbit of the rest of the book. She is a personification of the Natural. Fetishism and other deviations of the book take a minor place in the last chapter. It is true that a good many sexual practices which have been called perversions appear, such as fellatio and cunnilingus, but in this context these are simply innocent techniques for increasing pleasure. Joyce has tried to make sexual behaviour no longer a cause for anxiety and guilt, and to recreate a vision of the Earthly Paradise.

# 5

## Dubliners

This collection of short stories contains some masterly writing, but some of it at least is apprentice work. Because the stories are fairly easy to understand, they have been seized on by many critics who are unable to cope with *Ulysses* or *Finnegans Wake*; these critics, knowing that Joyce is in some sense a symbolic or allegorical writer, have grossly over-interpreted the simple and sometimes touching pieces of fiction, finding hidden meanings where most likely none were intended. 'The Dead', of course, is an exception, the earliest masterpiece in Joyce's mature idiom. Joyce explained modestly, in a letter to his publisher, what he was trying to do in the book:

> My intention was to write a chapter of the moral history of my
> country and I chose Dublin for the scene because the city seemed
> to me the centre of paralysis. I have tried to present it to the
> indifferent public under four of its aspects: childhood, adolescence,
> maturity and public life. The stories are arranged in this order.
> I have written it for the most part in a style of scrupulous
> meanness.

The style of scrupulous meanness is that employed by Flaubert in parts of *Madame Bovary* and in the short story 'Un Coeur simple' in *Trois Contes*, which Joyce admired almost as much as Flaubert's more romantic style in the *Tentation*. In his adaptation of Flaubertian naturalism Joyce had been anticipated in Anglo-Irish literature by George Moore; but the *Dubliners* stories are mainly based on the techniques invented and perfected by Chekhov.

The first three stories proceed roughly through childhood and adolescence in a kind of autobiography — 'The Sisters', 'An Encounter', 'Araby' — while 'Eveline' is about a girl just emerging from adolescence. The next seven stories are about people in their 'maturity', though few in Joyce's Dublin seem to be properly grown up. After my warning against over-interpretation, I have to admit that these stories may correspond to the Seven Deadly Sins, a not very complicated ironic use of an ethical framework, as follows: 'After the Race' (Pride), 'Two Gallants' (Avarice), 'The Boarding House' (Lechery), 'A Little Cloud' (Envy), 'Counterparts' (Anger), 'Clay' (Greed), and 'A Painful Case' (Sloth). The last four stories, which deal with public life, may be based on the four cardinal virtues: 'Ivy Day in the Committee Room' (Courage), 'A Mother' (Justice), 'Grace' (Temperance), 'The Dead' (Wisdom). Whether this is true or not does not greatly matter: it would only be Joyce amusing himself with an extra layer of irony.

The meaning of Dublin's 'paralysis' has recently become much clearer, thanks to a paper written jointly by a physician and a literary scholar, a kind of collaboration which might prove fruitful in many other literary fields.[1]

'The Sisters' is concerned with a boy's first experience of death, the death of an old priest who has taught him. He hears his elders talking about the priest, how his breakdown is connected with the accidental breaking of a chalice: evidently Father Flynn was mad and paralysed before the end. It seems certain that the kind of physical and mental illness described is 'general paralysis of the insane' or, as it used to be called, 'paresis', a consequence of tertiary syphilis. This is 'softening of the brain', the condition into which Oswald falls at the end of Ibsen's *Ghosts*, but Joyce, with his medical training, is much more precise than Ibsen: there are several precise parallels between Joyce's description and the symptoms of GPI as laid down in a standard textbook, Osler's *Principles and Practice of Medicine* in the edition of 1902, which Joyce might well have read. The last symptom quoted is 'important indications of moral perversion, manifested in offences against decency', which has echoes in the story: 'I wouldn't like children of mine . . . to have too much to say to a man like that.' There is therefore something much more sinister than ordinary paralysis (which usually results from a cerebral haemorrhage) about the old

---

[1] Burton A. Waisbren, MD, FACP, and Florence L. Walzl, PhD, Milwaukee, Wisconsin, 'Paresis and the Priest: James Joyce's Symbolic Use of Syphilis in "The Sisters"', *Annals of Internal Medicine*, vol. 80, pp. 758–62, 1974. I am most grateful to Dr Walzl for sending this paper to me.

priest, and, by extension, the paralysis that affects nearly all the characters in the book and indeed the whole of Dublin is the result of a
moral infection.

Paralysis does affect most of the characters: they are unable to move
out of their social milieu or to take any decisive action to improve
their lot — a condition, it should be remembered, in which the
majority of the human race has always found itself. The stagnation of
Dublin is caused by corrupt politics and British rule ('Ivy Day'), by
nationalism in the arts as well as politics ('A Mother') and above all
by the hold of the Roman Catholic Church ('Grace') — Stephen/Joyce
elaborates on all these forces in *A Portrait*.

'The Sisters' is a beautifully written story which evokes a powerful
atmosphere of piety and decay. Some of the other early stories are
rather slight, for example 'An Encounter', 'Araby' and 'After the
Race' (the weakest of all), but 'Eveline' contains more than meets
the eye. Eveline has at her mother's death been left in charge of the
other children and of her drunken father: her life is boring and oppres-
sive. She meets a young man called Frank who urges her to go abroad
with him to South America where he has prospects. Her father
distrusts the young man, but Eveline loves him and agrees to go with
him. At the last moment, when he is on board the boat and she is at
the quayside preparing to join him, she hesitates and refuses to go,
caught in yet another variety of the Dublin paralysis. At least that is
how most critics, including myself, have read the story until very
recently, when Professor Hugh Kenner put another interpretation on
it. This does not change the accepted view of Eveline's character and
motivation: she is caught in the net of family, and since she does love
Frank the pathos of her situation is real enough. But most readers
have missed the very Joycean irony: she was wrong about Frank, who
has deceived her. There is no reason to take his talk about prospects
and marriage at its face value. If you are unfamiliar with Dublin, you
might think that the boat at the quay is the one that is to take her to
South America; not so, for Atlantic liners sail from Liverpool or other
British ports, not from Dublin. It is likely that, as Kenner explains,
Frank merely wants to get Eveline to go with him to Liverpool or
perhaps London, where he will seduce her and probably abandon her,
as many a smooth-talking rogue has done to many a simple Irish girl.
This reading has been objected to, but it is in accordance with Joyce's
Ibsenic bluff, delivered with the sternest poker face.

Of the stories of 'public life' the funniest is 'Grace'. Mr Kernan, a commercial gentleman, falls drunkenly in a public-house lavatory, injuring himself slightly; in the next episode a group of his friends call on him when he is recovering in bed, headed by the pious Martin Cunningham, an official of the Castle: they tell him that they are going to take part in a 'retreat' (a temporary retirement for the purposes of devotion and spiritual refreshment) for businessmen, and ask him to join them. In the third section, which is quite short, the group are seen sitting in church, where they are sermonised by a popular preacher, one Father Purdon (apparently based on a well-known Dublin priest, Father Vaughan). For the first time Joyce, almost certainly, uses an allegorical framework: the three sections correspond to the three parts of Dante's *Divine Comedy*, the filth of the lavatory representing Hell, the cheerful but edifying conversation with the repentant Mr Kernan figuring Purgatory, and the gathering of the faithful, with the possibility of salvation, representing Paradise itself. The last three books of *Ulysses*, as we shall see, have a similar structure. The chief source of humour in 'Grace' is that almost every fact in the theological discussion is wrong. (I believe that Robert Adams was the first to notice that, as Marvin Magalaner was the first to notice the Dantesque pattern.)

'Ivy Day in the Committee Room' is the first of the stories of public life, and the first in the collection with decided literary merit. It is about an undistinguished event in local politics, a municipal election, which happens to take place on the anniversary of Parnell's death, 6 October, when nationalists wore a leaf of ivy to keep the great leader's memory evergreen. The story sets new standards of naturalism but is also rich with complex symbolic meaning. The long story of Joyce's dispute with the publishers over the text of this story can be followed in Ellmann's edition of the *Letters*, volume ii; they centred on the use of the word 'bloody', as in 'Here's this fellow come to the throne after his bloody owl' mother keeping him out of it till the man was grey' which he altered under pressure to read 'Here's this chap come to the throne after his old mother keeping him out of it till the man was grey', but he did not change the other occurrence of 'bloody' in *Dubliners*. Joyce's appeal to King George V about the passage dealing with his father Edward VII is described in his letter to the newspapers of 17 August 1911, published by *Sinn Fein* and, with the controversial passage omitted, in the *Northern Whig* (Belfast) in the same year. After 'till the man was grey' Joyce added a sentence for the version as finally published: 'He's a man of the world, and he means well by us.' It is hard to say if this was meant to be conciliatory.

The story is presumably intended to be a commentary on the whole of Dublin political life in the early 1900s. It does not describe a particular election, but is based on the experiences of Joyce's brother Stanislaus. The passage from Stanislaus's book *My Brother's Keeper* is worth quoting in full:

> Before I entered the accountant's office, my father was temporarily engaged as election agent and canvasser for a candidate in the municipal elections in Dublin, and I was his clerk. Writing to Jim in Paris, I described the committee room and the people who frequented it just as they appeared in 'Ivy Day in the Committee Room'. The old caretaker and his family woes, Mr Henchy (a sketch of my father toned down to the surroundings), the other canvassers, the unfrocked priest, the wastrel who recites the poem, everything, in fact, except the poem, he got from my letter or from my verbal description when he came home at Christmas. My brother was never in a committee room in his life. I unwittingly supplied all the material for the story except, as I have said, the poem, which strikes a faint note of pathos and saves the story from being cynical. It is introduced in such a way, that as Padraic Colum observes in his preface to the American edition, despite the hackneyed phrases and the tawdry literary graces, one feels in it a loyalty to the departed chief and a real sorrow.
>
> Of all the stories in *Dubliners*, 'Ivy Day' was the one my brother said he preferred. As for my part in it, I had written and spoken of the committee room and its canvassers and callers in a mood of sour disgust. It had never entered my mind that there might be material for a story in all that many-faceted squalor. I thought that not only were those Dubliners below literary interest but even below human interest except for hardened philanthropic societies. Still less had it occurred to me that by making a story of it in a spirit of detachment and in a style of 'scrupulous meanness', one could liberate one's soul from the contagion of that experience and contemplate it from above with tolerance, even with compassion.

That adds weight to the argument that James Joyce was not a satirist in the tradition of Swift and did not feel disgust at any part of humanity.

To return to the historical background, 1902 would seem to be the notional date of the story, the year before King Edward VII's visit to Ireland. Parnell had therefore been dead for eleven years, and the background is the slough of despond into which Irish nationalist politics had fallen after the great split. In 1900 Redmond had been elected leader of the re-united parliamentary party which kept its hold on the electorate: but little of interest to Ireland was taking place at Westminster during the long rule of the Tories. There was a general air of defeatism and cynicism over Home Rule; the Dublin electorate was quietist, and the country people were no longer engaged in militant action over land reform. Radical nationalism was kept alive only by a small group of the IRB (Fenians), by Gaelic Leaguers and Gaelic Athletic Association enthusiasts and by journalists like Arthur Griffith in *The United Irishman* and D. P. Moran in *The Leader*. Hynes belongs to this minority, which Mr Henchy calls 'hillsiders and fenians'. Griffith's periodical *Sinn Fein* did not appear until 1906, in which year the Liberal victory in the general election helped the upsurge of serious nationalism that led to Easter 1916. The political implications of the story are clear: almost every Irishman engaged in Dublin politics is a time-server, a sycophant of the British government; every one is unfaithful to the memory of Parnell. A key passage concerns Edward VII's visit:

— But look here, John, said Mr O'Connor. Why should we welcome the King of England? Didn't Parnell himself . . .
— Parnell, said Mr Henchy, is dead. Now here's the way I look at it.

In this superbly ironical indictment no one is spared, not even the nationalist Hynes: he is a hopeless waster, whose political idealism is spilled out in bad verse. Dublin is the centre of political paralysis. In this election to the office of City Councillor, the Conservatives have withdrawn their candidate and are supporting as the lesser of two evils the Nationalist Tierney, and the Conservative canvasser Crofton has been engaged to work for him — that is sufficient comment on Tierney's brand of nationalism. We are not told what party the rival candidate Colgan belongs to; it is presumably something vaguely Liberal or Labour but fairly innocuous to the Anglo-Irish Ascendancy. The battle is about nothing and will lead to nothing.

The 'plot' could not be simpler, and observes the Aristotelian unities of time and space. There is a desultory conversation between eight persons, centring on the topics of politics and parenthood (old Jack and his son, Hynes's father and son, Victoria and Edward) and ending with the recital of a ludicrous poem. But it is remarkable how many people are brought into the short action, and by the end the stage is crowded with presences. The characters in order of appearance or of being mentioned are as follows:

1 (Present) Old Jack, caretaker; Matthew O'Connor, canvasser; Joe Hynes, journalist; John Henchy, canvasser; 'Father' Keon, occupation unknown; the boy from Tierney's public house; Crofton, canvasser; Lyons, canvasser.

2 (Absent, living) Richard J. Tierney, publican and Nationalist candidate; Old Jack's son; Colgan, bricklayer and rival candidate; King Edward VII; Grimes, voter; Father Burke, nominator; Fanning, sub-sheriff of Dublin; 'a certain little nobleman with a cock-eye' (unidentified); Kavanagh, publican; Cowley, alderman; the Lord Mayor of Dublin; Wilkins, Conservative candidate; Parkes, Atkinson, Ward, voters.

3 (Absent, dead) Larry Hynes, father of Joe Hynes; Jesus Christ; Charles Stewart Parnell; Queen Victoria; Judas.

4 (Mythological or personified) Dublin; Erin; the Phoenix.

There are also references to groups of people and institutions, all absent, such as the Christian Brothers, Freemasons, Dublin Corporation, the Castle (short for the British government in Ireland), 'hillsiders and fenians', the Conservative Party, the Nationalist Party, the Roman Catholic Church and its priests, (living), Jewish priests (dead). Some of the fictional characters have real counterparts, as is usual in Joyce's fiction. Mr Henchy's style of talking is modelled, as we have seen, on that of Joyce's father. Crofton (who with Hynes appears again in *Ulysses*) has been identified by Robert Adams in *Surface and Symbol* (1962). There was a real Royal Exchange Ward and a councillor called Cogan, near enough to Colgan, was elected in 1904. The Lord Mayor whose frugal or plebeian pound of chops is jeered at must have been Timothy Charles Harrington, MP, who held office from 1901 to 1904; he came of humble origins and was a loyal Parnellite. Fanning is the same as the Long John Fanning of *Ulysses*, modelled on Long John Clancy, the sub-sheriff. I mention these trivia because they were the sort of thing Joyce concerned himself with. But whoever the characters may represent, one thing stands out: the absent are more powerful, both politically in real life and symbolically in the story; and the dead are more powerful than the living. The absent and the dead are summoned up like the ghosts in Homer's Hades (perhaps they come to smell the warm Guinness), but they have the effect of reducing the present and the living to the condition of twittering, bat-like shades. The king of the ghosts is Parnell, who ends by dominating the whole scene and all Dublin.

This is Joyce's most moving treatment of the theme of Parnell, who haunted him all his life. The theme can be followed through the Christmas Dinner scene in the *Portrait*, the 'Aeolus', 'Hades', 'Oxen' and 'Eumaeus' chapters of *Ulysses*, and in all parts of *Finnegans Wake*. Joyce early came to identify Parnell, the Uncrowned King of Ireland with Christ the King: each was delivered to his enemies by the treachery of his friends. In his article in the *Piccolo della Sera* of 16 May 1912, 'L'Ombra di Parnell' (that 'shade' again suggests a ghost, as in Yeats's poem about Parnell), he wrote of Parnell's melancholy conviction 'that in his hour of need, one of the disciples who dipped his hand in the same bowl with him would betray him . . . that he fought to the very end with this desolate certainty in mind is his greatest claim to nobility.' Joyce followed a current cliché in identifying Parnell with Moses, as we shall see in 'Aeolus', while the myth of the lost leader who will return from the tomb is developed in 'Hades' and further in *Finnegans Wake*. Joyce's identification of Stephen Dedalus, the ideal Artist, the God of Creation, and Parnell ('indifferent, paring his finger-nails') is crucial in the *Portrait*. One need not suppose that all these associate ideas were in Joyce's mind when he wrote 'Ivy Day', but the notion of Parnell as the Lord betrayed 'to the rabble-rout of fawning priests' is central.

Richard Ellmann notes that, as Joyce hinted, one of the main devices of 'Ivy Day' comes from another story about Christ: Anatole France's 'The Procurator of Judea' describes Pontius Pilate reminiscing to a friend about the days when he ruled Palestine. There is no mention of the obvious subject until at the end the friend asks him if he remembered anyone called Jesus, to which Pilate replies, 'Jesus? Jesus of Nazareth? I cannot call him to mind.' The dead and forgotten Jesus becomes the most important character in the story, since without His presence Pilate himself would be forgotten.

The process by which a dead man takes the centre of the stage and gradually reduces the living to shadows appears again in 'The Dead', where it is used with even greater subtlety and power. Another literary antecedent of 'Ivy Day' can be found in Flaubert. The last sentence — 'Mr Crofton said that it was a very fine piece of writing' —

is modelled on the classic anti-climactic and unemphatic last sentence of Flaubert's 'Herodias' in *Trois Contes*; the Essenes carry away the severed head of John the Baptist — 'Comme elle était très lourde, ils la portaient alternativement.' Hynes's poem, possibly modelled on one written by Joyce's father, is a masterpiece of bathos, a deadly parody of the sentimental patriotism typical of Irish popular verse. Yet it does convey Hynes's genuine feelings, to which the audience cannot help responding, and it sums up the basic themes of the story: Christ, traitors, priests and resurrection 'like the Phoenix from the flames'. Throughout the story the cold and damp of an October evening have been emphasised: the fire of life is almost out. 'Old Jack raked the cinders together'; O'Connor lights his feeble cigarette with an election card; there are only 'a few lumps of coal' for the fire and two candles. Everyone comes in cold, Mr Henchy 'rubbing his hands as if he intended to produce a spark from them'. The fire kindled by Parnell has been quenched: 'Musha, God be with them times!' said the old man. 'There was some life in it then.' The talk circles round bad fathers and errant sons; Parnell, unlike Old Jack, Larry Hynes, or Queen Victoria, was the just and stern parent who could have kept Erin's children in order: 'Down ye dogs!' The characters, especially Mr Henchy, present a microcosm of Irish treachery: each politely agrees with the other to his face, only to turn on him with wit and malice behind his back — a notable Irish trait observed by Bernard Shaw and others. But through the absurdities of Hynes's poem there shines, obscurely but unwaveringly, an image of the heroic and lonely who sacrificed themselves to the cause, to bring about 'the dawning of the day'.

'The Dead'

'The Dead' is Joyce's earliest masterpiece and is one of the greatest short stories in the English language. The first sentence gives a clue as to how it is to be read: 'Lily, the caretaker's daughter, was literally run off her feet.' That is a deliberate misuse of English: poor Lily could hardly have been *literally* run off her feet. Of course, it could be part of her interior monologue: Lily might have said in her own idiom 'Oi was lutherally run off me feet . . .', but this is not continued in the next sentence. So Joyce is telling us *not* to take the story literally: we are therefore to take it symbolically or allegorically, despite its painstaking realism. It is a poetic statement about the power that the dead have over the living, the past over the present, a theme that Joyce had already presented in 'Ivy Day in the Committee Room'. The vehicle for this general theme is a personal statement: Gabriel Conroy, a minor literary man and journalist, is James Joyce as he might have been; Gretta is closely based on Nora, a simple girl from the west where she is said to have been courted by a man who died young. At the end Gabriel is cuckolded (not 'literally') by a dead man: his strange jealousy is modelled on Joyce's. Finally, the story deals with more than Dublin, although like the rest it is set in Dublin. Joyce for the first time is trying to say something important about the whole of Ireland: the east–west axis which is not only geographical but cultural and historical is fundamental to the story.

Gabriel and Gretta Conroy have been happily married for some years, and have young children; in his middle thirties, Gabriel is still in love with Gretta. He is of the Dublin Catholic middle class, a university graduate, an intellectual, with some reputation as a writer; she is a much simpler person, from a west of Ireland, Galway City, background. They go to the annual party of his maiden aunts, the Misses Morkan. There is much eating, drinking and gaiety: Gabriel makes a speech proposing the health of his aunts. Towards the end of the evening Gretta hears a singer called Bartell D'Arcy (a real person) sing a popular ballad about death called 'The Lass of Aughrim'. It is a wintry night, with snow — rare for Ireland. Gabriel and Gretta are staying for the night in a hotel nearby: he is consumed with physical passion, but she is far away from him in thought. Finally she tells him that she has been thinking about the song and about the young man, Michael Furey, who used to sing it, who loved her and died; she then falls asleep. When Gabriel's emotions, a mixture of frustrated passion and jealousy, have calmed, he muses on the subject of death, then falls asleep himself.

The narrative plots the graph of Gabriel's increasing discomfiture and the disintegration of his confidence. He is slightly snubbed by Lily the caretaker's daughter, and more severely put out by Miss Ivors, a nationalistic young woman, clearly a member of the Gaelic League. She tries to persuade him to go with her friends on an excursion to the Aran Islands next summer; when he says that he usually prefers to travel to Europe she quizzes him:

And why do you go to France and Belgium, said Miss Ivors, instead of visiting your own land?

Well, said Gabriel, it's partly to keep in touch with the
languages and partly for a change.

And haven't you your own language to keep in touch with —
Irish? asked Miss Ivors.

Well, said Gabriel, if it comes to that, you know, Irish is
not my language.

Their neighbours had turned to listen to the cross-examination.
Gabriel glanced right and left nervously and tried to keep his
good humour under the ordeal, which was making a blush invade
his forehead.

And haven't you your own land to visit, continued Miss
Ivors, that you know nothing of, your own people, and your
own country?

O, to tell the truth, retorted Gabriel suddenly, I'm sick of my
own country, sick of it!

Because he writes for the *Daily Express* Miss Ivors calls Gabriel
'West Briton', i.e. the Irish equivalent of a non-nationalist Scot or
'North Briton'. This exchange is not wholly serious, but it makes
Gabriel unsure of himself, and no longer proud of his European
sophistication. From then on the evening becomes a disaster for
him. His speech is well received, but even while giving it he thinks
his triumph trivial. Despite the jollity of the evening, which is beautifully described with Dickensian richness, there are sinister undertones:
the conversation keeps drifting towards the subject of death, monks
who sleep in their coffins, Patrick Morkan and his horse and the
like. Inside the house all is solid comfort, food, drink, song and talk
of song; but outside the cold is menacing:

The piercing morning air came into the hall where they were
standing, so that Aunt Kate said: Close the door, somebody.
Mrs Malins will get her death of cold.

After Gretta has evoked the shade of her old suitor Michael Furey
in simple words, Gabriel's thoughts turn towards death, and gradually
the story moves out of naturalism into poetry. He begins realistically
enough:

Poor Aunt Julia! She, too, would soon be a shade with the shade
of Patrick Morkan and his horse. He had caught that haggard
look upon her face for a moment when she was singing *Arrayed
for the Bridal*. Soon, perhaps, he would be sitting in that same

drawing-room, dressed in black, his silk hat on his knees. The
blinds would be drawn down and Aunt Kate would be sitting
beside him, crying and blowing her nose and telling him how
Julia had died.

That is fairly prosaic, in keeping with Gabriel's not highly imaginative personality. But soon it shifts to something very different:

His soul had approached that region where dwell the vast hosts
of the dead. He was conscious of, but could not apprehend,
their wayward and flickering existence. His own identity was
fading out into a grey impalpable world: the solid world itself
which those dead had one time reared and lived in was dissolving
and dwindling.

This interchange of reality between the everyday world of the living
and the world of the dead was to become one of Joyce's greatest
themes, which he had already treated in 'Ivy Day in the Committee
Room' and was to treat more brilliantly in the 'Circe' chapter of
*Ulysses* and throughout *Finnegans Wake*. But Gabriel's vision is not
just of death; he is thinking, not logically, for his mind is getting blurred
with sleepiness, of the *unity* of the living and the dead. The motif
of the snow provides the link here: Joyce is alluding to a very famous
simile about snow in Homer's *Iliad*, which magically stresses the
unifying power of the snow, which covers the whole earth like
a blanket: it falls first on the high mountains, then on the lowlands,
then on the fields and the coastal town of Ionia, finally into the
Mediterranean. So Gabriel thinks of the snow falling over all Ireland,
and unifying the strange land of the west with the familiar cosy
eastern Dublin world. The west, even more than Dublin, is the
territory of ghosts, of myth and legend and old far off unhappy
things; the ancient Gaelic language, which Gabriel has rejected,
has long been spoken by natives almost entirely in the west. The
west is in another sense the land of the dead: to 'go west' is to die.
Ireland is a land of the dead, where the ghosts of the past have a
terrible hold on the living, where tradition leads to bigoted religion
and terrorism. But Gabriel, like his creator, must come to terms
with this Ireland, and must respond imaginatively to Ireland's dead.

The time had come for him to set out on his journey westwards.
Yes, the newspapers were right: snow was general all over
Ireland. It was falling on every part of the dark central plain, on

the treeless hills, falling softly upon the Bog of Allen and, farther
westward, softly falling into the dark mutinous Shannon waves.
It was falling, too, upon every part of the lonely churchyard
where Michael Furey lay buried. It lay thickly drifted on the
crooked crosses and headstones, on the spears of the little gate,
on the barren thorns. His soul swooned slowly as he heard the
snow falling faintly through the universe and faintly falling,
like the descent of their last end, upon all the living and the dead.

# 6

## *A Portrait of the Artist as a Young Man*

The last page gives the dates 'Dublin 1904. Trieste 1914', though in fact Joyce was still completing the *Portrait* in 1915. When it was published in the following year he was still only thirty-four. Therefore the book is a young man's book, in date of composition as well as in subject-matter. It was written slowly, re-drafted, abandoned for several years, and finished in a burst of energy; but in it Joyce is still uncertain as to whether his vocation as an artist has been confirmed. Even at the end he does not know if he will be able to complete a *major* novel of the order of *Ulysses* (which he had already begun). He knows he is capable of writing English prose as well as anyone living; that he had proved to himself with 'The Dead' and the early chapters of *A Portrait*; but there was still a huge gap between brilliant stylist and massive creator. When we meet Stephen again in *Ulysses* he still does not know if he will reach fulfilment as an artist, and this uncertainty persists until the penultimate chapter. So *A Portrait* is a prologue rather than a complete and rounded work, and it is a prologue cast in the form of an Ibsenic tragedy with the dénouement missing and the last act unwritten. It ends with question, hope and prayer.

Ibsen's view of the artist, which Joyce implicitly follows, is that he is a man separated from other men by his vocation, and he must strive to separate himself still further from all ties of family, community, nationality which would hold him to the everyday, bourgeois world. The artist must *transcend* the environment in which his fellow-men are immersed or 'immanent'; he must pursue the truth with the detachment of a scientist. The truth he tells will always be unpleasant to the people, who will persecute him as an 'enemy of the people'; the artist may then become damaged by society and end as a tragic hero, like Oswald, Eilert or almost any of Ibsen's chief characters of the younger generation. But there is a possibility of an even greater tragedy than persecution by society. In breaking the ties of family and ordinary, creaturely affection, the artist may fatally injure a vital part of himself. By denying ordinary affection he may poison the wellsprings of his being, and die as lover, husband or parent; and this will sooner or later entail his death as an artist, before physical death comes on him. John Gabriel Borkmann (an artist in the medium of capitalism and development) is a case in point, but the grandest example is the sculptor Rubek in Ibsen's last play *When We Dead Awaken*, who had paid the price of spiritual death for denying the love of his model Irene. We can be certain that Joyce not only saw this as a major theme in Ibsen, but also took it as a fundamental pattern of life, since in his youthful published essay on *When We Dead Awaken* he wrote with subtlety and at length what I have tried to put crudely and briefly.

It is essential to see that in the Ibsen–Joyce view there is no simple conflict between the artist and society. The artist may be an enemy of the people, but he is also his own worst enemy, and therefore deserves to be the target of his own irony. When Arthur Miller adapted Ibsen's highly political play, he made it into an effective parable about freedom, relevant and stirring, in which Dr Stockmann is a wholly admirable political martyr. But Ibsen's Dr Stockmann is faintly ridiculous as well as heroic, and this is true of most of his other characters: there is no play, even *Rosmersholm*, lacking in cruel irony. This is a pointer to the way we ought to read *A Portrait*. Stephen *is* an heroic figure, forging the uncreated conscience of his race, but he cannot cease to be a creature of his time and place, and that means he is also a rather affected and conceited young provincial, trying to be a colder fish than he can ever be. Joyce tried to hit a balance between self-glorification and self-criticism, and I think that he succeeded in doing so. But he perhaps did not make his attitude clear enough for the majority of readers. Some critics see the book as an expression of self-pity, others, like Hugh Kenner, as a satirical attack on an absurd young man.

On the simplest level, the book is a *Bildungsroman* ('Novel of Education'), which could have been subtitled 'Ireland Made Me'. It is an unparalleled study in the forming of a young man by excessively powerful forces of nationalism and religion. Ireland almost unmade Stephen, by submitting him to the tyranny of these forces, which would have made it impossible for him to write freely. The third part of the book describes how Stephen gradually began to cast off the shackles of Church and State, while remaining for ever a Catholic Irishman. Although the Catholic Church has changed a great deal in the last few years, the book remains the best account of a Catholic education ever written, some say, in any language, and young people from emerging nations have told me that it still speaks very strongly to them; as for example, Egyptians trying to free themselves from the traditions of Islam. Apart from religion and politics, there is a background theme of social pride. Stephen and all his school-fellows are the sons of Catholic gentlemen, some belonging to the small landed gentry but most to the professional and business middle-class. This class had feelings of inferiority *vis-à-vis* the Protestant Ascendancy, which was made up of the greater landed magnates and the top ranks of government, the professions and business; and because of this feeling it had all the greater pretensions to gentility. Simon Dedalus gives his son this advice:

> When you kick out for yourself, Stephen — as I daresay you
> will one of these days — remember, whatever you do, mix with
> gentlemen, When I was a young fellow I tell you I enjoyed
> myself. I mixed with fine decent fellows. . . . We kept the ball
> rolling anyhow and enjoyed ourselves and saw a bit of life and
> we were none the worse of it either. But we were all
> gentlemen, Stephen — at least I hope we were — and bloody
> good honest Irishmen too.

It is for this reason that Stephen had to be educated by the Jesuits and no one else. The Jesuits created at Clongowes Wood a copy of the great Catholic public schools of England, especially Stoneyhurst, which were themselves copies of the Protestant boarding schools of the nineteenth century, apart from their greater emphasis on religious education and practices. They were trying to cater for the needs of the Catholic middle class, and train up by a Spartan regime of games and classics a new ruling class. Belvedere College was a cheaper version of the same thing, created for the Dublin middle class who could not quite afford boarding school fees. The rest of the nation's boys who got beyond primary school were looked after by the socially less gifted or ambitious teaching orders of the Church, especially the worthy Christian Brothers:

I never liked the idea of sending him to the christian brothers myself, said Mrs Dedalus.

Christian brothers be damned! said Mr Dedalus. Is it with Paddy Stink and Micky Mud? No, let him stick to the Jesuits in God's name since he began with them. They'll be of service to him in after years. Those are the fellows that can get you a position.

And they're a very rich order, aren't they, Simon?

Rather. They live well, I tell you. You saw their table at Clongowes. Fed up, by God, like gamecocks.

At this point in his autobiography Joyce is lying: he actually did go to the Christian Brothers for a few months' schooling when his father could no longer afford to send him to Clongowes. Joyce did not mind confessing to his going with prostitutes at a tender age, but he did mind the shame of Micky Mud. To that extent he shared his father's pride, even though he was aware that his father and many other would-be Irish gentlemen like him were hopelessly vulgar. The idea of the gentleman remained purely Platonic, yet it was one to which Joyce was always attracted. His father's absurd snobbery is transmuted into the élitism of the intellectual prodigy. The principal subject of Joyce's work is vulgarity in its infinite comic variety: nearly all of *Dubliners* and half of *Ulysses*, including the last chapter, is about vulgarity, which Joyce loved deeply as a spectacle, but detested as a way of life that he himself was capable of leading.

One of Joyce's greatest discoveries in the *Portrait* was the modulation of style. He put his tremendous gifts for parody to service by writing each section in a different style, each appropriate to the stage of his hero's development. This is obvious in the first chapter, written in baby-talk; it is less obvious in the later sections, which some readers have imagined to be written in Joyce's mature style. The first chapter, in which Stephen is ill and in the sickroom at school, is written mostly in a naïve style suitable for a little boy, but the end of the sickroom episode shows a brief advance in maturity: 'And he saw Dante in a maroon velvet dress and with a green mantle hanging from her shoulders walking proudly and silently past the people who knelt by the waters' edge.' It seems that this is a true vision of Parnell's death, which must have taken place exactly at that time, before Stephen could have read or heard of it; and so the boy artist must have real visionary powers, and the premonition of the grand style is appropriate.

The next section, describing the Christmas dinner and the quarrel between Mr Dedalus and Dante, is flat reporting: it derives its energy only from the wonderful dialogue, which the little boy may be supposed to have remembered verbatim. The last section of the first chapter, although it centres on the important theme of justice (Stephen is unjustly beaten and has the courage to complain to the rector-headmaster), is told in the style of a schoolboy's story: 'And they gave three groans for Baldyhead Dolan and three cheers for Conmee and they said he was the decentest rector that was ever in Clongowes.'

The second chapter which traces the growth of the boy's imagination, shows a gradual though not regular evolution of style, and culminates in a romantic-erotic prose in the scene where he goes with the prostitute: this roughly corresponds to the kind of immature erotic fiction which the boys would then be reading secretly. In the next chapter, the tremendous sermon on hell, which scares Stephen nearly out of his wits, is a magnificent piece of rhetoric, but is still not mature: Joyce did not think that the Christian religion, however rich in rhetoric and poetry it might be, was productive of or representative of mature art. There is something childish, in Joyce's view, about all that hell-fire and damnation, a myth used to terrify the young and impressionable. After his repentance Stephen thinks of becoming a priest: now the style takes on the tones of Cardinal Newman's prose, of which Joyce remained a great admirer all his life. But he rejects the false religion of Christianity for the true religion of art: he will become a priest of the eternal imagination. In the scene on the beach, when a girl becomes a symbol of his new-found religion, the style parodies Pater and other writers of the late-nineteenth-century aesthetic movement, without ceasing to be beautiful in itself.

The episode at the University, with long discussions on aesthetics between Stephen and his friends, is written in imitation of late-nineteenth-century naturalistic fiction; the dialogue is more or less modelled on Ibsen. A great deal of criticism and scholarship has been expended on Stephen's theories of art, allegedly based on Aquinas. This has been largely a waste of time, since the theories do not represent Joyce's mature views on art, as they have sometimes been held to be, but are just the kind of thing that an intelligent undergraduate of that background and period would be likely to produce. At one point Stephen plagiarises Ruskin without acknowledgment, which is exactly what such a young man would do: 'These forms are: the lyrical form, the form wherein the artist presents his image in immediate relation to himself; the epical form, the form wherein he presents his image in immediate relation to himself and to others; the dramatic form . . .', etc. I do not propose to discuss Stephen's exposition of Aquinas ('Three things are needed for beauty, wholeness, harmony and radiance') since his theories have little bearing on Joyce's mature art. The second-to-last chapter, in which Stephen discusses religion with Cranly, is almost pure dialogue in the Ibsenic vein; while the very last, ostensibly extracts from Stephen's diary, is in fact a transcript of his stream of consciousness like the first chapter of *Ulysses*. It is quite likely that this chapter was written after Joyce had begun *Ulysses*, when he had been encouraged to complete the abandoned *Portrait*.

Like *Ulysses*, the *Portrait* uses a variety of styles, one modulating into the other; and like *Ulysses*, it employs a number of central or 'pillar' symbols, though not of course in such density. The principal symbol is again Joyce's hero, Charles Stewart Parnell: here he appears not so much as Moses as Lucifer, who fell from grace. Parnell's fall and death are most important in the early chapters, where he is overtly discussed, but Lucifer remains throughout. Joyce develops the Romantic notion of the artist as a rebel against society and then against God Himself; hence the adolescent Stephen defends and identifies himself with Byron, one of the first Satanist rebels among poets. But Lucifer incongruously means the 'light-bearer', and his fall in Milton is from light into darkness. Joyce takes the derivation literally and makes the 'fall' of the artist one from darkness into light. It is in fact a negative fall, which means an escape and flight upwards. This is the myth associated with Stephen's strange surname, Dedalus (in Greek Daidalos): this artist-hero–demigod, the 'old artificer' built the labyrinth of Crete but contrived to escape from it by inventing wings and flying out of the maze. His son Icarus also flew but his wings failed and he plunged to his death. This is the question left unresolved at the end of *A Portrait*: will the young hero prove to be a creative artificer or will he die with his promise unfulfilled?

The labyrinth is, first and almost literally, the slums of Dublin itself: 'He had wandered into a maze of narrow and dirty streets.' (Dublin is in fact a city of fine and large streets, but the prostitutes' quarter, to appear again in *Ulysses*, serves very well as a symbol of confinement.) Second, the labyrinth is the symbol of all the forces that confine the artist, of nationality, religion and family. He must reject all these and fall upwards into life, even though his flight will be dangerous: 'It was folly. But was it for this folly that he was about to leave the house of prayer and prudence into which he had been born and the order of life out of which he had come?' A labyrinth is a network of passages, and nets of religion and patriotism hold down the aspiring artist. He must go into exile, and exile will mean the solitude of the damned; but in 'silence, exile and cunning' he will create himself as an artist.

These themes are reinforced by a chain of poetic imagery, sometimes open and sometimes concealed. When the priest talks to Stephen about a possible calling to the Church, he stands 'in the embrasure of the window, *his back to the light*, leaning an elbow on the brown crossblind . . . the priest's face was a total shadow, but the waning daylight from behind him touched the deeply grooved temples and the curves of the *skull*.' (my italics) Although Stephen has not decided this consciously, he will soon know that for him Christianity is the religion of death (the priest also makes a hangman's knot out of the blind-cord) and he must not conform. The imagery is here proleptic and functional, as the images of birds and flight that appear throughout. The meaning of the last symbol in the book is not revealed until well on in *Ulysses*: Stephen is also the young Siegfried, according to Wagner himself the type of the young artist-rebel, who must reforge the fragments of his father's sword *Nothung*, or Needful, which must stand him in good stead in his fight against the dragon. He is leaving 'to forge in the smithy of my soul the uncreated conscience of my race. *April 27*: Old father, old artificer, stand me now and ever in good stead.'

# 7

## *Exiles* and Other Works

*Exiles*, Joyce's only play (1918), is a tribute to his great master Henrik Ibsen, and an exploration of his marital problems. Beyond that, there is not a great deal to say: although it is occasionally performed on the stage, it lacks dramatic force and literary charm. The most interesting part of the edition of 1952 consists of the comments, in some 4,000 words, that Joyce wrote on his own play, in a notebook unpublished until then. These notes reveal many of Joyce's ideas about women, which were to find richer expression in *Ulysses*, and about the artist's relationship with society. Richard Rowan is an imaginary portrait of the artist returned from exile to a job in Dublin (which Joyce thought of doing but did not). He has brought back with him Bertha, the young woman he eloped with almost a decade earlier, still unmarried; in some ways she is a portrait of Nora. He half falls in love, unless that is too simple a term for the relationship, with an educated young woman called Beatrice, while Bertha attempts a love affair with Richard's old friend Robert Hand. When he finds out about this Richard's jealousy is acute, but at the same time he seems to want to share his partner with another man. This theme is further pursued in *Ulysses*, where Bloom hints more than once that he would like to share his wife. After many masochistic complications Richard and Bertha are reconciled in the end; her last words are:

> 'Forget me, Dick. Forget me and love me again as you did the first time. I want my lover. To meet him, to go to him, to give myself to him. You, Dick. O, my strange wild lover, come back to me again!'

The elaboration of these words in the last passage of *Finnegans Wake* is much finer. There they are combined with operatic arias of death scenes, in the final monologue of the old woman-river. Evidently

Joyce still treasured at least one part of *Exiles*, even though he must have known that it was a failure as drama. Its greatest weakness is that it lacks humour, and Joyce's greatest achievements are all humorous. More interesting than the play are the author's notes, possibly not intended for publication, but now printed in about a dozen pages at the end of the 1952 edition. These are mainly of biographical interest, and point to the close identification of Joyce with Richard: but they also suggest a long unwritten novel about the female psyche; fortunately Joyce abandoned this and invented Molly Bloom instead.

Another autobiographical work, committed to a notebook but again possibly not intended for publication, is *Giacomo Joyce*, written about 1914 and recording his unfulfilled love for a Jewish girl, one of his language pupils in Trieste. I find this much more attractive than *Exiles*, partly because it is ironic and witty, and partly because it is written in the elaborate and highly finished style of the early chapters of *Ulysses*, with which it is probably contemporary. Joyce even used some of the paragraphs and phrases in *Ulysses*: this evocation of the Elizabethans is very like some of the pseudo-Shakespearean writing of 'Scylla and Charybdis': 'Here are wines all ambered, dying fallings of sweet airs, the proud pavan, kind gentlewomen wooing from their balconies with sucking mouths, the pox-fouled wenches and young wives that, gaily yielding to their ravishers, clip and clip again.' Another passage reappears in Stephen's meditations, transferred to Paris: 'Belluomo rises from the bed of his wife's lover's wife; the busy housewife is astir, sloe-eyed, a saucer of acetic acid in her hand.' There is no continuous narrative: the work is better described as a sequence of prose-poems. The presence of the lady, rich, frail and shy, is delicately but firmly suggested; her admirer Giacomo emerges as a poet in his early thirties, erudite and oblique, *irlandese italianato*, incarnate Lucifer in rebellion against a libidinous and epileptic lord and giver of life, a Renaissance soul in a Prufrock coat. Most of the text is quoted in Richard Ellmann's biography, but it was also published complete in 1968, with introduction and notes by Ellmann.

There are many writers, the most recent of whom is D. H. Lawrence, whose letters are themselves works of art; but Joyce is unfortunately not one of them. His correspondence is most valuable when he is explaining chapters of *Ulysses* to Frank Budgen or of *Finnegans Wake* to Miss Harriet Weaver: these explanations are only too few and too short, but they give by far the best clues as to what Joyce was about, and I have used them frequently in this commentary. The other letters are chiefly of biographical interest, but of two very different kinds. The later letters are usually about Joyce's personal miseries — his endless trouble with his eyes, the anguish of his daughter's mental illness, the endless negotiations over the publication of *Ulysses* in America and England. There are occasional flashes of humour, but it would be wearisome to reread most of them. The early letters, up to about 1912, are very different. Those to his brother Stanislaus are intellectually vigorous, and from them various stages in the composition of the *Dubliners* stories can be traced. The letters to Nora Barnacle are the most extraordinary in the whole collection, especially those written in 1909 when he was temporarily parted from her and visiting Dublin on business. He had not been there long before his false friend Vincent Cosgrave told him that Nora had been unfaithful before they had left Dublin in 1904: Joyce believed this lie and wrote back bitter accusations to Nora. The tone of these is extremely cruel and unpleasant; Nora replied with simplicity and dignity, protesting her innocence, but also threatened at one point to leave him. Eventually Joyce was mollified and then he began to write extremely sentimental letters to Nora. He identified her with Gretta in 'The Dead', but whereas the handling of emotion in the *Dubliners* story is beautifully controlled, in the letters it is crude and distasteful. The alternation between cruelty and submissiveness, to the point of overt masochism, is a striking clue to Joyce's personality, but the letters showing it add little or nothing to literature. After a while sentimentality turns into sensuality, and Joyce writes a set of highly erotic letters, urging Nora to reply in the same vein. Some of these are almost literature, since Joyce could not help being funny on any subject. When he is Rabelaisian in the strict sense, describing sex and other bodily functions without restraint, he anticipates some of the comic effects of *Ulysses*, approximating to Bloom's fantasies in 'Circe'. But the 1909 set of letters as a whole is unpleasant. I first read these in the Cornell university library, where many of Joyce's papers are kept: at that time (1961) they could not be printed, but since then the ban has been lifted. Joyce's letters were first edited very badly by Stuart Gilbert in a one-volume selection (1957); most of the extant letters not contained in Gilbert's volume were edited by Richard Ellmann in two more volumes (1966): these contained most of the 1909 letters, but not all of the most offensive ones. The missing ones are given in Ellmann's recent *Selected Letters of James Joyce*, so that there is no longer any mystery about this aspect of Joyce's emotional life.

Great writers often indulge, to a greater or lesser degree, in literary criticism which though it may not be systematic or scholarly is nevertheless highly valuable for the light it shows on the writer's intuitions and perceptions. Again Lawrence is a good example, and again Joyce is the exception. He began brilliantly with the essay on Ibsen of 1900 of which the Master approved, but thereafter did only a small amount of lecturing and journalism, and even this activity ceased in his thirties. None of the articles and lectures that have survived (apart from the Ibsen one) is of great interest. An article on Parnell, which cannot be called literary criticism, is profoundly felt and explains much of the symbolic importance of Parnell in 'Ivy Day in the Committee Room', *A Portrait* and the later works. This article should be read by everyone who seeks understanding of Joyce. Of the other pieces in the 'collected criticism', edited by Ellmann and Mason, the best is a prose-poem in the style of the *Wake*, a tribute to the Irish tenor Sullivan called 'From a Banned Writer to a Banned Singer'. There are dozens of operatic allusions in it, not too difficult to work out, and it is a good practising ground for those who want to decipher *Finnegans Wake*, as well as possessing wit and charm of its own.

There is a very funny piece of light verse about Ibsen's play *Ghosts*: the ghost of Captain Alving comes forward when the curtain has fallen and gives his explanation of the play, both ribald and profound. This, like all Joyce's other pieces of light verse such as his satire 'The Holy Office' is masterly. Joyce is also a *prose* poet of the highest order, whose art reached its culmination in the last passage of *Finnegans Wake*. But his serious verse, published in *Chamber Music* and *Pomes Penyeach*, has never received critical acclaim. These few dozen short lyrics are tenuous and delicate, but seem to be lacking in intellectual content, and to be at the opposite pole from the poetry of Joyce's near-contemporary T. S. Eliot. 'A flower given to my daughter' is an expansion of two sentences in the *Giacomo Joyce* notebook:

Frail the white rose and frail are
Her hands that gave
Whose soul is sere and paler
Than time's wan wave.

Rosefrail and fair — yet frailest
A wonder wild
In gentle eyes thou veilest,
My blueveined child.

That is hardly more striking than the original: 'Frail gift, frail giver, frail Blue-veined child.' 'Sere', 'paler', 'wan' are cliché adjectives, such as Joyce would normally use in one of his parodies. It seems likely that this and most of the other lyrics were written, not to record significant personal experiences, but to satisfy Joyce's love of song and singing. He was particularly fond of the uncomplicated melodies of the Elizabethans, the 'airs' of Dowland and Campion, in which there is a highly intimate relationship between words and music. I believe that he hoped some composer would set his lyrics for single voice and accompaniment, preferably on the lute or another traditional instrument revived by Dolmetsch. Many composers, of course, have been attracted to these poems: the *Joyce Book*, a tribute to the Master edited by Herbert Hughes and published in 1932, included settings by Antheil, Bax, Bliss, van Dieren, Goossens, Howells, Hughes, Ireland, Moeran, Albert Roussel and Sessions. Unfortunately none of these is a composer of the first rank, with the possible exception of Roussel, who in fact set 'A Flower Given to my daughter'. There was no English composer of the epoch equal to Fauré or Debussy, who left such perfect settings of Verlaine's poems; the nearest was the younger Vaughan Williams, whose *On Wenlock Edge* seriously rivals Ravel, and it is a pity that he was not drawn to Joyce as well as to Housman. The best settings so far are probably those by the American Samuel Barber: his version of 'I hear an army' is highly successful. I am not suggesting that Joyce the lyricist should be taken as seriously as Verlaine or even Housman; but if his verse is placed in this musical context, it becomes much more significant.

# 8

## *Ulysses*

*Ulysses* is above all a great comic novel. The reader who does not find the adventures of Mr Bloom funny will be well advised to leave the book alone. It is also touching, even sentimental, bawdy and satirical. This combination of qualities, which is also found in Sterne, is repulsive to some readers, but highly attractive to others; fortunately I find myself among the latter, for *Ulysses* has added more to my enjoyment of life than any other book of this century. The notes on the book's chapters that follow may seem to be inconsistent with this view, since they are detailed, schematic and in places, I fear, pedantic. But that is partly Joyce's fault, since as well as being a great humorist *he* is obsessed with minute details, schematic and, at times, pedantic. To begin with the schematic: every chapter has its own title (which Joyce suppressed on publication), its own hour of the day, dominant colour, Homeric correspondences, technique, science or art, allegorical sense, organ of the body and set of symbols. In 1920 Joyce sent his first schema with all these things in it to Carlo Linati; he then revised it slightly after 1921 and circulated it privately among a few critics, finally authorising its publication in Stuart Gilbert's *James Joyce's Ulysses* (1930). These schemata must be the starting point for all readings of *Ulysses*, and my notes in the following pages are largely elaborations of Joyce's own hints about the symbolism and imagery of each chapter.

One of the difficulties in approaching the book is to see it as a whole, over and above the multitudinous details. Here again Joyce's own comments are the most helpful. He wrote to Linati that *Ulysses* was the epic of two races (the Jews and the Irish), the cycle of the human body, and a kind of encyclopaedia; and to those aspects of the book I shall return. He did not mention the most obvious fact about the book, namely that it is his autobiography in a thin covering of fiction. The

continuation of *A Portrait of the Artist as a Young Man*, *Ulysses* presents
a day in the life of Stephen Dedalus, not much older than when we
last saw him; and of Leopold Bloom, an ironic self-portrait of the
artist as a middle-aged man, husband and father.

Bloom and his wife Molly are purely fictional characters, although
Joyce used something of his wife Nora for Molly, but everyone or
almost everyone else in the book is real or closely based on a real
person. Like *A Portrait* it is highly structured autobiography, but more
heavily disguised by parody, outright fantasy, and digressions. Because
Bloom is so inferior to Stephen and to his creator in literary and
philosophical culture, it takes some time and effort to understand that
in all the essentials of his emotional life, and even in his fondness for
pseudo-scientific general knowledge, he really is Joyce himself.
Stephen is still Joyce as a young intellectual of immense promise, but
one who has not yet created anything of value, and fears that he may
never do so. Before Joyce could become a creator, he had to pass
through the major experience of falling in love with a mature woman
and becoming a spouse and father. Of course, nothing of the sort
happens literally to Stephen in the narrative of *Ulysses*. Even his
meeting with Bloom is short, their conversation perfunctory. Nevertheless the experience necessary for becoming a creator is passed
symbolically from Bloom to Stephen, and that is sufficient. All men
are sons and most men are fathers at some time in their lives; the mature
man is he who discovers the son and the father inside himself.

Despite his oddities and anomalous position of being one of the few
Jews in Dublin, Bloom is Everyman, and meant to be a universal
figure: hence the great emphasis throughout the book on the human
body and all its processes. But Stephen is not an Everyman: he is a
very rare kind of person, a potential creator of art. Artistic creation is
a major theme of the book, and is presented, I believe, in religious
terms. The Holy Ghost, Who descended at Pentecost and made men
speak with tongues, is the symbol of artistic and literary creation; and,
as I shall try to show, the story illustrates the relationship between
God the Father (Bloom), and God the Son (Stephen) who must in
some sense be united before the Trinity is completed by the Holy
Ghost and the miracle of creation can begin. I must admit that this
interpretation of *Ulysses*, and the view that there is a Biblical story
corresponding to every chapter, is somewhat controversial.

That there are correspondences with the Homeric epic of Odysseus
is, of course, not a controversial view, since Joyce made this clear from

the start. He indicated the chapter titles in the Linati scheme, but cut them out of the text before publication. He chose Odysseus as the archetype of his hero, because he too is a kind of Everyman. Joyce told Frank Budgen (who quotes him in *James Joyce and the Making of 'Ulysses'*) that Ulysses was his 'complete man in literature', more so than Hamlet, who is only a son:

> Ulysses is son to Laertes, but he is father to Telemachus, husband to Penelope, lover of Calypso, companion in arms of the Greek warriors around Troy, and King of Ithaca. He was subject to many trials, but with wisdom and courage came through them all. Don't forget that he was a war dodger who tried to evade military service by simulating madness. He might never have taken up arms and gone to Troy, but the Greek recruiting sergeant was too clever for him, and, while he was ploughing the sands, placed young Telemachus in front of his plough. But once at the war the conscientious objector became a jusqu'auboutist. When the others wanted to abandon the siege he insisted on staying until Troy should fall.

The hero of the *Odyssey* is in fact very different from the Odysseus who appears in the *Iliad* as one of the warrior chieftains, just as the tone and narrative technique of the *Odyssey* is different from those of the *Iliad*. The *Odyssey* is much more of a domestic than a heroic poem, and it presents Odysseus and his family in a fairly realistic way. But it combines a kind of realism with extremely fantastic episodes, which are based on ancient European folktales about cannibals and witches. The first four books are called the Telemacheia, describing Telemachus at home in Ithaca, persecuted by his mother's suitors; this is followed by his journey to the mainland in search of news about his father. Most of this is realistic, except for the narration of the tragic story of Agamemnon, which is its first appearance in literature. The next eight books describe the wanderings of Odysseus, from his departure from the nymph Calypso's island to his arrival at the palace of Nausicaa and her father; there Odysseus recounts his adventures over the twenty years since the fall of Troy. The encounter of the shipwrecked and naked hero with the princess Nausicaa is realistic enough, but the stories of Polyphemus and Circe are not intended to be anything but marvellous. The last twelve books are called the Nostos, or home-coming, and tell how Odysseus against terrible odds won back his kingdom: these books are partly domestic-realistic, as in the famous encounter with the old nurse, and partly in the epic mode, as in the description of the shooting contest and the fighting. Joyce follows this plan, with considerable modifications. His first three chapters, before Bloom appears, correspond to the Telemacheia, and the last three to the Nostos, roughly in sequence. The central chapters, which make up his second 'Book', are based on the wanderings of Odysseus but in a different order from Homer's. The most fantastic episodes in Homer are treated by Joyce in the most fantastic manner, using parody, hyperbole, dreams and visions; this reaches a climax in the 'Circe' chapter, which forms the end of Book II.

Since *Ulysses* contains so much fantasy it cannot be taken literally. Yet realism does appear in some of the book's levels: first, in the minute descriptions of Dublin, its buildings, streets, the conversation of its citizens and so on; and secondly, in the 'interior monologue' of Stephen, Bloom and Molly, which gives the illusion of psychological reality. In fact this 'stream of consciousness' is highly structured and full of symbolism; far from having the random nature of ordinary thought, everything is carefully arranged, but the arrangement is concealed by an ingenious pretence of free association. The creation of this illusion is perhaps Joyce's greatest technical feat: as the reader becomes immersed in the ruminative flow of Bloom's thought he may have a complete suspension of disbelief and imagine that he is really entering another mind.

Despite the brilliant psychological realism, Bloom does not become a 'real' character: he is too much of a composite of the early-middle-aged Joyce and a stock comic figure of a Jew. Joyce certainly did much research into Judaism and Zionism, and observed the traits of Jewish friends and acquaintances; he is careful to note Jewish family feeling and paranoia ('When in doubt persecute Bloom'), but I do not believe that any Jewish reader is convinced by the authenticity of this hero. There is an approximation to realism, achieved only by the piling on of historical detail. Rather than think of Bloom as a real Jew, it is better to follow Joyce's lead and think of the book as an epic of the Jews and the Irish, who are people with a similar history of oppression, a theme which is worked out most fully in the 'Cyclops' chapter. In 'Aeolus' and elsewhere in the book Charles Stewart Parnell appears as the Irish Moses, leading his people out of the Egyptian bondage towards the Promised Land of Home Rule. This theme is filled out with an enormous mass of historical detail on the Irish side: Joyce shared his countrymen's obsession with the minutiae of centuries of grievances. When Joyce called his book an encyclopaedia, he meant that it was chiefly an historical encyclopaedia, and this is perhaps the hardest part for a non-Irish reader to follow. The abundance of popular science and general knowledge, which reaches an absurd climax in the 'Ithaca' chapter, is much easier to understand and consequently much funnier. You have to know quite a lot of Irish history to follow the comic inaccuracy of Mr Deasy in the second chapter and of the Cyclops-Citizen. It is also an encyclopaedia of Dublin topography, with which Joyce was also obsessed; but this does not present the reader with too many difficulties, although for a full understanding it is better to follow Mr Bloom's wanderings on the site.

When Joyce said that his book presented the cycle of the human body, and in the chart named a different organ for each chapter, he had, I think, one principal purpose. He wished to make the creatures of his imagination as *creaturely* as possible, that is, as much like God's own creatures in their mortal integuments as is possible in the artistic medium of words. He therefore shows the shining intellect of Stephen and the immortal spirit of Bloom in their fleshy and transient vessels: mind and body are inextricably linked as they are always in the real universe and hardly ever in fiction. The references to bodily processes are dense and systematic, from Bloom's eating and defecating on his first appearance to Molly's urination and menstruation at the end. This is not meant to be disgusting, although there is always some irony and mockery. There is of course a good deal about sex in *Ulysses* and I suppose some of this could be called pornographic technically in that it might tend to increase sexual desire (just as Bloom's hunger tends to increase hunger in the reader). But sex takes place as just one of the bodily functions, and not, as for example in D. H. Lawrence, as a pre-eminent experience of mystical value.

In the commentary on the several chapters that follows, these points are explained. Each chapter can be taken as a complete prose-poem, which is organised like a tone-poem by Richard Strauss or Schoenberg. In each there are the *leitmotifs* of colour, organ, symbol, etc. undergoing continuous transformations to produce a satisfying imaginative unity. But in addition there are *leitmotifs* running through-out the whole book, like those that run throughout the whole of Wagner's *Ring*. Some of these are Homeric and Biblical but not all are: quotations from Mozart's *Don Giovanni* hint at Bloom's cuckoldom, quotations from *Hamlet* adumbrate the father–son theme; eventually in 'Circe' hundreds of earlier phrases are recapitulated, in dramatic form. The best way of getting to know the inner structure of *Ulysses* is to note in the margin the references to pages where phrases are repeated. Gradually one learns the point of the repetitions, as one learns the motifs of the *Ring*. Although it would be idle to maintain that *Ulysses* is a masterpiece of form — it is still a loose and baggy monster like all long novels — nevertheless these repetitions do give the narrative a degree of coherence.

Finally, *Ulysses* has a moral theme, which is fairly deeply concealed at first and is only fully revealed in the last chapter. The moral of the book is the rejection of violence, whether the violence of Fenian terrorism or that of Don Giovanni's *machismo*. Bloom, for all his imperfections, is at length praised as the ideal non-violent man.

I.i. 'Telemachus'

It is 8 a.m. on Tuesday 16 June 1904, at Sandycove, on the coast a few miles south of Dublin. Stephen Dedalus is sharing the Martello Tower (built during the Napoleonic Wars and still extant today as a Joyce Museum) with Malachi 'Buck' Mulligan, a medical student; they have as a guest a visiting Englishman called Haines. Mulligan shaves, teases Stephen about his gloomy behaviour, and begins his stream of blasphemous witticisms. They have breakfast, say a few words to an old woman who delivers their milk, and set out for Dublin. Mulligan goes for a swim, but Stephen never bathes: it is unnecessary, he says, since 'all Ireland is washed by the Gulf Stream'. Stephen's interior monologue is as gloomy as his appearance, since he is thinking a great deal about his mother's recent death. The ruling art of this chapter is theology, and Stephen's theological speculations centre on heresies about the Trinity, that is about the relationship of God the Father to God the Son. He is a son in search of a spiritual father, just as Telemachus is in search of his father Odysseus. In Book I of the *Odyssey* Telemachus is threatened by the suitors of his mother Penelope, the chief of whom is Antinous. The goddess Athena appears in disguise and advises him to go on a journey to seek his father. The Homeric correspondences in this chapter are not very important, apart from the identification of characters: Stephen is Telemachus, Mulligan is Antinous, the milk-woman is Athena. But the theological correspondences are very important: Stephen is Jesus at his baptism, Mulligan is John the Baptist and Haines is the Devil, who is shortly to tempt Jesus. The chapter contains the opening phrase of the Latin Mass,

'Introibo ad altare Dei', and various sections of the Mass are alluded to later in the chapter, according to A. M. Klein. Since Mulligan makes his blasphemous parodies, there is also a hidden Black Mass, which reappears at the end of 'Circe' with a vision of Mulligan and Haines as celebrants in the Martello Tower. Mulligan's word 'Christine' implies a feminine version of Christ's body: the Black Mass is traditionally celebrated over a woman's body lying on the altar. The key phrase in the New Testament for this chapter and indeed for the whole of *Ulysses* is 'Hoc est enim corpus meum' (Matthew 26: 'this is my body', which Jesus commanded his disciples to take and eat at the Last Supper). Joyce pronounced the phrase over a birthday cake at an anniversary of *Ulysses*, thus hinting that he intended the book to be his own body and the Body of Christ. But he probably meant that if he were Christ, so was everyone: the Christian story is used because it is universally true, if interpreted non-religiously, just as the *Odyssey* is universally true. Every son is in search of his true father.

In the development of Stephen as the artist, this is an early and crucial stage. Mulligan is John the Baptist, up to this point, possessing more prestige and confidence than Stephen: he has the advantage of wealth, education at Oxford, great energy and wit, to which he gives free play in this chapter. Mulligan baptises Stephen with his verbal wit (literary inspiration as a symbol of the Holy Ghost). But Stephen must henceforth leave Mulligan behind, and go on to create finer things than the 'Ballad of Joking Jesus'. As the book goes on Mulligan becomes less important to Stephen and indeed less attractive; he is finally even treacherous, in Stephen's view, when he deserts Stephen at Amiens Street Station at the end of 'The Oxen of the Sun'. If he is to become an artist and even an adult, Stephen must become free of Mulligan's influence.

There are other forces from which Stephen must free himself. 'I am the servant of two masters, Stephen said, an English and an Italian. . . . And a third . . . there is who wants me for odd jobs.' The obtuse Englishman Haines does not understand, until Stephen explains: 'the imperial British state ... and the holy Roman catholic and apostolic church.' He does not bother to explain that the third is his Muse, to whom alone the writer must always be a devoted servant. Stephen must also free himself from morbid guilt about his mother — he knows rationally that cancer killed her, but feels irrationally that he himself killed her, by refusing to kneel down at her bedside in prayer. At this point another figure appears in the mythology of

*Ulysses*: Orestes the matricide haunted by the Furies. His mother's ghost, associated with a *leitmotif* from 'Prayers for the Dying' ('liliata rutilantium'), is not laid to rest until the end of Book II, after the climax of 'Circe'.

The first chapter is remarkable for the brilliant contrast it makes between the gloomy involutions of Stephen's consciousness and the vivid external world of the Tower and coast. His erudite display of theological learning only serves to deepen his gloom — neither religion nor the abandonment of religion for atheism is liberating. Yet all the time Stephen is perfectly conscious, and through him the reader, of the bright morning, the sea, the pleasures of literary quotation and parody, the high spirits of youth: the experience of these things has hardly ever been more brilliantly evoked.

### I.ii. 'Nestor'

At 10 a.m. Stephen is teaching at a small private school for boys, evidently Protestant boys, in Dalkey, about a mile south of the Martello Tower. He gives them a short history lesson (history is the art of this chapter) and an even more perfunctory poetry lesson. Then he goes to the headmaster's study to receive his monthly pay and has a long conversation with Mr Deasy, an Ulsterman, about Irish history, in which a rich set of parallels between past and present is drawn. Mr Deasy thinks Stephen must be a Fenian: he is mistaken, but this is not a surprising opinion, since Stephen is a recent graduate of what is now University College, Dublin, at that time a hot-bed of extreme nationalism. Mr Deasy knows that Stephen has literary and journalistic connections, and asks him if he can get a letter, on the subject of foot-and-mouth disease in cattle, placed in one of the Dublin newspapers — a commission which Stephen duly carries out. As Robert Adams has pointed out, Deasy makes a great many mistakes in his discussion of Irish history, not the least of which is his assertion that the Irish never let the Jews in — there had in fact been a small but quite thriving Jewish community in Ireland during the later nineteenth century. But Deasy, though garrulous, is not a totally bigoted Ulsterman, and shows politeness and tolerance.

In the Homeric parallel Mr Deasy stands for Nestor, the oldest of the Greek heroes in the *Iliad*, who had a high reputation for wisdom, though it is possible that Homer is mocking him for garrulity, as Shakespeare certainly did. After the war Nestor has returned to his kingdom in sandy Pylos, where he is a famous breeder of horses: the sport of horse-racing is loved by Mr Deasy, as by most Irishmen. Telemachus approaches him for advice about the suitors and his absent father. Nestor does not in fact give very good advice nor does he know what has happened to Odysseus, but he does tell him much about the fate of the Greek heroes when they returned from the war. Nestor's recital is the oldest source for the tragedy of King Agamemnon, slain on his home-coming by his faithless wife Clytemnestra. This story is not irrelevant to the *Odyssey*, for it seems to suggest that a similar tragedy could happen at Odysseus' home-coming in Ithaca. Homer may be trying to say that this must not happen, although the happy ending will not be achieved without violence and danger. So in Joyce's *Ulysses*: we are to believe that the book will end as a comedy but both Stephen's and Bloom's courses are beset with perils.

The Homeric parallel is pursued further with the story of yet another unfaithful wife, Clytemnestra's sister Helen. In Book IV Telemachus goes to the court of Menelaus, her husband; she is now repentant of the elopement that started the war. Mr Deasy draws the Irish parallel inaccurately: correctly, it should be one with Devorgilla, the wife of O'Rourke Prince of Breffny, who ran off with Dermot MacMurrough, King of Leinster in 1152; MacMurrough, by asking the aid of King Henry II of England, helped to bring about the first Norman invasion of Ireland. Yet another instance of the political trouble caused by a woman is produced: Parnell's political career collapsed after his affair with Mrs Kitty O'Shea had been revealed in a divorce case. But here the parallel is rather with Agamemnon, as we shall see in the 'Hades' chapter.

The Gospel correspondences are easy to discover if it is remembered that this is the *second* chapter of *Ulysses*. Matthew chapter 2 describes the gold brought by the Magi, and gold is a recurrent theme of 'Nestor', from the sovereign paid by Mr Deasy to the last sentence: 'On his wise shoulders through the checkerwork of leaves the sun flung spangles, dancing coins'. Mark chapter 2 describes the healing of a paralytic and Jesus's conflict with the scribes and Pharisees. The former appears in the feeble boy Sargent who writes 'in long *shaky* strokes' ('shady' is a misprint; note the paralytic stroke as well as the spastic shake). The conflict, polite enough, is between Stephen and Mr Deasy. Luke chapter 2 is even closer: the boy Jesus is in the Temple, sitting among the teachers. Mr Deasy says, ' "You were not born to be a teacher, I think. Perhaps I am wrong." "A Learner, perhaps," Stephen said.' John chapter 2 is the closest of all, since it is about Jesus driving the money-changers out of the Temple. When Mr Deasy says that England is in the hands of Jews, who are 'wanderers on the earth to this day', Stephen has a memory of the Jewish money-changers he saw in Paris: 'On the steps of the Paris Stock Exchange the gold-skinned men quoting prices on their gemmed fingers. Gabbles of geese. They swarmed loud, uncouth about the Temple, their heads thickplotting under maladroit silk hats.'

In terms of Stephen's development as an artist these parallels can be interpreted as follows: he was born with great gifts, and he was a boy prodigy, but he must now face and overcome the temptations to abandon his vocation as a writer for teaching or banking (professions which Joyce had to take up under duress). These are not, however, the most serious temptations for this young bohemian; a more deadly one faces him in the next chapter, already hinted at here. He must not be drawn into politics, like so many of his Irish contemporaries; and as a first step must free himself from the webs of Irish history. 'History, Stephen said, is a nightmare from which I am trying to awake.'

This can be read in two ways: first, obviously, that Irish history has been a nightmare; second, that Irish nationalistic historiography is also a nightmare, and has been the mother of Irish violence — as will be seen in the 'Cyclops' chapter, in which the extreme Fenian view of history is expressed most powerfully, and as has been proved over and over again in Irish life.

## I.iii. 'Proteus'

Stephen is walking on the beach (Anglo-Irish 'strand') at Sandymount, between 11 a.m. and noon. The chapter consists almost entirely of his interior monologue, which is here extremely learned and complex: a set of annotations is essential for every reader, and fortunately several are available. The monologue is a philosophical and aesthetic meditation on the subject of the ever-changing material world. Stephen is always thinking about mortality and the possibility that he may die before he has achieved anything of lasting value; and now his thoughts go beyond human mortality to the flux and reflux of the physical universe (the chapter's symbol is the tide) and to the never-ceasing metamorphoses of language (the chapter's art is philology). The central puzzle is how it is possible for any artist to produce anything permanent in the endless cycles of birth and death that make up this universe. Stephen does not solve this puzzle by logical means either here or during the 'Oxen of the Sun' chapter, where it is the subject of his discourse, but as we shall see it perhaps solves itself before the end of the story. The Homeric parallel is hardly a narrative, but offers a symbol of metamorphosis in Proteus, the Old Man of the Sea. Menelaus, becalmed in Egypt on his way home from Troy, wrestles with this divine being who takes on the shapes of several animals and of water and fire; when Menelaus succeeds in holding on to him throughout these changes (a motif well-known in folktales), Proteus gives him some valuable information, including the news that Odysseus is stranded on Calypso's island. When Menelaus tells this story to Telemachus, it is the first the latter has heard of his father's whereabouts. Proteus is allegorised in this chapter as Nature herself, who can be made to yield answers if grasped firmly enough. That is a scientific way of putting it; the mystical equivalent is Jakob Boehme's theory that God has left his signature on all created things, for man to read with his spiritual eye. ('Signatures of all things I am here to read', reflects Stephen.)

The Gospel parallel is the Temptation. Jesus spent forty days in the desert; the Devil appeared to him and offered him the kingdoms of the world, which he refused. This corresponds liturgically to the season of Lent, and is the prelude to Jesus's Ministry. It has already been hinted in 'Nestor' that Stephen must reject the temptation of money; now he must reject political power, and more specifically the achievement of power through violence. Stephen thinks in 'Nestor' of 'the ruin of all space, shattered glass and toppling masonry, and time's one livid final flame', which is a vision of the Fenian's terrorist bombs. This is developed in 'Proteus'. Stephen even imagines himself as a murderer, if only of a post office employee who has shut the door in his face: 'Shoot him to bloody bits with a bang shotgun, bits man spattered walls all brass buttons.' The Devil appears in human form as the exiled Kevin Egan, whom Stephen met in Paris two years ago; even Egan's cigarette is like a bomb: 'The blue fuse burns deadly between hands and burns clear.' The theme of political violence, which is also associated with the Phoenix Park Murders, rises to its height at the end of 'Circe', where it is clearly associated with the Devil.

The Devil also appears in disguise as the dog seen by Stephen on the beach. 'Dog' is 'God' backwards in the Black Mass of 'Circe' where everything runs backwards. Is the artist a young god or creator, or just a young dog (as Dylan Thomas thought himself to be)? Between God above and the Devil below stands Man. Stephen thinks of the first man in Eden, where in Traherne's words, 'the corn was Orient and Immortal wheat'. Adam must have been created without a navel, and Stephen imagines us all being connected to him by a series of ancestral navel-strings like telephone wires. The theme of birth is associated with the two midwives that Stephen sees on the beach. Later they turn up in 'Aeolus' as the two old women on Nelson's column when their meaning becomes clearer: they assist the process of artistic creation. The birth theme, or rather complex of themes, including that of Moses in the bulrushes, is given its fullest treatment in 'The Oxen of the Sun'. All the remaining themes connected with Stephen make their first appearance: e.g. his walking-stick or 'ash-plant', his potential homosexuality (Wilde's 'love that dare not speak its name'), his self-identification with Hamlet. But they are set in such an opaque matrix (the word means 'womb') of references to Aristotelian philosophy, the annals of Dublin, Fenian anecdotes, medieval heresies and so on, that the chapter can only be understood after many readings.

## II.i. 'Calypso'

Mr Leopold Bloom now makes his appearance, in a breakfast scene in his house at 7 Eccles (pronounced 'Eck-less') Street. This is synchronised with the beginning of 'Telemachus' at 8 a.m.: at one moment Bloom sees the same cloud, briefly dulling the bright morning, that Stephen does. Bloom goes out to buy a kidney for himself, gives his wife breakfast in bed, having a brief conversation with her, eats his kidney, defecates and contemplates the day before him. This corresponds with Book V of the *Odyssey* which is the first after the prologue of 'Telemacheia', and shows the beginning of Odysseus' voyage home to Ithaca. He has been for seven years on the island of the nymph Calypso, at first enjoying but later wearying of her love and unable to escape. He gets away only because the goddess Athena, his protectress, sends Hermes to instruct Calypso to let him go. Though Bloom's wife Marion (Molly) is Penelope in the final chapter, she is here the nymph, la Belle Dame Sans Merci who hath him in thrall; she has other roles to play before she is finally transformed into the Earth Mother. The physical image of Calypso appears in a print titled 'The Bath of the Nymph' which hangs above the Blooms'

marital bed. The breakfast that Bloom brings to his lazy wife is a symbol of his servitude, from which he must free himself by embarking
on the male pursuits of business and pleasure.

If Stephen's day is told in terms of the Gospel story, Bloom's is
told in terms of the Old Testament or Jewish Bible, with approxi-
mately a different book for every successive chapter up to 'Circe'.
Here at the outset the book must be Genesis (a Greek word meaning
'birth' — the Hebrew title means 'in the beginning'). Bloom is
presented as one or all of the patriarchs, Abraham, Isaac or Jacob,
much-married men. Like them he is enjoying possession of his own
tents and flocks, but like most Jews throughout their history he is an
exile, thinking of Zion from afar. This ties in neatly with exiled
Odysseus. Athena sends Hermes to recall Odysseus to Ithaca and his
own people, and the recall of Bloom to true Jewish thoughts about
Palestine is performed by Dlugacz, the pork-butcher from whom
Bloom buys his kidney, and who, according to Gifford and Seidman
(*Notes for Joyce*) is Hermes or Mercury. Now, Dlugacz seems intended
to be a deliberate impossibility: for his name proclaims him an
Eastern-European Jew, and he is not an apostate Jew like Bloom,
since he is a recipient of Zionist propaganda, that is, sheets of Zionist
literature which he uses to wrap up his meat. It is almost unthinkable
that such a man could be a pork butcher or that Joyce could have
slipped up on this point, since he knew about the Jewish dietary laws
as well as anyone else. It is better to suppose that Joyce introduced
an impossibility to deceive the careless and to warn the more perceptive
reader that *Ulysses* is a work of fiction, not of fact; although fantastically realistic, laboriously researched and documented, it remains a
parable, not to be taken literally. That is the point of the first sentence
of the chapter — 'Mr Leopold Bloom ate with relish the inner organs
of beasts and fowls' — we are being told to look inside, at the spiritual
symbol, not just at the surface. ('Beasts and fowls' also suggests the
language of Genesis.)

Dlugacz's sheets carry an advertisement for fruit farms in Palestine:
this is how Zionism began, not very long before 1904, with Jews
buying up land from Arabs. The organisation of farmers is called
'Agendath Netaim', apparently an error for 'Agudath Notim' (association of planters). Bloom is not a Zionist and is vague about the
religion of his ancestors, but the advertisement sets him dreaming
about the East. There is from now on an oriental flavour about
Bloom's stream of consciousness, which sometimes brings in the

*Arabian Nights*. When the sun goes behind a cloud his happy thoughts of Palestine change to desolation: he thinks of the Dead Sea, the Cities of the Plain, Sodom and Gomorrah, thus confirming his association with Abraham.

His short conversation with Molly introduces another minor theme. She has received a letter from Blazes Boylan, her agent and lover, about the next concert, when she is to sing 'La ci darem la mano' from Mozart's *Don Giovanni*. This and other fragments of the opera enter Bloom's thoughts from time to time, with a sad irony: although he would like to see himself as a Don Juan, he is only one of the cuckolds. A more explicit pointer to a basic idea in *Ulysses* occurs when Molly asks him the meaning of 'metempsychosis' in a novel she is reading. Bloom translates it correctly as 'transmigration' and then has to explain that term 'in plain words'. Are we to believe that Bloom really is Ulysses reborn? Not literally, any more than we are to believe that Stephen is Jesus Christ reborn. But Joyce does seem to believe that if Ulysses and Jesus (and Hamlet) are figures of universal significance, their experiences must be repeated over and over again in human history, and in that sense they can be said to be reborn.

## II.ii. 'Lotus-eaters'

On leaving home between 9 and 10 Bloom makes his way to the Westland Row Post Office, where he picks up from the 'Poste Restante' a letter from a girl he has never seen, one Martha Clifford, with whom he is carrying on a flirtatious correspondence. He goes to a pharmacist to order some face lotion for Molly (in 1904 such things had to be prepared specially) and buys a cake of soap. He is approached by a gambling acquaintance called Bantam Lyons, who asks to see the sporting pages of his newspaper. 'You can keep it,' Bloom says, 'I was just going to throw it away.' We learn later that Lyons takes this as a tip for today's big race, and intends to back 'Throwaway'. Bloom then walks towards the Leinster Street Baths, seeing himself prophetically in the bath, which he takes after the chapter ends.

The episode in the *Odyssey* is only a brief part of Odysseus' recapitulatory narrative in Book IX: he tells how he lost some of his men because they decided to stay with the friendly Lotus-eaters, 'eating that native flower and forgetting their homelands'. It is not known what land Homer had in mind nor what they ate — it must be assumed to be one of the many narcotics known to mankind from primitive times, and is treated as such in this chapter. Here almost every kind of drug is mentioned with some indication of its pleasurable effects. Furthermore, nearly all the pleasures of the senses (sight, touch, hearing, taste and above all smell) are evoked to add to the lotus-eating effect. If the mood of 'Calypso' is one of fubsy cosiness, that of 'Lotus-eaters' is one of enlightened if drowsy hedonism. Joyce calls the technique 'narcissism' and Bloom himself is Narcissus even to the contemplation of his own image in the pool. The organ of the chapter is the male genitals: Bloom's mood is gently masturbatory, and suggests Freud's 'genital age'. He is not alone in his day-dreaming, self-titillating state of pleasure, since the whole of Dublin on this fine morning seems to be lost in an agreeable trance. It is a day of wine and roses; the various types of narcotics and narcotic-users have a delicate background of sweetly-scented flowers (botany and chemistry are the arts of this chapter). A small slummy boy is smoking, and Bloom reflects: 'Tell him if he smokes he won't grow. O let him! His life isn't such a bed of roses.' Bloom thinks of tea, inhales his own hair-oil, thinks of the East and the hot-house in the Botanic Gardens. The castrated cabhorses have achieved a kind of peace, as they chew their oats, like oriental eunuchs. Bloom's only narcotic habit is to smoke an occasional cigar, which 'has a cooling effect'; like most Jews he is a very moderate drinker, but the Irish consume 'millions of barrels of porter'. Bloom enters a church, where the Irish receive their religion, the opium of the people, at all hours of the day: he reflects sceptically on the eucharistic bread and wine and dreams of heaven, to the accompaniment of sacred music, another drug. The chemist's shop makes him think of 'chloroform. Overdose of laudanum. Sleeping draughts. Lovephiltres. Paregoric poppysyrup bad for cough.' (Such opiates were sold very freely in Britain in the 1900s.) The last and most apt example of lotus-eating is watching cricket.

Lotus-eating fits neatly into the structure of Biblical correspondences, if it is assumed that this chapter deals with the Egyptian captivity of the children of Israel. This was evidently not a wholly unpleasant experience: the sons of Jacob went to Egypt sponsored by their brother Joseph, a high official of Pharaoh. It was only later that they had to suffer forced labour, but when they were in the desert they regretted 'the fleshpots of Egypt'. The lotus is also a flower of the Nile.

Moses had to lead the Children of Israel into austerity before they could win the Promised Land, and his leadership was sometimes unpopular. This chapter is a prelude to the Mosaic theme which is sounded so loudly later in the novel, with an explicitly political meaning. The Irish, let it be remembered, were not all unhappy all of the time under British rule. Dublin enjoyed considerable prosperity during the second half of the nineteenth century, when a great deal (then pronounced 'a gradle') of money was made by exporting agricultural goods to Britain. Many of the southern Irish in 1904 were happy to be ruled by King Edward VII and to be economic and political 'West Britons' (see 'The Dead'). Many continued to accept the status quo even when they voted for the Parliamentary nationalist party, which, in fact, after Parnell's death had lost most of its energy. Ireland had been promised but did not yet enjoy Home Rule; Bloom, as we have seen in 'Calypso' did not enjoy home rule, but servitude had its own pleasures.

The last image is of Bloom, the patriarch who has signally failed to carry out the divine command 'be fruitful and multiply'; a lazy oriental god resting from the labours of creation. He 'saw the dark tangled curls of his bush floating, floating hair of the stream around the limp father of thousands, a languid floating flower.'

## II.iii. 'Hades'

At 11 a.m. Bloom attends Paddy Dignam's funeral, travelling in a coach with the modest funeral procession from Dignam's house in Sandymount, south-east of the city centre, to Glasnevin in the north. With him in the coach are Martin Cunningham (a minor official in the British Administration), Stephen's father Simon, and a Mr Power. They meet other mourners at the Catholic burial service, performed by Father Coffey; afterwards some of them pay a short visit of respect to Parnell's grave.

In Book XI of the *Odyssey* Odysseus visits Hades on the advice of Circe, to consult the shade of the seer Tiresias about his home-coming. He kills an ox and the famished dead come to drink the blood. He meets the ghost of Elpenor, one of his crew who had recently died by falling off the roof of Circe's house; then that of Tiresias, who warns him that if his men kill the Oxen of the Sun God they will be lost and Odysseus' difficulties increased. According to some scholars, a later hand added more to this episode, showing Odysseus on a tour of the Underworld where he meets the ghosts of many famous people, as in Virgil's imitation (*Aeneid* VI). Odysseus meets his former commander-in-chief Agamemnon, and learns of his death at the hands of his wife Clytemnestra; Ajax, who refuses to speak to him because of a quarrel; Hercules, and others. There are mythological characters whom he sees but does not meet, such as Sisyphus, condemned to the eternal punishment of rolling a stone uphill: his modern equivalent is Martin Cunningham, married to a hopeless drunkard who keeps selling their furniture for drink. Agamemnon, as in 'Nestor', is paralleled by Parnell, brought low by a woman. Ajax is a solicitor called Menton, who snubs Bloom because of a tiff they once had at a game of bowls. Elpenor is Paddy Dignam, the most recently dead. Cerberus, the guardian dog at the gates of hell, is Father Coffey, 'with a belly on him like a poisoned pup'. The four rivers of Hades (Styx, Acheron, Cocytus, Phlegethon) are represented by the River Dodder, the Grand and Royal Canals and the River Liffey, all of which are crossed by the funeral procession. The other correspondences are not certain, but it may be assumed that the caretaker of the cemetery, whom Joyce called the 'symbol' of the chapter, is Tiresias. This man tells a comic story to cheer up the mourners, about two drunks who mistake a statue of Christ for that of their friend Mulcahy (*'Not a bloody bit like the man. . . . That's not Mulcahy . . . whoever done it.'*) This is an important message couched in parable, concerning the identity of Christ with Everyman, in parallel with the message from the seer Tiresias which will 'cheer up' Odysseus.

Although the Homeric episodes do not appear in their correct order, the Biblical episodes seem to do so more precisely. After the Egyptian captivity, there is the Exodus in which Moses leads the chosen people into the wilderness. This is a time of hardship for them, and many, including Moses himself, die before they enter the Promised Land of Canaan. The figure of Parnell, leading the Irish people out of captivity through adversity towards Home Rule, dying himself before it was reached, is powerfully evoked in this chapter, and closely tied in with the Mosaic references in 'Aeolus'. Not only the cemetery but the whole of Dublin is described as a stony wilderness like the Sinai desert: the word 'stone' occurs frequently; they pass the scene of the Childs murder case, a 'tenantless, unweeded garden', and so on.

Joyce called the technique of the chapter 'incubism', a hitherto unknown word. An incubus is an evil spirit who causes nightmares and worse by lying on top of the sleeper, so one supposes the writing is intended to produce a nightmarish effect by heavy repetition and emphasis on death. It is certainly successful in this: not only is every aspect of death and decay discussed gruesomely and vividly, but there are many oblique or hidden references to death, especially to the failure of the heart, which is the organ of the chapter. The late Frank O'Connor pointed out an example of 'piling on' which I and doubtless many other readers had missed. Bloom thinks of the day he begat his dead son Rudy, after he and Molly had been watching two dogs copulating in the street: 'And the sergeant grinning up. She had that cream gown on with the rip she never stitched.' The policeman is Shakespeare's 'fell sergeant death' and the rip in Molly's dress is 'R.I.P.'. I can perhaps add to O'Connor's explanation that the grin is that of a death's head; 'cream' suggests semen, and 'rip' the female genitals; this would be in order, since the chapter is a compressed metaphysical poem full of conceits not only about death, but about life-in-death. It is hinted that someone has been making love in the undertaker's coach. Bloom remembers Molly on the above occasion asking him to make love: 'Give us a touch, Poldy. God, I'm dying for it. That's how life begins.' That suggests the seventeenth-century use of 'to die' for sexual intercourse; the chapter might be centred on the traditional rhyme of *womb* and *tomb*. 'In the midst of life we are in death', as 'The Burial of the Dead' in the Prayer Book puts it; but here in the midst of death there is lots of life.

## II.iv. 'Aeolus'

A short prologue evokes the transportation system of Dublin: of people (the Dublin United Tramway Company), of post (the Royal Mail) and of porter (Guinness drays). Bloom is first seen in an office of the *Freeman's Journal and National Press*, then in the printing works, talking about an advertisement; next he goes to the editorial office of the *Evening Telegraph*, an associated paper. Inside a group of hangers-on — 'Professor' MacHugh, Simon Dedalus and Ned Lambert, and later J. J. O'Molloy — are discussing the first specimen of rhetoric, a newly reported speech by one Dawson. The group is joined by the editor Myles Crawford and the parasite Lenehan. Bloom comes in to make a telephone call and then leaves. MacHugh makes a short speech, on the subject of Rome (equals England) versus Greece (equals Ireland). Accompanied by Mr O'Madden Burke, Stephen enters and asks the editor to publish the letter of Mr Deasy. The main debate then begins, on the topic of the Ancients versus the Moderns: Crawford asserts that there are no modern journalists or orators as good as the old ones, instancing Ignatius Gallaher's coup in reporting the Phoenix Park Murders, and the eighteenth-century orators. There is a reply by J. J. O'Molloy, who produces as the second specimen of rhetoric a speech by the barrister Seymour Bushe. MacHugh caps this with what he considers an even finer speech by John F. Taylor (third specimen). Stephen puts the motion 'that this house now adjourn' to a pub. As they walk to Mooney's Stephen delivers his own speech, 'The parable of the Plums'. Bloom approaches the editor in the street, fussing about his advertisement, and is rudely rebuffed ('K.M.R.I.A.'). Stephen finishes his parable to an uncomprehending audience. The whole tramway system of Dublin comes to a halt because of a short circuit; at the centre of this system, Nelson's Pillar (now, sadly, no more), Stephen and his companions also halt, the professor peering aloft at the 'onehandled adulterer'.

In Book X of the *Odyssey* Odysseus describes how he was entertained by Aeolus, King of the Winds, on his floating island. When he left Aeolus gave him a bag containing all the winds likely to be dangerous to his voyage and sent him on his way with a favourable breeze. Odysseus sailed nearly home to Ithaca and then fell asleep. His companions, thinking that the bag contained treasure, undid it and the winds broke out and drove the ship back to Aeolus. The wind god lost his temper, refused to help Odysseus again and drove him away. Crawford the editor is the King of Wind, who first dismisses Bloom in a kindly manner, but rebuffs him at the end. The newspaper office is full of winds and draughts, and there are many metaphors of which 'wind' is the vehicle, e.g. flatulence, balloon, zephyrs, gale, windfall, what's in the wind, reaping the whirlwind, veer about, get the wind of, weathercocks, breath, blows over, windbag, blowing out, blow, the draught, there's a hurricane blowing, on the breeze a mocking kite, first puff, storm, wheeze, fanned, breath of fresh air, Inspiration, Windy Arbour, breath of life, shape of air, trees blown down by that cyclone, *il vento*, divine afflatus, belch, spirit, gone with the wind, the four winds, take my breath away, windy Troy, breathless, caught in a whirl, bellows, a little puff, squalls, raise the wind.

This metaphor suggests one of the basic allegorical structures of the novel, which is literary creation. English and other languages play into Joyce's hands, as they did into Rabelais's and Swift's. For example, Hebrew *ruach* can mean 'breath, wind, air, breeze, blowing, animal life, spirit, ghost, soul, mind, intellect, passion'. Greek *anemos* has many Indo-European cognates in the same semantic field, such as Latin *anima*, 'air, breeze, breath, principle of animal life', *animus*. The etymology of 'spirit' and 'inspiration' shows the same confusion of literal and metaphorical, by which primitive religious beliefs have been fossilised in language: Latin *inspirare* 'to breathe into, blow upon, excite, inflame, arouse by divine influence'; *spiritus* 'breath, breeze, breath of life, life, soul, mind, spirit, energy, courage, pride, arrogance'. Wind, therefore, may be flatulence, over-blown rhetoric or false inspiration; but it may be the true inspiration of religion and of art. A central theme in *Ulysses* is that of the Trinity, God the Father, God the Son and God the Holy Ghost (Old English *gast*, 'life, spirit, soul'): here and elsewhere religion provides metaphors for the process of artistic creation. At the beginning of the book, the Trinity is separated; Bloom the Father (and the Body) and Stephen the Son (and the Intellect) are separated and consequently sterile; only in the 'Ithaca' chapter do the two come together mystically, and the Trinity is completed, made Holy and Undivided, by the Holy Spirit, the Inspiration of the book itself. In 'Aeolus' Stephen is still uncreative: Myles Crawford gives him another reminder that he has done nothing yet.

But just as the Old Testament in the view of traditional theology contains prophecies of the Trinity and of the triumph of Christ, so in 'Aeolus' there are foretastes of the god-like creative power to come. This chapter corresponds to the Ministry of Jesus and in particular to the Sermon on the Mount, to which there are references: 'sufficient for the day is the newspaper thereof' (Matthew 6), and weeping and gnashing of teeth (Matthew 7); other gospel references are to the wise and foolish virgins (Matthew 25), while Stephen's teaching falls on deaf ears, just as the seed falls on stony ground (Matthew 13) and as the plum-stones of his parable fall on the pavements of Dublin. The Old Testament correspondences are obviously Mosaic. Bloom thinks about the Passover, two of the speeches are about Moses, and the Parable has the subtitle 'A Pisgah Sight of Palestine'. The entry into the Promised Land is frustrated by the paralysis of the Dubliners, of which the becalmed tramcars are an emblem; so Odysseus gets a glimpse of his own promised land of Ithaca before the wind blows him away. The figure of Moses is central to the political theme of *Ulysses*, the sustained parallel between the Jews and the Irish. Again Joyce uses the old cliché that compared Parnell to Moses, leading his people out of British bondage. Joyce also equates Parnell with Christ, the uncrowned king, whose kingdom was not of this world. The implication is that there can be no true victories in the world of politics and the only triumphs are those of the creative imagination.

Joyce's use of medieval 'typology', the method of making fanciful comparisons between the Old Testament and the New, was supposed to have been invented by Jesus himself; in the mysterious words of John 3:14, 'And as Moses lifted up the serpent in the wilderness, so must the Son of Man be lifted up.' The comparison between Moses and Christ is used in the Good Friday Reproaches, which Stephen parodies in the 'Oxen of the Sun'. The art of the 'Aeolus' chapter is rhetoric, which the Romans took to mean the whole art of writing; and by his emphasis on Moses Joyce is saying something about the way in which *Ulysses* is written and in which it ought to be read. When he made the first gramophone record of his work, he chose a passage from 'Aeolus', namely, his own freely and beautifully written version of a speech he had heard John F. Taylor deliver in 1901 at his university Law Students' Debating Society. Ironically, Taylor was defending the revival of the Irish language, an issue on which Joyce's views were negative. The passage is transformed into a truly inspired statement of Joyce's artistic credo:

> But, ladies and gentlemen, had the youthful Moses listened to and accepted that view of life, had he bowed his head and bowed his will and bowed his spirit before that arrogant admonition, he would never have brought the chosen people out of their house of bondage nor followed the pillar of the cloud by day. He would never have spoken with the Eternal amid lightnings on Sinai's mountaintop nor ever have come down with the light of inspiration shining in his countenance and bearing in his arms the tables of the law, graven in the language of the outlaw.

Rhetoric is a subject that now seems to be tedious to most readers, critics and writers — but it was not so to Joyce and his contemporaries. The art of making persuasive speeches is an ancient and much-loved tradition of the Irish, especially making political speeches, whether at the graveside of dead leaders or from the dock. I have read that until recently every Irish barman in London kept under the bar a collection of the speeches of condemned felons; a selection of Irish oratory was edited by Joyce's friend T. M. Kettle. Most of the great orators in the English language have been Irish, from the days of

Burke and Sheridan, and speeches have played an important part in Irish politics.

Joyce calls the technique of 'Aeolus' *enthymemic*, thus producing one of the most irritating minor problems in the interpretation of *Ulysses*. For neither Joyce nor anyone else seems to know exactly what an enthymeme really is. The Greek *enthymema*, 'a thought, argument', is derived from *enthumesthai*, 'to consider, reflect upon', and that in turn from *thumos*, 'mind'; but its special meaning comes from Aristotle, who discusses it under the heading of *logos*, that is of arguments possessing rational appeal. In one view it is the rhetorical equivalent of the syllogism: in logic, the syllogism is a device for proceeding from two premises, major and minor, to a conclusion, e.g. all Ms are Ps (major), all Ss are Ms (minor), therefore all Ss are Ps (conclusion), or supplying examples, 'All men are mortal', 'Socrates is a man', therefore 'Socrates is mortal'. To ask a rhetorical question, what can be the rhetorical equivalent of that? One answer is that it is 'an argument based on what is true for the most part: good men do not commit murder; Socrates is a good man; therefore Socrates did not commit murder.'[1] It is not certainly true that good men do not commit murder, but only very probably true. So 'the essential difference is that the syllogism leads to a necessary conclusion from universally true premises but the enthymeme leads to a tentative conclusion from probable premises.'[2]

Hence, more loosely, the enthymeme may be an argument based on probable premises as distinct from a demonstration (*O.E.D.*). But the word has come to have a second and very different meaning, that is, of a truncated syllogism, with one premise suppressed, the simplest example being Descartes's *Cogito, ergo sum* (which omits the major 'all thinking beings exist', a ridiculous tautology); another example is 'we are beggars and therefore cannot be choosers'. The second meaning presumably came from Aristotle's statement that 'the enthymeme must consist of few propositions, fewer often than those which make up normal syllogisms'.[3] I suppose his reason for saying that is

---

[1] G. A. Kennedy, *The Art of Persuasion in Greece*, Princeton University Press, 1963, p. 97, cit. Brian Vickers, *Classical Rhetoric in English Poetry*, London, Macmillan, 1970, p. 62.

[2] E. P. Corbett, *Classical Rhetoric for the Modern Student*, New York, Oxford University Press, 1965, p. 61, discussing Aristotle, *Prior Analytics*, II 27.

[3] *Rhetoric* I, 2, cit. Corbett, op. cit., p. 62.

that it is tedious for an orator to take his audience step by step through an entire syllogism. It could be that Joyce meant that the whole chapter was enthymemic in sense 1, in that nothing is certainly demonstrated; it cannot be proved by syllogisms that Irish = Hebrew or Stephen = Christ. But he also used sense 2, e.g. 'We were weak, therefore worthless' (suppressing the major, 'all those who are weak are worthless' — which the Gospel says is untrue in any case). The example of an enthymeme given by Gilbert seems to me to be wrong: 'If you want to draw the cashier is just going to lunch', says Bloom to Hynes; but that is just an elliptical sentence, from which the words 'you had better hurry, because' have been deleted; and in fact Bloom has tactfully deleted another, undeniably true, proposition, 'and since you owe me three shillings, will you please repay me' — which is an intolerably difficult sentence to say to anyone. The chapter abounds with these tactful ellipses; everything is left hanging in the air. The richest example of reasoning is the following: I cannot decide whether it is an enthymeme or a true syllogism. Bloom and Red Murray see the publisher Brayden enter:

— Don't you think his face is like our Saviour? Red Murray whispered.
. . . Our Saviour: beardframed oval face: talking in the dusk Mary, Martha. Steered by an umbrella sword to the footlights: Mario the tenor.
— Or like Mario, Mr Bloom said.
— Yes, Red Murray agreed. But Mario was said to be the picture of Our Saviour.

That seems to be a way of proving rhetorically, if not logically, that not only Stephen = Christ, but Brayden = Christ, Mario = Christ, and by extrapolation every human being = Christ, a proposition set out in 'Circe'.

The structure of the chapter follows the traditional rhetorical structure of a speech. The authoritative formulation for this is given in the treatise *Ad Herennium*; I quote from Brian Vickers's lucid exposition.[1] There are six sections within a speech: *exordium, narratio, divisio, confirmatio, confutatio*, and *conclusio*. 'The narration is the beginning of the discourse, and by it the hearer's mind is prepared for attention.' This is the prologue, with trams, mail, porter drays in circulation.

---

[1] *Classical Rhetoric in English Poetry*, London, Macmillan, 1970, pp. 65ff.

'The narration or statement of facts sets forth the events that have occurred or might have occurred'; or, as Red Murray says, 'There it is.' The narration beginning with Bloom in the newspaper office is summarised above. 'By means of the Division we make clear what matters are agreed upon and what are contested, and announce what points we intend to take up.' The first matter agreed on is that Dawson's is a poor specimen of rhetoric. The second matter agreed on is that in all things except plumbing the Romans (British) were inferior to the Greeks (Irish). The matter disagreed on is that the modern journalists and orators are inferior to the ancient or those of the recent past. The next heads in the *Ad Herennium* are *confirmatio* (proof) and *refutatio*: 'Proof is the presentation of our arguments, together with their corroboration. Refutation is the destruction of our adversaries' arguments.' Crawford presents his argument, corroborating it with the story about Ignatius Gallaher; he is refuted first by O'Molloy and then by MacHugh, whose only proof is to produce outstanding specimens of modern rhetoric. 'The Conclusion is the end of the discourse, formed in accordance with the principles of the art.' There would appear to be no conclusion to the debate, since the point at issue, like the 'enthymemes' and elliptical sentences of the chapter, is left hanging in the air. But this inconclusiveness is only apparent, since the fragmented discourse is in fact brought to a conclusion by Stephen's Parable of the Plums.

The discourse is taken on to a higher plane, since the Parable, for all its absurdity, is true imaginative art, in contrast to merely brilliant oratory; and because Stephen speaks with Christ-like simplicity. The Fathers contrasted the high style of the pagan rhetoricians unfavourably with the *sermo humilis* of the Gospel, the only proper style for the spreading of God's word. The Parable contains in its ludicrous narrative dark sayings and hidden mysteries which are close to the heart of the book. The two Dublin vestals (Martha and Mary) are the two midwives seen by Stephen on the beach in 'Proteus', where he first names one of them Florence McCabe. Her gamp is named after the famous umbrella of Sarah Gamp, who was not only midwife but layer-out of corpses. Representing the two phases of Woman that preside over birth and death, they reappear in 'The Oxen of the Sun'. 'The aged sisters draw us into life . . . over us dead they bend. First saved from the waters of the Nile, among bulrushes.' The Mosaic reference suggests that they are the midwives of the New Ireland, but are also the layers-out of its stillborn corpse. They spit out the plumstones, which will die on the stony ground, unless fertilised by the urine of Bloom's humanity and Stephen's art. Thus they exemplify the major wasteland-fertility theme, which receives its fullest treatment in 'The Oxen of the Sun'. At the end, they are too tired to move 'or to speak' (no more rhetoric); static on a phallic monument, they gaze up in paralysis at the phallic Nelson, the one-handled adulterer.

— . . . That tickles me I must say. [says J. J. O'Molloy]
— Tickled the old ones too, Myles Crawford said, if the God Almighty's truth was known.

But God's truth *is* at last, in the fullness of time, known; and the debate on old versus new is concluded. The midwives have presided over the birth of a miraculous Child, and now a great modern writer is among us.

## II.v. 'Lestrygonians'

At 1 p.m. Bloom is getting hungry and looks for somewhere to lunch; but he is revolted by what he sees in various restaurants, where customers are guzzling coarse food. Eventually he settles for a simple cheese sandwich and a glass of burgundy in Davy Byrne's 'moral' pub at 21 Duke Street. Then he goes to the National Library to look up an advertisement in the files of a newspaper. He also does much window shopping in this chapter; but even when he is looking at his favourite fetish, women's underclothes, his thoughts turn to food; 'Molly's legs are out of plumb', he thinks, making one of the many unconscious puns connected with food. Joyce calls the technique of the chapter 'peristaltic'; which seems to mean that Bloom's thoughts are like the 'rhythmic involuntary constrictions of the intestinal canal, whereby the contents are mixed with the digestive juices, and forced along the canal', as a dictionary defines *peristalsis*. The organ of the body is naturally the oesophagus.

The Homeric correspondences are concerned with food. Odysseus loses all his ships but one at the island of the Lestrygonians. These people are cannibals and their king Antiphates sends his daughter to lure the sailors ashore to their death; all are eaten except Odysseus' own crew. The Biblical correspondences have nothing to do with food, however. Continuing with the outline of Jewish history, Joyce takes us to the era of Solomon and the building of the great Temple at

Jerusalem. There are many references to stones and building, including the first words, 'Pineapple rock'. Bloom is thinking about food and rock, as in 'Brighton rock', means hard candy; but it also means the foundation of the Temple, proleptically the foundation of the Christian Church; as Jesus said to Peter in a famous pun, 'thou art Peter (i.e. rocky) and on this rock' he would found the Church. Physically St Peter's Church is the Vatican, in the gardens of which there is a famous *pine*-cone. The running theme of masonry invokes poetically the beautiful public buildings of Dublin, and also points to the major subject of Freemasonry, which will turn out to be the religious centre of Bloom's life.

Freemasonry is a half-secret association based allegedly on the traditions of the working stone-masons, although in fact it was largely invented in the early eighteenth century. Since the early nineteenth century Catholic have been forbidden to become Freemasons, but the movement has always been strong among Protestants, and will not refuse admission to anyone who believes in God of any kind; Jews were certainly eligible. The fact of Bloom's membership, which is asserted confidently by Nosey Flynn in this chapter, adds to the religious tension surrounding him, which is greatly increased in the 'Cyclops' chapter. The Masonic brethren are philanthropic and look after their less successful fellows: Nosey Flynn says that they have rescued Bloom from awkward situations, the most serious of which seems to have been a swindle involving lottery tickets. Apart from its practical and charitable side, Masonry is concerned with ritual and esoteric lore, centring on the building of Solomon's Temple: the initiation rite is based on a death-and-resurrection myth about one Hiram, supposedly one of the architects of the Temple. The occult side of Freemasonry is several times suggested in this chapter, as for example by the appearance of the poet-mystic George Russell or AE, who is overheard talking mystically to a disciple. 'Under the apron' refers to the Masons' uniform, as does 'lay it on with a trowel'.

The practical work of the stone-masons is also prominent in 'Lestrygonians', and the art of the chapter is architecture. Dublin is a city of splendid buildings in brick and stone, and this chapter pays a special tribute to this aspect of the city. It also describes many of the statues and monuments of Dublin: 'He crossed under Tommy Moore's roguish finger. They did right to put him over a urinal: meeting of the waters.' Joyce tells us that the symbol of the chapter is 'constables'.

Dublin was a densely policed city, with many of the Dublin Metropolitan Police, who later became the 'Garda' and are there today, and many of the Royal Irish Constabulary, a paramilitary force who were disbanded at once after the Treaty. The police are the embodiment of law and order: 'A squad of constables debouched from College street, marching in Indian file. Goose step. Foodheated faces, sweating helmets, patting their truncheons.' If the D.M.P. stands for the inevitable order of civilisation, the R.I.C. stands for the brutality of conquest: their phallic truncheons are associated with the overheated penis of Blazes Boylan, Molly's conqueror.

Despite its grotesque humour, this chapter reaches a great intensity of pathos. Bloom is intensely aware of his cuckolding by Boylan, which is figured by a ridiculous image of copulation: 'Stuck on the pane two flies buzzed, stuck.'

II.vi. 'Scylla and Charybdis'

The subject-matter of this chapter is Shakespeare and very little else. It describes a discussion in the National Library on this subject between Stephen, Lyster the Librarian, Magee ('John Eglinton') the assistant librarian, Best — another assistant, and George Russell the mystic poet (AE); later Buck Mulligan joins in briefly. Most of this discussion is a highly unspontaneous lecture by Stephen on the biographical interpretation of Shakespeare's plays — it is unlikely that any young man of twenty-two could have delivered such a polished discourse off the cuff, especially since it is so closely dependent on books of Shakespearean scholarship. Stephen's theory is not to be taken seriously as Joyce's mature views on Shakespeare, but it is vital to the central ideas of *Ulysses*. The core of the theory is that all literature is in a very real sense autobiography and that the father–son relationship is as important in *Hamlet* as in Homer and the Bible. On the other hand, the conversation must be taken as a nearly real one: the things the speakers say are either reported verbatim or are wholly characteristic of them. Frank O'Connor told AE in his later years that Joyce had made him say in this chapter, 'The supreme question about a work of art is out of how deep a life does it spring', to which AE replied, 'How clever of Joyce: I might have said something like that.' 'He said it every day,' O'Connor comments. The discussion is forthright but hardly ever rude; the technique is dialectic, i.e. thesis, antithesis and synthesis as the three stages of the quest for truth.

The Homeric correspondences are again in this chapter symbolical rather than narrative. One of the perils Odysseus has to undergo is to sail through a narrow channel: on one side is a six-headed monster called Scylla, who lives on a rock and is able to snatch sailors from their ships if they get too close; on the other is Charybdis, a raging whirlpool. Circe advises Odysseus to keep to the side of Scylla, which he does and escapes, though not without some loss of men. Scylla represents materialism, Aristotle's philosophy and the biographical kind of literary criticism; Charybdis represents idealism and mysticism, Plato and the theory that literature consists of 'formless essences'. Stephen argues for the first, Russell for the second; each has its perils, but the biographical-materialist has fewer. A second set of correspondences consists of the equations Stratford = Scylla, Charybdis = London. It may have been more boring for Shakespeare to retire to Stratford, but it was safer than getting lost in the whirlpool of London.

The Biblical correspondences are rather obscure, but as before they occur in the correct sequence. Bloom is off the scene, except for brief appearances at the beginning and end of the chapter, when he turns up at the Library in search of the files of a newspaper, and even then he is hardly seen or heard. Since it is Stephen's chapter, we return to the life of Christ. His Ministry finished, Jesus enters Jerusalem, riding on a donkey and greeted by the populace, who are strewing palms. This is liturgically Palm Sunday and the beginning of Holy Week; the service for this day includes the opening of the west door of the church (normally kept closed) and a procession through it. This is reflected in the business with doors in the chapter, as the librarian comes and goes. There are several *palms* in the chapter, notably 'Antisthenes . . . took the palm of beauty from kyrios Menelaus . . . brooddam, Argive Helen, the wooden mare of Troy in whom a score of heroes slept, and handed it to poor Penelope' — a neat pointer to various Homeric themes. The donkey appears in Stephen's use of the Commandment:

— No sir smile neighbour shall covet his ox or his wife or
his manservant or his maidservant or his jackass.
— Or his jennyass, Buck Mulligan antiphoned.

Antiphonal singing, like the Creed and the plainchant printed on the page point to the liturgical framework of the passage. The participants are high priests of literature, as is appropriate to the Temple of Jerusalem; and at the end they are also 'the druid priests of Cymbeline, hierophantic: from wide earth and altar'. The final repetition of 'altar' in the quotation from *Cymbeline* invokes Christ's sacrifice at the end of the Week.

## II.vii. 'Wandering Rocks'

*Ulysses* is a book about wanderers; Bloom the Wandering Jew and Stephen the searcher cover many miles in the day, and so do many of the other characters. Dubliners, despite their paralysis of the spirit, are continually on the move, if only from church to church or pub to pub. This chapter is an attempt to portray the whole city on the move, groups of citizens corresponding to the Homeric 'Symplegades' or 'clashing' (rather than 'wandering') rocks. These rocks do not appear in the action of the *Odyssey* but are mentioned by Circe to warn Odysseus of their danger. They have sometimes been identified with the two banks of the Bosphorus, and as such they correspond to Father Conmee SJ (Church) and the Viceroy (State). The chapter begins with Father Conmee, who travels by tram and on foot to the suburbs, first to the east and then to the north-east, and it ends with the Viceroy, who travels by carriage from his Lodge in Phoenix Park roughly east to open a charity bazaar. Nearly all the other characters travel parallel to the Viceroy's path, but throughout the chapter the sandwich-men, bearing the letters HELY'S to advertise a department store, shuttle to and fro north and south. Conmee goes parallel at first, and then turns at right angles; in history Church and State sometimes agree and are sometimes at cross purposes. Stephen is the servant of both Church and State, as he explains to Haines in the first chapter; they both make intolerable demands on him and they may end by crucifying his art. But in the event he escapes by avoiding them, just as Odysseus avoids the Symplegades. Bloom, thanks to his cool indifference to religion and politics, runs no great danger from Church or State.

The New Testament correspondences point to the arrest and trial of Jesus, in particular his appearances before the High Priest (Conmee) and before Pontius Pilate (the Viceroy, Rome once again being represented by Britain). Conmee is chosen because he was once Stephen's headmaster and in authority over him; he is personally a kind and just man, as can be seen from the *Portrait*, but his claims to power over the spirit mean the death of art. The technique of the chapter is called 'labyrinth', and it evokes the physical labyrinth of

Dublin streets, while the *Portrait* symbolises the spiritual labyrinth from which Stephen must escape.

There are nineteen sections, each consisting of a rather simple narrative with a small amount of interior monologue; each is interrupted by one or more of the other sections; the events are simultaneous in time but separated in space. One interpolation is not drawn from the other sections but from a later chapter: the 'bronze and gold' Sirens watch the Viceregal procession in the next chapter. The principal actors, apart from 1 and 19, are as follows: (2) Corny Kelleher (carriage hirer and undertaker); (3) one-legged sailor, to whom the invisible Molly Bloom throws a coin; (4) the Dedalus girls in their poverty; (5) Blazes Boylan on his way to Molly; (6) Stephen in conversation with his singing teacher Artifoni; (7) Miss Dunne, Boylan's secretary; (8) Lambert, showing the historic Abbey of St Mary to Hugh Love; (9) Lenehan and M'Coy, admiring a gadget invented by one Tom Rochford, and Lenehan telling an erotic anecdote about Molly Bloom; (10) Bloom buying secondhand pornography; (11) Mr Dedalus being unkind to his daughter Dilly; (12) Tom Kernan of 'Grace' in *Dubliners*, a little drunk; (13) Stephen looking in at a lapidary's window, then talking to his sister Dilly; (14) Cowley, Dollard, and Simon Dedalus meet on their way to the Ormond Hotel; (15) Martin Cunningham at his charitable work of raising a subscription for poor Paddy Dignam's wife and children, with his friends; (16) Mulligan and Haines eating afternoon tea in a tea-shop and discussing Stephen; (17) Artifoni, the eccentric Farrell and the blind piano-tuner; (18) Paddy Dignam's son. Nearly all these appear in section 19 to salute the Viceroy, but there is one significant addition: 'In Lower Mount Street a pedestrian in a brown mackintosh, eating dry bread, passed swiftly and unscathed across the Viceroy's path.' He is Death himself, the mysterious man in the mackintosh at Paddy's funeral, who symbolically foretells the death of British rule in Dublin. Several of these sections point to Stephen as he might have been: if he had followed his teacher's advice and taken his singing more seriously, he might have been a successful tenor; on the other hand, if his eyesight had got worse he might have ended up as a blind piano-tuner. Mulligan discusses Stephen cogently:

> — They drove his wits astray, he said, by visions of hell. He will
> never capture the Attic note. The note of Swinburne, of all
> poets, the white death and the ruddy birth. That is his tragedy.

He can never be a poet. The joy of creation. . . .

But he is too anxious to write Stephen off as uncreative. Mulligan himself, despite his flow of quotation and parody, will turn out to be sterile.

## II.viii. 'Sirens'

*Ulysses* is structured on musical principles throughout, and contains many references to opera and song; but the 'Sirens' is by far the most musical of the chapters. It begins with a set of fifty-eight fragments, the first of which is 'Bronze by Gold Heard the Hoofirons, Steely-ringing' — which means literally that Miss Lydia Douce, with bronze hair, and Miss Mina Kennedy, with gold hair, the barmaids at the Ormond Hotel, hear the Viceregal procession go past. This introduction is best described as a catalogue of motifs, like those printed at the beginning of the scores of Wagner's *Ring*; for the convenience of performers and audience the list gives the motifs or themes called 'Rhine-maidens', 'Loki', 'Siegfried', etc. The beginning of 'Sirens' is there to remind us that the whole of *Ulysses* is based on the verbal equivalent of the *leitmotif*, which is a phrase associated with a character or an idea and reappearing in various transformations throughout the work. The fragments as printed here also make up a mysterious prose poem, which cannot be understood at first reading, but which gradually yields its meaning as the context of each phrase in the chapter becomes clear. Joyce described the technique of the chapter as a 'fugue' and this has given the critics some trouble. The phrase that Joyce gave Gilbert, *fuga per canonem* ('fugue according to rule') is archaic and adds nothing: all that matters is that a fugue is a contrapuntal composition for a given number (usually three or four) of parts or 'voices': the voices enter successively in imitation of each other; the opening entry or 'subject' is in the tonic key, the next entry or 'answer' is in the dominant. A fugue is not a strict musical form; still less is 'Sirens' in strict musical form, but with its echoing repetitions, it does offer ingenious equivalents to counterpoint and imitation.

There are also equivalents to other musical devices, such as variations of tempo, rhythm, volume and orchestral colour. Two songs are sung in the music room adjoining the bar: 'M'appari' from Flotow's *Martha* in the sweet tenor voice of Simon Dedalus, and a nationalistic ballad 'The Croppy Boy' sung by baritone Ben Dollard; the latter gives yet another version of Irish violence, even in this lyrical context.

The text of 'The Croppy Boy' weaves in and out of Bloom's interior monologue, and he begins to think of another famous nationalist text, Robert Emmet's last speech, 'When my country takes her place among the nations of the earth, then and not till then let my epitaph be written.' Unfortunately Bloom has an attack of flatulence and his wind instrument adds a fifth voice to the counterpoint:

> *Then and not till then.* Tram. Kran, kran, kran [the sound of the tram]. Good oppor, Coming. Krandlkrankran. I'm sure it's the burgund. Yes. One, two. *Let my epitaph be.* Karaaaaaa. *Written.* I have.
> Pprrpffrrppfff [This includes the signs for pianissimo and fortissimo].
> *Done.*

The Homeric counterpart is musical. Circe warns Odysseus about the perils of the Sirens, who lure sailors to their deaths. If he wants to hear their beautiful song, he must stick wax in the ears of his crew, and get them to tie him to the mast. He does this and is able to hear the dangerous ladies in safety. The Sirens are the two barmaids, their isle is the bar: a place of danger, where many Dubliners, though not Bloom, ruin their health. The two singers, Dedalus senior and Dollard, are both alcoholics; poor Paddy Dignam's death was indirectly caused by drink, and there are many other instances of alcoholic excess in the book, including Stephen's. Bloom, prudent as usual, drinks very little; a glass of cider with his dinner in the hotel was all, though combined with the glass of burgundy he enjoyed three hours earlier, it was enough to give him flatulence. Bloom likes music, but he is not seduced by it as most of the Irish in this chapter seem to be. He remains cool and unravished even by Dedalus's final and triumphant high note. Drink also may increase venery, but Bloom, writing a letter to his unseen friend Martha Clifford, is indifferent to the charms of the barmaids.

The Biblical counterpart is the Song of Songs (Song of Solomon, or Canticles), the only book in the Bible that is called a song, and the only one which is a scarcely disguised pagan erotic poem. In Christian tradition it is allegorised into the marriage of Christ and the Church, an absurdity that must have delighted Joyce and encouraged him to invent even stranger allegories.

## II.ix. 'Cyclops'

Joyce was often called a satirist when *Ulysses* first appeared but the term was gradually dropped by the critics as being too narrow to describe the whole book. Nevertheless parts of *Ulysses* are certainly satirical, most notably the 'Cyclops' chapter. Satire is not a literary form but the expression of an attitude to experience, a militant and critical attitude. It involves an attack on folly or vice or both by means of ridicule, always employing some degree of wit and humour, since straightforward invective is hard to take except in very small doses. Parody, exaggeration and reduction are normal techniques of the satirist, and Joyce was a master of these. In other chapters his parodies are purely comic, as in the 'Oxen of the Sun' but in 'Cyclops' they are used with propagandist intent, in a deliberate rejection of violence and especially the violence of nationalist Ireland. This, as we have seen, is a running theme in *Ulysses*, but at this point Joyce focuses his attack with venom on the figure of the Cyclops-Citizen, who stands for all that is worst about Ireland. The chapter also examines the problem of nationalist politics in general, and the freedom of small nations, which remains one of the greatest problems of our day. The violence of British imperialism is satirically attacked, and Bloom asserts the values of liberalism, pacificism and tolerance. He is absurdly humiliated, but is finally spiritually victorious. His is the triumph of mind over body, of love over hatred.

Bloom comes to Barney Kiernan's pub on an errand of mercy; he wants to see Martin Cunningham about the insurance for Paddy Dignam's widow. He neither accepts nor buys drinks, but engages in conversation with a group of customers. The conversation centres on politics, but turns also to such subjects as hanging, sport, boxing, flogging in the British Navy, lynching in America — all connected with muscular violence. When Bloom goes out for a while, feeling rises against him, especially since he is wrongly believed to have won a bet on 'Throwaway', in which case it would have been etiquette to stand drinks all round. The discussion becomes more and more political, embracing anti-semitism and that most inflammatory of topics, religion. On his return, Bloom has to face the drunken rage of the Citizen: he courageously stands up for the Jews, and only just escapes physical assault. As Martin Cunningham drives him off the Citizen throws a biscuit tin after him, but misses.

A major motif in *Ulysses* is the similarity between the Jews and the

Irish: both are oppressed people struggling for independence (e.g. Parnell as the Irish Moses, see 'Aeolus'). The irony of this chapter is that no one except Bloom is able to see this similarity. 'Only connect' is E. M. Forster's advice: the Citizen and his friends cannot 'connect', and thus their legitimate nationalism has become barbarous insularity, as tyrannical as the foreign rule to which it is opposed. This is one of the reasons why Joyce rejected the demands of nationalism on himself as artist and went into exile.

The chapter is a wonderfully comic and accurate recreation of Dublin pub talk. The anonymous narrator is the authentic voice of Dublin, speaking the purest demotic idiom. The conversation reflects the main obsessions of the Irish (whom Joyce calls in *Finnegans Wake* 'phillohippic theobibbous') — religion, politics, horses, drink and song. The narrator's flow is interspersed with digressions which do not reflect his voice or thoughts, but take off tangentially from the topics he raises. These contain the finest parodies and the most telling satire in the book: Rabelaisian burlesque, mock-heroic, and grossly inflatory travesty. Joyce ridicules bad journalism, fake versions of epics like *Ossian*, and the apocalyptic tone of nationalist rhetoric. Incidentally, the version of history given by the Citizen is hardly at all exaggerated from that favoured by the IRA today and only a little more from that taught in some Irish schools. It is not, however, a totally false view: the account of the English attitude to the Famine has some basis in truth. 'Perfectly true, says Bloom. But my point was. . . .' He is not allowed to finish this sentence, but by the end of the chapter Bloom makes his point: the only means of waking up from the nightmare of history is 'Love . . . I mean the opposite of hatred.' Bloom speaks with the voice of Christ, and narrowly avoids crucifixion; other theological meanings are suggested at the end of the notes. But he is also in his moment of humiliation a triumphant representative of humanism.

In Book IX of the *Odyssey* Odysseus and his men land on the island of Polyphemus, the Cyclops, one of a race of one-eyed giants, who do not obey the laws of the gods of men. Some are caught by the Giant, carried off to his cave and eaten one by one. Odysseus makes Polyphemus drunk, blinds him with a heated stake, and escapes from the cave by clinging to a sheep's belly. Odysseus has told Polyphemus that his name is *Outis* (Nobody): when Polyphemus cries out in pain and the other Cyclopes ask who has hurt him he replies 'nobody', and so they do not come to his aid. Once he has escaped to his ship Odysseus rashly taunts Polyphemus, who throws a huge rock at him and nearly sinks his ship. 'Nobody' is the anonymous narrator of the episode, the voice of demotic Dublin, who could as well be Everyman. Bloom shows the same qualities as Ulysses, resourcefulness, prudence as a rule but occasionally rashness which goes beyond courage. Minor correspondences include the blinding in the first sentence — 'I was just passing the time of day with old Troy of the D.M.P. at the corner of Arbour Hill there and be damned but a bloody sweep came along and he near drove his gear into my eye' — and when the Citizen throws the biscuit tin (rock) at the end — 'Mercy of God the sun was in his eyes or he'd have left him for dead.' Bloom's cigar is the glowing stake used for the blinding. In the first sentence 'D.M.P.' means Dublin Metropolitan Police and this combined with the legal rigmarole of a few pages later reminds us that the Cyclops does not care for law; Bloom, a man of peace, is all in favour of law and order. When Bloom escapes he is called 'sheepface' to remind us of Odysseus under the ram's belly.

The Cyclops-Citizen rejects established law and offers only the violence of terrorism and muscle. He is based on Michael Cusack, the founder of the GAA (Gaelic Athletic Association) and a member of the IRB (Irish Republican Brotherhood, or Fenians). The IRB was an ancestor of the modern IRA and used bombs and other forms of murder to assist the liberation of Ireland. They did not recognise the law-courts of the established government, or indeed any authority except their own elected leadership. The art of the chapter is politics; this means revolutionary and violent nationalism set against the violence of British imperialism; the political overtones of religion, which are all-important in Ireland; anti-semitism as a particularly disgusting form of political prejudice; and finally Bloom's mild liberalism. The Gaelic Athletic Association was also a political organisation and played quite an important part in the liberation, as I have mentioned in an earlier chapter. Joyce is also making the point that the Irish people in his time were fond of violence in sport and in other forms of entertainment, as Synge shows brilliantly in *The Playboy of the Western World*. Violence also goes with heavy drinking and Irish *machismo*, which are the themes of 'Counterparts' in *Dubliners*. (Bloom in these respects too is an outsider.) The 'Cyclops' chapter, by introducing the sports movement and its founder, neatly combines the art of politics with the bodily 'organ', which is 'muscle'. Interwoven with many detailed references to the history of Irish nationalism are descriptions of sports and in particular a boxing match. Hardly less barbarous and Cyclopean are the discussions and fantasies about corporal and capital punishment.

The Biblical correspondences are mainly Old Testament, since Stephen is totally absent. They hang on the prophet Elijah, who ascended to heaven in a chariot of fire, and whose second coming is said in Jewish tradition to precede the coming of the Messiah. But since in Christian belief the Old Testament Prophets all forecast the coming of Jesus Christ as Messiah, there are foretastes of Christ in this as in all other chapters, especially in the public execution episode. But the full meaning of the various religious motives does not become clear until the end of the chapter.

The technique of the chapter is called 'gigantism', another nonce-word, which can be taken to mean exaggeration, or hyperbole. The narrative of Noman is interrupted by thirty-three parodies each of which takes off at a tangent from the last subject he has mentioned, and exaggerates the subject fantastically. The effect is like 'mock-heroic', which was one of the main vehicles of satire in the eighteenth century: *Ulysses* in general and 'Cyclops' in particular can be compared to Pope's *Dunciad*, where trivial events in the literary life of Grub Street are given heroic status. The point of this inflation is that the victim will eventually blow up with his own flatulence. The parodies in 'Cyclops' are of bad translations of Homer, Macpherson's *Ossian*, Irish legends used by nationalists, various kinds of sensational journalism, and a pseudo-scientific account of an earthquake. The change of scale is derived from the Brobdingnag section of *Gulliver's Travels*.

The scene is 'the Tavern', that is Barney Kiernan's pub in Little Britain Street. Everyone is drinking hard throughout the action, and at the end everyone is fairly drunk, except Bloom. The first sight of the Cyclops-Citizen is as he is sitting with his dog, 'that bloody mangy mongrel Garryowen, and he waiting for what the sky would drop in the way of drink . . . and his load of papers, working for the cause.'

> The figure seated on a large boulder at the foot of a round tower was that of a broadshouldered deepchested stronglimbed frankeyed redhaired freelyfreckled shaggybearded widemouthed largenosed longheaded deepvoiced barekneed brawnyhanded hairylegged ruddyfaced sinewyarmed hero.

(That should be recited in one breath, if possible and *crescendo*.)

The conversation turns on Paddy Dignam's death and the possible appearance of his ghost, with a parody of a Yeatsian spiritualist séance; and then on to hanging. Bloom begins his political argument with the Citizen, who silences him with an appeal to patriotic song ('The memory of the dead') and the slogan *Sinn Fein* ('Ourselves alone', suitable for the barbarous insularity of the Cyclops). The next long parody is of a journalistic description of an imaginary public execution: the victim is one of the heroes of 1798, who is to be hung, drawn and quartered in Elizabethan style.

> [Near the public executioner] were neatly arranged the quartering knife, the various finely tempered disembowelling appliances (specially supplied by the worldfamous firm of cutlers, Messrs John Round and Sons, Sheffield), a terracotta saucepan for the reception of the duodenum, colon, blind intestine and appendix etc. when successfully extracted and two commodious milkjugs destined to receive the most precious blood of the most precious victim.

The quotation of the liturgy indicates that this hero is a Fenian Christ; there are two religions in Ireland, nationalism and Catholicism, but the latter always gives way to the former under pressure.

After talk about sport and the revival of the Irish language the British are attacked in the funniest part of the chapter. Bloom tries to put in a good word for them, with 'moderation and botheration and their colonies and their civilisation'.

> — Their syphilisation, you mean, says the citizen. To hell with them. The curse of a goodfornothing God light sideways on the bloody thicklugged sons of whores gets! No music and no art and no literature worthy of the name. Any civilisation they have they stole from us. Tongue-tied sons of bastards' ghosts.
> — The European family, says J.J. . . . .
> — They're not European, says the citizen. I was in Europe with Kevin Egan of Paris. You wouldn't see a trace of them or their language anywhere in Europe except in a *cabinet d'aisance*.

To understand the joke one has to know that in the late nineteenth century lavatory porcelain made by Shanks of Paisley was widely exported to Europe; and that the next passage parodies Irish legend, Ossian and Homer himself: a *medher* is a pail, and the other piece of Irish means 'Up the Red Hand' (of Ulster).

> He said and then lifted he in his rude great brawny strengthy

hands the medher of dark strong foamy ale and, uttering his
tribal slogan, *Lamh Dearg Abu*, he drank to the undoing of his
foes, a race of mighty valorous heroes, rulers of the waves, who
sit on thrones of alabaster silent as the deathless gods.

Bloom soon compares the Irish to the Jews, who are a persecuted
minority, and then says pathetically 'it's no use . . . Force, hatred,
history, all that' and recommends 'Love . . . I mean the opposite of
hatred.' Nothing could be flatter than that. He leaves and is mocked
by all present. Just before he returns the fatal subject of religion has
come up. When Martin Cunningham says before drinking 'God bless
all here is my prayer', there is the finest and most Baroque interlude
of all: a huge procession of saints advances through Dublin to bless
Barney Kiernan's pub. In the list of saints the names of all the customers
appear, including Bloom (Leopold) and even Garryowen the dog
(Owen Caniculus) and the narrator (S. Anonymous).

When Bloom returns the Citizen is very drunk, truculent and now
openly anti-semitic. Bloom finally turns to defend his religion just
as Martin Cunningham has got him into a carriage.

And says he:
— Mendelssohn was a jew and Karl Marx and Mercadante and
Spinoza. And the Saviour was a jew and his father was a jew.
Your God.
— He had no father, says Martin. That'll do now. Drive ahead.
— Whose God? says the citizen.
— Well, his uncle was a jew, says he. Your God was a jew.
Christ was a jew like me.
Gob, the citizen made a plunge back into the shop.
— By Jesus, says he, I'll brain that bloody jewman for using
the holy name. By Jesus, I'll crucify him so I will. Give us that
biscuit-box here.

The Citizen throws the tin, but misses; the penultimate parody is the
only one to combine the voice of the anonymous interpolator with
that of the anonymous narrator:

When, lo, there came about them all a great brightness and they
beheld the chariot wherein He stood ascend to heaven. And they
beheld Him in the chariot, clothed upon in the glory of the
brightness. . . . And they beheld Him even Him, Ben Bloom

Elijah, amid clouds of angels ascend to the glory of the brightness at an angle of forty-five degrees over Donohoe's in Little Green Street like a shot off a shovel.

There are just thirteen customers in the pub, making a kind of Last Supper. Counting one way, Bloom is Judas and the Citizen is a Fenian Christ; counting another way, the Citizen is Judas, and Bloom the type of a humanist Christ.

II.x. 'Nausicaa'

Tired after his escape from the Cyclops-Citizen, and after a visit of sympathy to the widowed Mrs Dignam in Sandymount (an episode not recounted) Bloom stops for a rest on the rocks of Sandymount Strand. This is just where Stephen stopped during his morning walk ('Proteus'). It is notionally 8 p.m. at the beginning of the chapter: 'The summer evening had begun to fold the world in its mysterious embrace. Far away in the west the sun was setting and the last glow of all too fleeting day lingered lovingly on sea and strand.' As far as I can make out, the sun does not set in the latitude of Dublin on Blooms-day until 9 p.m. G.M.T. (there was no 'summer time' in 1904) — perhaps Joyce slipped up here. He is careful to point out that Bloom is facing the east, away from the setting sun; it is easy to visualise the scene incorrectly in this highly pictorial chapter. On the beach are three young women, looking after twin infant boys and a baby: two of the girls are playing with the baby but the third, Gerty MacDowell, sits on the rocks. Bloom admires her and she him, at a discreet distance. After dark there is a firework display on the horizon, during which Bloom, his gaze fixed on Gerty's underwear, masturbates. When Gerty gets up to go, Bloom sees that she is lame. He daydreams for a while, then dozes quietly until the end of the chapter.

Nausicaa is the princess who encounters Odysseus on the beach of Phaeacia, where he had been shipwrecked. After the storm he is naked and penniless, but covering himself as best he can he makes a speech eloquent enough to convince Nausicaa that he really is the Prince of Ithaca; she gives him clothes and takes him back to her royal parents. Clothes are a basic theme in this chapter: Nausicaa is laundering the palace linen with her maidenly companions, and Gerty and Bloom have many thoughts about underwear. Samuel Butler had a theory that a woman wrote the *Odyssey*, leaving a concealed self-portrait in the character of Nausicaa. Joyce uses this theory and writes the first half of the chapter in the most sickening style of the popular lady-novelists, as found in the cheap women's magazines of the day. This half Joyce calls 'tumescene' in technique, and in it he used every sentimental cliché and journalistic vulgarity he could find. By comparison, the second half, in the technique of 'detumescene', is sad and sober.

The theological level is fairly explicit where Gerty is concerned: 'the voice of prayer to her who is in her pure radiance a beacon ever to the storm-tossed heart of man, Mary, *star of the sea*', in the first paragraph, announces the themes (as well as referring to Odysseus in the storm). The background to the mysterious encounter of Gerty and Bloom is the Litany of the Blessed Virgin Mary which is being sung in a nearby church. Direct quotation of this Litany is interwoven with allusions to it in the sickly description of Gerty herself: 'The waxen pallor of her face was almost spiritual [*vas spirituale*] in its ivorylike [*turris eburnea*] purity though her rosebud [*rosa mystica*] mouth was a genuine cupid's bow [*foedera arca*] . . . a languid queenly hauteur [*regina angelorum*]', etc. The identification of Gerty and the Virgin is fully worked out: blue is Mary's colour and Gerty's eyes 'were of the bluest Irish blue', she wore a 'neat blouse of electric blue', a hat with an underbrim of 'eggblue chenille' and on her underclothes 'she was wearing the blue for luck, hoping against hope, her own colour'. 'Star of the sea' in the first paragraph refers to the hymn 'Ave, maris stella'; the image of the star is developed in the fireworks episode. The whole chapter centres on the concepts of *woman, moon, tide, sea* (introducing the erroneous connection between the moon and menstruation), just as Molly Bloom's monologue in 'Penelope' does, but with an obvious difference: Molly is a powerful and realistic earth-mother, Gerty a feeble creature living in a world of fantasy.

The autoerotic confrontation with Bloom can only mean one thing: the impregnation of the Virgin Mary by God the Holy Ghost, sent from God the Father. Bloom in this chapter is the Old Testament God, who has decided to begin the New Dispensation by creating a son on earth with a mortal mother. Since there is no physical contact with the mother, the act can blasphemously be linked to onanism (as in the Egyptian creation myth that is used in *Finnegans Wake*). At the end God is naturally exhausted, and can only wait gloomily for the events of Holy week (the Last Supper and the Crucifixion), of which he can only be an impotent spectator. For the time being communication between heaven and earth is impossible. Bloom tries to write a message in the sand with his phallic stick, then gives up.

Mr Bloom effaced the letters with his slow boot. Hopeless thing sand. Nothing grows in it. All fades. . . . He flung his wooden pen away. The stick fell in silted sand, stuck. Now if you were trying to do that for a week on end you couldn't. Chance. We'll never meet again.

We are now in dead universe, ruled by pure chance; but it seems that a minor miracle has taken place.

II.xi. 'The Oxen of the Sun'

At 10 p.m. Bloom pays a call to the National Maternity Hospital in Holles Street to enquire after an acquaintance, Mrs Purefoy, who has been having a difficult accouchement. There he finds a number of medical students eating and drinking in a staff room, and Stephen with them; Mulligan later puts in an appearance. Most of the young men are fairly drunk at the beginning of the chapter and very drunk at the end, especially Stephen, although he is able to hold forth on literary, theological and medical topics with fluency. Bloom is as prudent and sober as ever, secretly pouring away his glass from time to time. A nurse comes in with the good news that Mrs Purefoy has successfully given birth, and soon afterwards the company leaves for Burke's public house, and then Westland Row railway station, where it splits up: Stephen and Lynch take a train for the very short distance to Amiens Street station, whence they will proceed to the brothel district; Bloom, worried about Stephen's helpless drunkenness, decides to follow.

The Oxen of the Sun are the sacred herd of the god Helios. Odysseus has been warned that his crew must not kill these beasts or they will come to deadly harm. When they land on the Sun God's island, Odysseus makes his men swear that they will spare the cattle; but the crew break their oath and when Odysseus is asleep they kill and eat them. Zeus personally avenges this blasphemy by sending a thunderbolt that destroys all the crew; Odysseus alone escapes in the keel of his wrecked ship and is carried to Calypso's island (where we first see him in the epic). The thunderclap occurs literally in the narrative, when a shower sends down its fertilising rain on drought-stricken Ireland. But the destruction of the crew (the medical students including

Mulligan) must be taken as prophetic: they will perish as *creative artists* because they have broken a vow. That goes for Mulligan too: he will never be a poet (as he says of Stephen) but will remain a poetaster, with the outward shell of style but not the inward spirit — a prophecy which was more or less accurate. But what was the vow they broke? It has been suggested that as good Catholics they are committed to fertility ('Be fruitful and multiply') but since they consort with prostitutes and use contraceptives they have sinned against fertility: as Stephen talks in Aristotelian terms of 'these God-possibled souls we nightly impossiblize'. Bloom has also sinned in this respect, since he has performed the 'rite of Onan' in the 'Nausicaa' chapter, and thinks sadly of his failure as a progenitor.

The point reached in the Biblical (New Testament) narrative is the Last Supper, which takes place liturgically on Maundy Thursday. The analogy between Stephen and Christ, sitting at table, eating and drinking with his disciples, is clear enough, and extends to Stephen's theological discourses, which are almost sermons, full of Biblical allusions that point to the imminent death of Christ on the Cross. Stephen's fear of death emerges powerfully through his learned jesting.

The most obvious fact about 'The Oxen of the Sun' is that it is written in a series of different English 'period' styles, arranged in roughly chronological order. These are always said to symbolise the growth of the child in the womb, in keeping with the gynaecological subject-matter of the chapter, and of course that must be correct. But if I am right in my interpretation of the theme of fertility, the historical parodies have a second meaning: they are the empty shells of literature. Literature in essence was to Joyce the same in every age: Homer is our contemporary, the character of Odysseus is eternally true to human nature, true poetry cannot date. What does change is the accidental part of literature, the language of the age, the conventions and clichés, the 'formulae' or repeated phrases of Homer: only in this relatively trivial sense can literature be said to evolve. Yet paradoxically, the creative writer whose final concern is with the unchanging part of experience and of art is forced to deal with the transient and inessential media of style and language, and must wrestle with them endlessly, since he has nothing else to use. This is the central literary paradox of *Ulysses*: just as Joyce had to immerse himself in the trivia of 1904, the advertisements, comic songs, gossip and other transient rubbish of the moment, so he had to master the language of his day, doomed to vanish as certainly as Anglo-Saxon. Perhaps

Joyce designed the set of pastiches to reassure himself that the writers
of every age have faced the same problems. Whatever his reason for
using so much effort and space, Joyce clearly enjoyed himself greatly:
he is a master of parody, as he has already demonstrated in the fake-
Elizabethan of 'Scylla and Charybdis' and the mock-heroic of 'Cyclops'.
The different styles of the masters of English prose are beautifully
taken off in the 'Oxen', which to students of the history of English
literature is one of the most amusing chapters.

A reason why the pastiches are so convincing has only recently
come to light: they are in part *centos* or mosaics, that is, compilations
using the actual words and phrases of the authors parodied. Joyce,
though very learned, was not omniscient: to save time in his quest
for authenticity he went to two well-known anthologies of English
prose, Saintsbury's *History of English Prose Rhythm*, and Peacock's
*English Prose from Mandeville to Ruskin* (World's Classics, 1903, a book
which I had on my shelves for many years without realising that Joyce
used it). The details can be found in Phillip F. Herring's edition of
*Joyce's* Ulysses *Notebooks in the British Museum* (University Press of
Virginia, 1972), in which there are acknowledgments to the earlier
discoveries of Janusko and Atherton. The main point is that Joyce
pillaged these two books thoroughly, rewriting whole paragraphs
only enough to make them fit the context of the 'Oxen' and leaving
as many of the original words as possible: he parodied little that is
not in these two books, except the Bible. After the prologue the
styles are as follows. First, Anglo-Saxon alliterative poetry, especially
the 'Wanderer'; the fifteenth-century morality play *Everyman*; *The
Travels of Sir John Mandeville* (fourteenth century); Malory, *Le Morte
d'Arthur* (the eulogy of Bloom and his soft hand under a hen is modelled
on the eulogy of Sir Lancelot towards the end of Malory). This is
followed by a series of sixteenth-century writers to be found in
Peacock's anthology, such as Elyot, Berners, Florio, North and
Hakluyt. But the splendid phrase about the Prodigal Son wasting his
substance, 'murdered his goods with whores', is drawn from Wyclif's
translation of St Luke's Gospel of the fourteenth century. The Autho-
rised Version of the Bible is used in the next passage, with more
Elizabethan prose. Then there is a major shift of style to the Latinate
masters of the earlier seventeenth century, especially Sir Thomas
Browne; this is one of Joyce's triumphs. It is followed by the plain
style of John Bunyan, and the Restoration diarists Pepys and Evelyn.
The next author is Defoe, with extensive use of the whole novel

*Colonel Jack* and of shorter extracts in Peacock. Joyce knew Swift's *A Tale of a Tub* too well to need to take it from an anthology: the story of the Irish Bull is very close to the first great Anglo-Irish writer in form and content. Addison and Steele's *Tatler* and *Spectator* are followed by Sterne, *A Sentimental Journey* (1768), with a set of indecent puns that would have delighted Sterne. The next originals are Goldsmith, *A Citizen of the World*; Burke's oratorical style; the prose of Alexander Pope; and Gilbert White of Selborne, from Peacock. Joyce's next parody is of the oratory of Richard Brinsley Sheridan rather than his plays. It is not accidental that Sterne, Goldsmith, Burke and Sheridan are, like Swift, Anglo-Irish writers, all interested in rhetoric and games with language. The next rhetoricians of the eighteenth century are English, 'Junius' and Gibbon. Romanticism begins with Horace Walpole's Gothic novel *The Castle of Otranto*, with echoes of the Anglo-Irish Le Fanu's *The House by the Churchyard*. Charles Lamb is followed by De Quincey, especially his 'Dream Fugue' from *The English Mail Coach*, which is a vision of death — death is very much at the centre of the characters' thoughts at this point in the chapter. The other nineteenth-century authors are, in order of their appearance, Landor (*Imaginary Conversations*); Macaulay; Thomas Henry Huxley, the naturalist, with a little Hazlitt; Dickens, especially chapter 53 of *David Copperfield*, with some passages of Thackeray from Peacock; Cardinal Newman, who was Joyce's favourite prose stylist; Ruskin; and, going slightly out of chronological order, Thomas Carlyle, with some passages of Lockhart, Scott's biographer, from Peacock. Carlyle's eccentric and exhibitionist prose is offered as the ultimate development of Victorian style. Thereafter there is no single literary style in the parody, but a mixture of slang, thieves' cant, and other specialised English, with fragmentary quotations, grotesquely imitating the drunken conversation of Stephen and the medical students. This messy epilogue also stands for the afterbirth.

The chapter symbolises the growth of the child in the womb in ways other than stylistic. Joyce wrote a longish account of his design in a letter to Budgen (*Letters*, vol. i, pp. 139–40), which shows that he structured the passage to imitate the growth of the human foetus, with oblique references to the nature of the foetus at various stages, using details culled from books on obstetrics and embryology. Believing with Haeckel that ontogeny repeats phylogeny (the embryo recapitulates the stages of faunal evolution, from tadpole through fish to monkey, etc.) he also worked in references to the phyla of the animal world in the order of their appearance on earth. Again, by references to earlier chapters of *Ulysses*, 'The Oxen of the Sun' illustrates the growth of the book itself up to this point. All this was worked out in an extraordinary article by A. M. Klein ('The Oxen of the Sun', *Here and Now*, Toronto, 1, January 1949), which many critics think is just too complicated. I personally do not think so: Klein, a Montreal lawyer and poet, was a genius who unfortunately did not complete his study of *Ulysses*; I think he understood the complexities of Joyce's mind very well. Another excellent but simpler treatment of the chapter is by J. S. Atherton (in the collection of essays edited by Hart and Hayman, 1974).

## II.xii. 'Circe'

At midnight Stephen, very drunk, with his friend Lynch, makes for the brothel quarter. They are pursued by Bloom, who had lost sight of them at the railway station, but is now determined to see that Stephen comes to no harm. He catches up with Stephen in Mrs Cohen's establishment at No. 82 Tyrone Street Lower. Joyce calls the district 'Nighttown', which was Dublin journalists' slang for the late shift on a newspaper; the local name was in fact 'Monto' after Montgomery Street (which no longer exists). After some desultory conversations Stephen dances a frenzied waltz, becomes giddy, has a vision of his dead mother, smashes the gas mantle with his walking stick, and rushes outside. Bloom pacifies Mrs Cohen, and finds Stephen in a meaningless confrontation with two drunken British soldiers: one of them believes that Stephen has insulted the King of England, so knocks him down and disappears. Bloom speaks tactfully to a policeman and says that he will look after Stephen. Standing over Stephen's unconscious body, he has a vision of his dead son Rudy.

The Homeric story is that of the witch Circe (Kirke) who transforms some of Odysseus' men into pigs. Odysseus is warned by Hermes of her, and given an apotropaic herb called 'moly'. He confronts Circe and conquers her magic with his moly; he then makes her swear that she will release his men and do him no harm. She keeps her word and entertains Odysseus and his men handsomely; she gives him good advice about his descent into Hades and about dealing with the Sirens and Scylla and Charybdis. The whore who turns men into swine is a magnificently apt correspondence: we are to remember that *syphilis*, though actually of unknown origin, has been derived from Greek 'swine' and 'love' in popular etymology. Bloom's moly that preserves him from enchantment is literally the piece of potato he carries in his pocket as a remedy for rheumatism; on another level, it is his sexual indifference after the evening's masturbation and his natural prudence which prevails over perverse lust.

In the Biblical narrative this chapter seems to have three parallels. Since it is at the end of Book II of *Ulysses*, the Old Testament or Jewish section, it refers to the last book of the Old Testament, that of the prophet Malachi and in particular Chapter 4, verse 5: 'Behold, I will send you Elijah the prophet before the coming of the great and dreadful day of the Lord.' The appearance of the American evangelist Elijah J. Dowie, which bears on the manifestation of Bloom himself as Elijah in 'Cyclops', is one of the most dramatic moments in the chapter. Malachi is also suggested by Mulligan's name. In parallel there is the last book of the New Testament, the Revelation of St John of Patmos: the apocalyptic theme resounds powerfully, from the building of the New Bloomusalem in the shape of a giant kidney to the scene of destruction ('Dublin's burning') at the end. The third set of Biblical references is to the Passion narrative. Stephen suffers at the hands of the British soldiers (British equals Roman throughout *Ulysses*) and is crucified on the 'pavement' (for the *Lithostroton* or Pavement see the Gospel of John). This corresponds liturgically to the Good Friday rites and especially to the 'Tenebrae' or 'darkness', which recalls Good Friday when the candles in the church are extinguished to symbolise the temporary loss of hope with the physical death of Christ on the Cross: hence the smashing of Mrs Cohen's gas lamp. At the end of the chapter Bloom as God the Father looks down sorrowfully from heaven at his crucified Son, who is a fusion of the unconscious Stephen and the dead Rudy. If there were any doubt about the liturgical significance of the chapter it would be banished by Stephen's drunken chanting of 'the introit for paschal time' as he enters: 'Vidi aquam egredientem de templo a latere dextro. Alleluia' ('I saw a stream of water welling forth from the right side of the Temple' — referring allegorically to the blood and water coming from Christ's side wound). This antiphon strikes a note of joy, and reminds us that *Ulysses* is to be a Divine Comedy.

The main difficulty about reading this very long and densely packed chapter is that it places three levels of discourse in apparent equality. Everything is printed as if it were a play, with characters' names, stage directions and dialogue. But only a small part of this is literal, giving the actual words and actions of Stephen, Bloom and a few other characters. A slightly larger proportion consists of interior monologue, mostly Bloom's but most dramatically Stephen's at the crucial apparition of his dead mother. The greater part of the chapter is, however, a dramatisation of *fantasy*. Each fantasy takes off at a tangent from some point in the conversation that touches on the ambitions, hopes and fears of Bloom and to a lesser extent of Stephen; each, however much action it may appear to contain, takes place almost instantaneously in the real time of the narrative. In this respect they are as dreams were once said to be (now I understand that dreams have been proved to take a measurable amount of time), or as is also said about the last thoughts of a drowning man. When the fantasies, interior monologues and literal narratives are put together, the chapter forms a five-act drama, with a prologue and epilogue, as follows.

Prologue — all literal. Stage directions: the 'Nighttown' scene. Enter Stephen and Lynch, who go into the brothel.

Act I — enter Bloom, in pursuit. He is worried about being seen in such disreputable surroundings and his anxiety produces a sequence of minor apparitions: his father, mother, wife and old flame Mrs Breen. Finally he imagines himself being arrested and put on trial for various offences: this long fantasy ends with the appearance of Paddy Dignam's ghost.

Act II — Bloom enters the brothel and talks to Zoe (Greek for 'life'), a young whore. He starts to hold forth in mock-serious, typically Bloomian style on the evils of smoking: Zoe says, 'Go on. Make a stump speech out of it', at which point Bloom's speech slides into fantasy. He becomes a famous orator, politician, lord mayor, king, builder of the New Bloomusalem, until his power collapses and he is martyred; at the end of the wonderfully comic delusion of grandeur Zoe says, 'talk away till you're black in the face', a direct continuation of her last words.

Act III — the literal action consists of desultory conversation between Stephen, Bloom and the whores: Bloom's fantasies concern his grandfather Virag, whose discourse is Jewish, clinical and obscure.

Act IV — enter the whore-mistress Bella Cohen. Bloom stares at her and starts a long train of masochistic fantasy, in which he and Bella undergo a sex change. This is the closest that Odysseus–Bloom gets to falling into Circe's power, since masochism is evidently a serious temptation; but one of Bloom's trouser buttons snaps and the spell is broken; when Bloom comes to his senses, Bella says, 'You'll know me the next time.'

Act V — mostly concerns Stephen and his fantasies: he dances drunkenly, is haunted by his mother's ghost and smashes the lamp (in fact, only the gas mantle). Bloom has little to do but pay for the damage, which is not serious, placate Bella, calm the whores, and follow Stephen into the street.

In the Epilogue Bloom can do no more; and the brothel is left behind for ever. Stephen must suffer his Calvary alone; and he brings on his own execution by his ambiguous and provocative remarks to the British soldiers. There are a few fantasies, nearly all concerned with violence, both British imperialistic and Irish nationalistic, with echoes of 'Cyclops'. At the apocalyptic climax of violence, 'Dublin's burning', a Black Mass is celebrated by Mulligan and Haines, with a recall of 'Telemachus'. The last words are more of a vision than a fantasy, when Bloom superimposes his dead son Rudy on Stephen.

These fantasies are obviously akin to dreams, and not only in their instantaneous duration: they are related to the dreams of anxiety, of sexual arousal and of wish fulfilment, that are the common experience of mankind. The whole chapter has a dreamlike logic and points forward to *Finnegans Wake*, even in the use of puns. The fantasies are meant to be interpreted in a broadly Freudian sense, in that they have a latent content in contrast to their manifest content; the latent content can only be divined by putting each piece of apparent nonsense in the context of the whole novel, just as Freud interpreted the apparent nonsense of his patients' dreams by placing them in the context of their lives. Joyce had evidently read Freud by the time of writing this chapter, although I do not think he wanted to interpret his material according to the orthodox Freudian theory of the Oedipus complex. Bloom does not seem to have Oedipal feelings about his father or his mother; Stephen has a special relationship with his dead mother, which he must break, but it does not appear to be specifically Oedipal.

If 'Circe' is Freudian in showing the immense capacity and power of the unconscious mind, it is also related to more orthodox forms of psychiatry. The fantasies are intended to be typical of the major types of mental disease, as described in the standard textbooks of the early twentieth century. Bloom begins with the clinical state of anxiety and proceeds in Act II to paranoia, which usually shows in combination delusions of grandeur (building the New Bloomusalem) and persecution mania ('When in doubt persecute Bloom'). Act III is difficult to place, but I think that the curious twitchings of Virag are related to locomotor ataxia and to general paralysis of the insane (GPI), both of which are consequences of syphilis. GPI is what Oswald calls 'softening of the brain' in Ibsen's *Ghosts*, which is one of the sources of this chapter. In Act IV Bloom suffers from systematic delusions, mostly connected with his imagined change of sex, which are characteristic of schizophrenia, then known as 'dementia praecox'. In Act V Stephen's delusions also seem to be schizophrenic, and in a sense so is the whole chapter. A symptom of one kind of schizophrenia is the endowing of inanimate objects with life; in 'Circe' there are remarkable examples of this process of hypostasis, by which objects like pictures, trouser buttons and cakes of soap, and even abstractions like the Hours and the End of the World have speaking parts in the drama on equal terms with human beings.

The dividing line between mental disease and sexual deviation is an obscure one, but Joyce evidently thought that there was some connection. Certainly 'Circe' is full of deviations (or 'perversions' if that is not too loaded a word for Joyce). All Bloom's hidden longings for unorthodox sexual practices come to light, with full details which are sometimes disgusting and sometimes hilarious. We are not to believe, of course, that Bloom really practised all these bizarre rituals, any more than his creator did. Joyce was indeed given to sexual deviation, as his letters to Nora and various anecdotes show, but he was not using this chapter as a confessional. We can be fairly sure of this because so much of the material is drawn straight from the main nineteenth-century authority, Krafft-Ebing's *Psychopathia Sexualis*. Bloom's sexual profile is notable for fetishism (women's underclothes are more arousing than their bodies), transvestism (which is not necessarily the same as homosexuality) and masochism, all of which are at their strongest in the Bella Cohen episode. Krafft-Ebing derives all sexual deviation from masochism and Joyce appears to follow him. But Joyce had a more literary source for some of his more picturesque details, namely *Venus in Furs* (*Venus im Pelz*) by the author who gave his name to the deviation, Count Leopold (!) von Sacher-Masoch (1836–95), his novel being published posthumously in Bloomsyear. This is also a *locus classicus* of fetishism, since fur is one of the principal objects of this deviation. The plentiful quotations from these two sources are fully documented by Gifford and Seidman (1960). *Venus in Furs*, is, by the way, hardly pornographic, and is rich with unconscious humour and Bloom-like clowning. As for the converse of masochism, Joyce did not seem to have much use for the Marquis de Sade, since the overt message of *Ulysses* is the rejection of violence and cruelty.

Psychopathology in more folkloric terms has been called possession by demons, and this is a major theme of 'Circe,' allied appropriately to that of witchcraft. The apparitions resemble the hideous demons who assailed the desert Saint Anthony (and his pig!), as painted by Breughel and Bosch: they are monstrous forms, suggestive of sexual perversion, floating through the air around the saint's head in a surrealist carnival of evil. Joyce probably had these paintings in mind, and certainly used a literary work inspired by them. Flaubert's *Tentation de St Antoine* is quoted several times, as when Molly appears in oriental costume and Stephen as a cardinal. Flaubert's work is cast in quasi-dramatic form, and presents the disembodied voices of the dead and the living alike; it is therefore a formal model for 'Circe'. The saint is tempted not only by the obvious fleshly lusts, but also by more sophisticated offers of worldly powers and intellectual conquest, which the unseen Devil holds out to him; is tempted even by recondite heresies and finally by science itself. In his erudition and humour Flaubert is very close to Joyce.

The apparitions are not all demonic: some resemble the ghosts of the dead or the phantoms of the living that have been studied by psychical researchers. One of Joyce's favourite plays was Ibsen's *Ghosts*: the Norwegian word is *Gjengangere*, better translated by 'revenants' or 'returners': the events of the past recur over and over again; Captain Alving is reborn in his son Oswald. This cyclical notion is very much more important in *Finnegans Wake*, but is already present in 'Circe': all the persons, objects and events of the previous chapters of the book recur in this chapter, emerging from the past to haunt the present. The spirits of the dead are supposed to come back on Hallowe'en (All Souls' Night). This was also one of the nights when witches held their sabbaths, dancing round in a circle, like the giddy dance of Stephen and the whores. The most famous witches' sabbath in literature is in Goethe's *Faust*, Part Two, which Joyce undoubtedly uses in 'Circe'. The most terrifying ghost in the whole chapter is that of Stephen's mother. She is based on the ghost of Clytemnestra who appears to her son Orestes and drives on the Furies to punish the matricide in the *Eumenides* of Aeschylus. Stephen feels irrationally that he has killed his mother, by refusing to pray at her bedside, although he knows this to be logically nonsense. From this point on her ghost ceases to trouble him.

## III The Homecoming — i. 'Eumaeus'

Odysseus returns to his island of Ithaca alone and in danger of being murdered by Penelope's suitors. The goddess Athena advises him to disguise himself as an old man and to ask for the hospitality of Eumaeus the swineherd, who does in fact treat him well. Telemachus also returns to Ithaca quietly and comes to Eumaeus for news of his mother. After testing his loyalty Odysseus reveals himself to Telemachus, and together they plan how they can recover the house (Books XIII–XVI). Eumaeus is here represented by the keeper of the cabmen's coffee-stall, who is alleged to be 'Skin-the-Goat' or Fitzharris, one of the Phoenix Park Murderers (another disguise). The drunken sailor is a pseudo-Odysseus, i.e. a pretender to his title; Corley the ne'er-do-well (from the story 'Two Gallants' in *Dubliners*) is Odysseus' disloyal and scurrilous goatherd Malanthios. This is a rather slow and tedious section of the *Odyssey* and this chapter is apparently in slow motion.

The Gospels' narrative ceases with the Crucifixion, except for the brief account in three of them of the Resurrection. But there is a great deal in the Liturgy after Good Friday, and this is followed closely in the last three chapters of *Ulysses*. In the Creed and in the apocryphal 'Gospel of Nicodemus' it is said that Christ 'descended into hell', where he rescued the souls of certain Biblical worthies. In the Liturgy he is assumed to be in hell until Easter Sunday: 'the third day he rose again from the dead' and 'ascended into Heaven', passing through Purgatory *en route*. 'Eumaeus' therefore covers the rest of Good Friday; 'Ithaca' is Easter Saturday until Mass on Easter Sunday; and 'Penelope' is all time after that, or rather Christ's sojourn in Heaven, which is eternal and outside time. The three chapters fit logically into the three parts of Dante's *Divine Comedy*, 'Eumaeus' being the inferno. Dante's hell is arranged geographically in ever-deeper circles, with the worst classes of sinners lower down. At the very bottom are examples of treachery, the traitors to lords and masters being Brutus and Cassius, political murderers, and Judas: '— And that one was Judas, said Stephen, who up to then had said nothing whatsoever of any kind.' With the motif of assassination we are brought back to contemporary Irish politics and especially to the Phoenix Park Murders; hence the literal presence of the alleged Fitzharris, and hence Stephen's remark to Bloom: 'But oblige me by taking away that knife. I can't look at the point of it. It reminds me of Roman history.' Dante is mentioned two pages later; and some Italian ice-cream vendors quarrel in their own language. There are references to circles, rocks and flames ('the heap of barren cobblestones and by the light emanating from the brazier'); the whole atmosphere is dark and gloomy.

It is in fact the darkest hour of the night, at 1 a.m. Stephen is still very drunk and groggy from his knockout, and has hardly come to his senses by the end of the chapter. The organ of the chapter is 'nerves' (by which I suppose Joyce meant the central nervous system), and the narrative and prose style suggest exhausted twitching. The art of the chapter is 'navigation': literally Bloom has to navigate the bewildered Stephen to the cabman's shelter, and thence to Eccles Street. On a symbolic level, navigation means the art of getting through the moral and political dangers of the world, such as faced Dante, 'Nel mezzo del cammin di nostra vita'. Parnell turns up again, this time as an example of shipwreck, or poor navigation; his career ran on to the rocks of the O'Shea divorce, which is discussed at some length.

### III.ii. 'Ithaca'

It is now 2 a.m. Stephen, by now fairly well sobered up, accepts Bloom's invitation to come home to 7 Eccles Street with him for a cup of cocoa. They walk from the cabmen's shelter, discussing various topics on the way. On arrival, Bloom finds that he has forgotten his key, so jumps down into the basement well and comes up to the front door to let Stephen in. He lights a fire and boils a kettle, and they drink cocoa. Their conversation continues, turning on their mutual acquaintance, Mrs Riordan of *A Portrait*, there known as 'Dante' (not a meaningless name in the context of 'Ithaca'). They discuss the Hebrew and the Irish languages, in which neither is skilled: Stephen is a bad Irishman, Bloom is a bad Jew. Stephen, with a singular lack of tact, softly sings a traditional ballad about the Jewish ritual murder of a Christian, but Bloom does not seem to be offended. He invites his guest to stay for the night, but Stephen amicably declines. They go out into the yard and urinate, looking up at the stars and at Molly's lighted bedroom window. The church bells ring out, then Stephen walks off into the night, to disappear from the book. Bloom gets undressed downstairs, and the interior of the house is described in immense detail: his accounts for the day are set out to the last penny, his small library is catalogued, and his private drawers reveal his pornographic and personal secrets. We now know that although he doesn't earn much Bloom has a modest private income that keeps him above the poverty line. He has, like everyone else, fantasies about money, first about making a vast sum and second about losing everything. He sees clear evidence that Blazes Boylan has been in the house, but is philosophical about the adultery that has certainly taken place. He goes upstairs to bed, gives his wife Molly a slightly shortened version of the events of the day (suppressing his visit to the brothel), curls up in the foetal position and goes to sleep.

This is the most beautiful chapter of the book, though at first sight the most forbidding. Joyce called it the 'ugly duckling' of the novel. It is apparently written in the driest of scientific or rather pseudo-scientific prose, as suits one side of Bloom's mind, and it contains just one striking poetic image: 'The heaventree of stars hung with humid nightblue fruit'. Stars and other heavenly bodies (planets, meteors, comets) form the principal metaphor of the chapter, but they are treated in an apparently literal, unmetaphorical way; it is only towards the end that the narrative turns out to be a powerful allegory of the human condition, like the narrative of Dante.

The Homeric story, occupying six books of the epic, is greatly condensed. Odysseus, disguised as a beggar, enters his own house. The suitors hold a competition to see who can string Odysseus' bow; none can do so, and then the beggar does it with ease, and at once starts to shoot the suitors. As prearranged father and son take other weapons from the armoury and kill all the suitors but two. Odysseus then purifies his house by fumigation. This slaughter takes place so swiftly that Penelope remains asleep upstairs. When her husband makes himself known to her, still in his disguise, she is at first unwilling to recognise him: but when he shows her that he alone knows one of the secrets of the house, namely the marriage bed partly made out of a living tree, she acknowledges him as her husband and celebrates the rites of wedded love.

Bloom as the non-violent man does not of course kill off Molly's many suitors, but he does at least think of violence. He has already 'disposed of' Mulligan (Antinous) in the previous chapter by telling Stephen not to trust him again, and now he thinks what to do about Boylan (Eurymachus):

What retribution, if any?
Assassination, never, as two wrongs did not make one right.
Duel by combat, no. Divorce, not now. Exposure by mechanical
artifice (automatic bed) or individual testimony (concealed
ocular witness), not yet. . . .

In fact, he deals with Boylan and the others simply by banishing
them from his mind. In a splendid passage on the next page he gives a
number of reasons for taking a passive and tolerant attitude to Molly's
affair, ending with the reflection that the universe simply does not
care about it: 'the apathy of the stars' has the last word. The bow he
uses for the conquest of the suitors is therefore Reason, or the Religion
of Science and Logic. The 'mechanical artifice (automatic bed)' is an
ingenious allusion to the Lay of Demodocus, the minstrel's song that
Odysseus hears in Phaeacia, about the adultery of Ares and Aphrodite,
and how the injured husband Hephaistos caught the guilty pair in the
act: he invited the other gods to see them trapped in his machine
and Olympus resounded with divine laughter. Homer has been cen-
sured for introducing so trivial and improper a story into his great
epic, and of course Joyce has been attacked on similar grounds of
impropriety. He earlier introduced Demodocus' song as the pornographic novel *Sweets of Sin* and again thumbs his nose at his prudish
critics. Other correspondences include the celestial portents that
abound in Homer: when Odysseus strings the bow Zeus sends an
encouraging thunderclap and so Bloom hears a 'loud lone crack
emitted by the insentient material of a strainveined timber table'.

The Christian correspondences are based, as I mentioned in my
notes on 'Eumaeus', on Christ's ascent to heaven at Easter. The chapter
begins with the liturgy for Easter Saturday. Bloom falls into the
basement well as Adam fell; but, as the Missal insists, this was a happy
sin or fortunate fall, since without it we should never have known
the inestimable blessing of our Redemption: 'O felix culpa' was to
become a major theme of *Finnegans Wake*. Bloom rises to his feet, as
Christ ascends from hell on the third day. He then lights a fire, pours
water into a kettle and makes two cups of cocoa. This business of
fire and water, described at length, corresponds to the ritual of the
Paschal Candle on Easter Saturday. The drinking of the cocoa equals
the Communion on Easter Sunday; this is celebrated by the ringing
of bells. The botanical name for cocoa is *Theobroma cacao*, the first term
being Greek for 'food of the gods', another divine coincidence. The

cocoa is 'Epps massproduct', made by modern mass-production but still the Eucharist. Bloom drinks it like the monk in Browning's 'Spanish Cloister', 'three sips to his opponent's one', a symbol of the Trinity. Stephen and Bloom have now mystically joined each other in the Holy Trinity. I do not know whether this is correct theologically, but Joyce's view seems to be that after the Resurrection God the Father is no longer separate from God the Son: the separation was only a temporary one during Christ's incarnation as Jesus. Hence they are now called 'Stoom' and 'Blephen'. The third member of the Trinity is the Holy Ghost or Spirit or the inspiration (for the meaning of which see 'Aeolus') that has enabled Joyce to write the book; or for that matter, any author to write any work of literature. But the nature and source of this inspiration is not yet fully explained.

That Bloom the Father is now also Christ the Son is proved by some delightful details. When he undresses he feels the scar of the bee sting for which he was treated in hospital seventeen days earlier: this is the side-wound which in traditional art Christ still carried after his resurrection and ascension. The feet-wounds follow in the shape of a lacerated toenail; the bang on the head when he collides with some furniture is a reminiscence of the crowning with thorns, as well as of the stool thrown by a suitor at Odysseus.

Dante continues to provide a framework for this chapter. If 'Eumaeus' is Hell, visited by Christ on Good Friday, 'Ithaca' must be Purgatory, which Christ like all the blessed must ascend on his way to Paradise. In Dante, Purgatory is a mountain, with a garden at the top known as the Earthly Paradise, where lost Eden is recovered. Bloom's earthly paradise is his dream house, described at length in the language of house agents and auctioneers, called 'Bloom Cottage, Saint Leopold's, Flowerville'. Towards the end of his fantasy about being a prosperous gentleman he imagines among possible light recreations 'house carpentry with toolbox containing hammer, awl, nails, screws, tintacks, gimlet, tweezers, bullnose plane and turnscrew'. These are of course the Instruments of Christ's Passion, as well as the tools of Jesus's father. Dante (whose name appears in connection with Mrs Riordan of the *Portrait*) uses an astronomical framework for the whole of the *Divine Comedy* and ends each book with the word 'stars'. Thus *Inferno* ends 'E quindi uscimmo a riveder le stelle' ('And thence we came out to see the stars again') — which is like Bloom and Stephen coming out of their dark house; leaving Purgatory Dante is 'Puro, e disposto a salire alle stelle' ('purified and prepared to ascend to the stars'). So Bloom, having purified his room with incense, is ready to climb up the stairs to bed.

Astronomy is the art of this scientific chapter, as befits the most elegant and imaginative of all the sciences. Bloom and Stephen become heavenly bodies and their movements are charted in a way that I found hard to understand until in the age of the satellite I began to grasp some simple Newtonian ideas. They are like two comets who are drawn into the earth's gravitational field from outer space, at first having very little physical effect on each other (Figure 1). (They had seen each other several times distantly during the day, then more closely in the hospital and brothel, but had not properly conversed until now.)

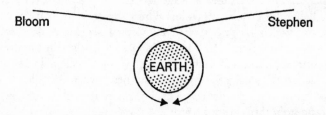

*Figure* 1

Now they go into orbit together for a few revolutions; but then Bloom becomes centripetal and drifts downwards to the earth's surface (in a manner that we can now understand from observing the return of moonships), while Stephen is centrifugal and, receiving a fresh boost perhaps, circles outwards until he takes off for outer space, never to return (Figure 2).

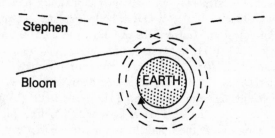

*Figure* 2

The technique of this chapter is called 'catechism-mature', in contrast to the naïve catechism of Stephen by schoolmaster Deasy in the second chapter. Everything is in the form of question and answer, and both are highly impersonal. There is no direct speech: the conversation between Stephen and Bloom is summarised like the minutes of a committee meeting; even Bloom's internal monologue, though obviously continuing with its rich mixture of sense and nonsense, is reduced to a bare skeleton: the organ of the body in this chapter is the skeleton. But who is the catechist? And whose is the voice of the answers? In a Catholic catechism it is the priest as instructor who asks the questions, the person under instruction who replies; and that is also true of formal and informal examinations. But throughout most of the process of education it is the pupil who asks, the teacher who answers, and that would seem to be the case in 'Ithaca', although sometimes the questioner seems to be setting problems. Another way of putting it is that the questioner is man the scientist, the answerer is the universe itself, which will usually give correct replies if asked the right questions by experimenters.

The procedure of 'Ithaca' is reductive. Everything is stripped away and reduced to the bare bone, or to the mathematical reality that lies behind all physical and ultimately social and psychological reality: hence the itemised budget for the day, the measurements of Bloom's body before and after doing Sandow's exercises, his bank balance, etc. 'Reduce Bloom by cross multiplication of reverses of fortune, from which these supports protected him, and by elimination of all positive values to a negligible negative irrational unreal quality.' This is a mathematical problem, to which the answer is the square root of minus one; but it is also a human problem — where would Bloom be without the money inherited from his father? The answer is a list of miserable occupations and conditions, which are all to be found somewhere in *Ulysses*, e.g. 'dun for the recovery of bad and doubtful debts . . . maimed sailor, blind stripling. . . . Nadir of misery: the aged impotent disfranchised ratesupported moribund lunatic pauper.' That is, as low as you can get without actually dying (and it is, incidentally, the condition of most of the characters in the works of Joyce's disciple Samuel Beckett). Not only is Bloom thus reduced but the whole cosy little world of Dublin is reduced to its physical components, and the great globe itself becomes a bare set of abstractions. The universe is purely physical, therefore morally meaningless: there are no gods or Santa Clauses or Friends behind Phenomena. This is what the existentialists mean by the universe being 'absurd': the galaxies drift through space without a goal, subject only to blind chance, and apart from individual human consciousness there is only what Joyce calls 'the void incertitude'. The astronomical universe is both a metaphor for the existentialist universe and also the literal cause of real terror: 'Le silence éternel de ces espaces infinis m'effraie', wrote Pascal ('The eternal silence of these infinite spaces terrifies me'). Space is empty, almost a perfect vacuum and very cold: 'Alone, what did Bloom feel? The cold of interstellar space, thousands of degrees below freezing point or the absolute zero of Fahrenheit, Centigrade or Réaumur.' All men are alone throughout much of their lives and all certainly die alone. Loneliness and death are the great underlying themes of this chapter. Bloom finally understands who the mysterious man in the mackintosh at Paddy Dignam's funeral really is (answer: death); and where Moses was when the light went out (answer: in the dark).

But at the lowest point of darkness and cold Bloom feels 'the incipient intimations of proximate dawn', and the chapter celebrates a triumph over death and extinction, though not the orthodox Christian one. Stephen, who has been worrying about his possible death before his talent could come to fruition, is mysteriously cured of his fears and of his hangup; he walks out of the book, at last able to write the book.

### III.iii. 'Penelope'

I am going to leave the last word with Molly Bloom, the final episode being written through her thoughts and tired Poldy being then asleep (Joyce to Budgen, 10 December 1920).

Penelope is the clou of the book. The first sentence contains 2500 words. There are eight sentences in the episode. It begins and ends with the female word *yes*. It turns like a huge earthball slowly surely and evenly round and round spinning. Its four cardinal points being the female breasts, arse, womb and cunt, expressed by the words *because, bottom, woman, yes*. Though probably more obscene than any preceding episode it seems to me to be [the essence of the?] perfectly sane full amoral fertilisable untrustworthy engaging shrewd limited prudent indifferent *Weib. Ich bin das Fleisch das stets bejaht*[1] (Joyce to Budgen, 16 August 1921).

---

[1] 'I am the Flesh that always affirms', parodying Goethe's 'I am the spirit that always denies'.

In Book 23 of the *Odyssey*, when Odysseus has conquered the suitors he still has to win the acceptance of his wife Penelope. She has been upstairs in bed during all the fighting, unaware that anything unusual has been taking place. Not having seen her husband for twenty years, she will naturally be suspicious of a stranger who claims the kingdom. So Odysseus has to convince her, by showing that he knows a secret that is otherwise known only to her husband: namely, that he formed one of the four posts of the marriage bed out of a living tree that still grows through the room. When he tells her this, she accepts him as her true husband and grants him his marital rights. So at the end of *Ulysses* Molly Bloom accepts Poldy as her true love (although it is not suggested that he will ever regain his rights, which have been suspended for some years).

The Christian and Dantesque story also comes to an end, in Paradise — where the story must end for each individual Christian who is saved and for the Church as a whole. Bloom, having ascended the Mountain of Purgatory (a memory of which appears as the Rock of Gibraltar) and having reached the Earthly Paradise in his fantasy towards the end of 'Ithaca', now enters the Paradise of Molly's mind: he achieves immortality and salvation because at the end she thinks well of him, and indeed only of him. He is also deified and is not only redeemed man but God in all three persons. In Canto XXXIII of the *Paradiso* Dante has a vision of all the blessed in heaven forming a rose (presumably an emblem of the Virgin Mary, 'rosa mystica', to whom St Bernard addresses the final prayer).[1] Molly thinks much of roses, among other flowers; and she repeats the words of a popular song, 'Shall I wear a red rose, or shall I wear a white?' The red rose must be a reference to her menstruation, which begins halfway through her monologue: we are meant to think of Dumas's *La Dame aux camélias*, whose heroine wears a red flower to warn her admirers of her periods. The red rose has of course a long history as a sexual as well as a religious symbol and provides a pivot for the ironic see-saw of earthly and heavenly love, *eros* and *agape*. Finally *eros* (personified by Blazes Boylan) is vanquished by *agape* (personified by Bloom).

Nothing could be earthier than Molly, of course. She is the great

---

[1] In forma, dunque, di candela rosa
Mi si mostrava la milizia santa.
(In fashion, then as of a snow-white rose Displayed itself to me the heavenly host. XXXIII)

globe itself, the round planet on which the meteor (or satellite) Bloom comes to rest. The Earth is not only the planet but the element from which all things grow, in traditional mythology (in reality life began in the sea, but that need not concern us here). So Molly is not only the deified planet, in Greek Gē or Gea, in Latin Tellus; she is also the Great Mother, the Fertility Goddess of the Mediterranean, who took precedence in prehistoric times and in the beginnings of civilisation over the male Olympians. One of the later descendants of the Mediterranean Great Goddess was the Egyptian Isis, with whom Cleopatra is identified by Shakespeare: Molly is Mediterranean (Spanish–Gibraltarean) and Cleopatran — age cannot wither nor custom stale her infinite variety. She has also more modern literary parallels, for example in Chaucer's Wife of Bath, from whom she draws some of her naturalistic and antinomian views of sex and morality: 'what else were we given all those desires for.' Still later is her namesake Moll Flanders, the heroine of Defoe's novel, which Bloom has given her to read: 'a whore always shoplifting,' she calls her.

Molly's unspoken thoughts reveal her to be little better than a whore, and she has apparently no misgivings about criminality. She thinks of a variety of sexual irregularities, such as fellatio, without any inhibitions. Throughout her monologue she seems to be incapable even of distinguishing one man from another: the word 'he' which she uses so frequently covers a wide range of past lovers and admirers, and in memory she shifts vaguely from one to another. She even considers the possibility of taking Stephen as a future lover. She thinks of Boylan, her latest bedmate, but in the end Bloom is the only 'he' who counts. As she goes to sleep she thinks of his courting her on the Hill of Howth:

> and I thought well as well him as another and then I asked him
> with my eyes to ask again yes and then he asked me would I yes
> to say yes my mountain flower and first I put my arms around
> him yes and drew him down to me so he could feel my breasts
> all perfume yes and his heart was going like mad and yes I said
> yes I will Yes.

Stephen and Bloom, the two parts of the artist, have finally become one: Stephen, symbolising their joint soul, disappears outwards from the earth's gravitational field into space, while Bloom, who represents their physical joint body, homes on the earth and is buried in her, as a seed or embryo: he assumes the position of the child in the womb before he goes to sleep. The meaning of the book is always to be looked for in terms of the artist's creativity. What this chapter says is that the artist, or at least the male artist, cannot fulfil himself and become truly creative unless he achieves a successful union with a woman, a relationship which is sexual and more than sexual.

# 9

## *Finnegans Wake*

*Finnegans Wake* is notoriously the most obscure book ever written by a major writer; at least, by one who was believed not to be out of his mind. The difficulties are truly appalling. While writing this chapter I am alarmed to count up the months and years of work I have put into its decipherment, with only partial success. I was quite well equipped to begin reading *Finnegans Wake*, since I am fond of puzzles, useless general knowledge, literary quotations and so on; but although from time to time my work has made some progress, it has several times ground to a halt well short of adequate understanding. There are now quite a few better readers of this book than I am, though none has reached the level of Mr J. S. Atherton, from whom I have learned most; but not even he would claim to have solved all the *Wake*'s mysteries. Why then do I go on wrestling with the angel, and why am I recommending this apparently hopeless task to readers, who, in years to come, will doubtless have more urgent things to do? Because the quest, though doomed to failure, is exciting in itself; and because many people seem to find reading the book, even through a cloud of uncertainty, to be a strange and moving experience.

*Finnegans Wake* appeals above all to lovers of the literature of fantasy, such as the Alice books, from which its punning language descends. As everyone knows, it is a dream book and is therefore somewhat akin to Kafka's visionary stories — but it lacks the metaphysical *angst* of Kafka or for that matter of Samuel Beckett. The humour carries more painful and even sinister autobiographical overtones than does that of Lewis Carroll; but Joyce takes a fairly happy view of the relationship of God to Man, and of the nature of the universe. Despite the occasional intensity of personal misery, the fantasy is continuously humorous and the humour usually runs sparkling if not clear. The book also seems to find sympathetic readers

among those who enjoy mythology and epic, fantastic stories of gods
and heroes such as are found in Wagner and Tolkien. It can be only a
small section of the publics for Wagner and Tolkien that will enjoy
the *Wake*; for if Wagner is Tolkien for grown-ups, then the *Wake* is
Wagner for rather learned and linguistically sophisticated grown-ups.

As we shall see, there is a lot of Wagner scattered about the *Wake*,
mainly *Tristan* but also much of the *Ring*. There is even more of the
Scandinavian myths, known from the *Edda*, that form the basis of
Wagner's *Ring*; and there is still more of the ancient Irish epic material,
such as the *Cattle Raid of Cooley* and other parts of the Ulster or
Cuchullin cycle, while the title and chief character of the book is
taken from the other heroic cycle, that of Finn MacCool. The first
chapter of Book I is especially rich in giants and battles which suggest
Homer's *Iliad* (rather than his *Odyssey*), and the wars of the Old
Testament. A reader of the *Wake* must enjoy Genesis as literature, and
probably he ought to know even more of the Bible than is necessary
for the understanding of *Ulysses*. The 'Cyclops' chapter of *Ulysses*,
with its background of folklore, legend and epic, burlesque and
scrambled, is the part of *Ulysses* which most resembles *Finnegans Wake*.

Third, the *Wake* is for those who truly love puzzles — and why
not? There is no need to apologise for this taste, since a great deal of
literature consists of puzzles and obscurities that must be deciphered:
Anglo-Saxon kennings, Old Norse skaldic verse, English metaphysical
poetry and so on. Puzzles are only a part of fantasy and 'nonsense'
literature: they demand translation from the unknown to the known,
like the riddles of folklore. A basic riddle runs throughout the *Wake*,
in its first version reading 'why do I am alook alike a poss of porterpease?', meaning (among other things) how can twins, as like as two
peas, be totally different; and how could Isolde have drunk the love
instead of the death potion? The whole book is a riddle, but so
notoriously is the universe: just as scientists laboriously decipher the
physical universe, so historical scholars decipher the records of the
past, to discover forgotten human and unique actions. I think that
Joyce deliberately overlaid his story with a mass of esoteric allusion
and multilingual puns, so that his text should be an analogue of the
mysterious universe; and I think that in this he made a fundamental
error, which has prevented the book from taking its place with *Ulysses*
among the world's greatest masterpieces. He made it just too hard for
any human mind to comprehend: too many languages are quoted
(some of them wrongly, to make confusion worse confounded), too

many pieces of junk from the past have been dumped. Everything in the book ought to be information, but much of it continues to be noise, and perhaps always will be. This is also true about the universe we inhabit, and it is discouraging.

I am a polymath, thou art eclectic, he/she is a dilettante: the three persons make up the 'ideal reader with an ideal insomnia' whom Joyce demanded. But a less than ideal reader will almost certainly possess some range of special knowledge which will enable him to make his own discoveries, since Joyce's encyclopaedic mind took in the jargons and vocabularies of so many different professions or skills. For example, until the other day I knew nothing at all of the language of heraldry. When I had acquired a smattering I found I could read off most of a couple of Joyce's burlesque coats-of-arms, and so enjoy a few more of Joyce's learned jokes. The acquisition of useless knowledge of this kind is irritating to the Philistines, but Joyce anticipated the great explosion of useless knowledge which can be witnessed in the paperback and coffee-table books of the Age of Affluence.

*Finnegans Wake* is a book entirely suited to the modern universe, as revealed by scientists in the decades before and after Joyce's death. It gave a name to a fundamental particle, postulated by theoretical physicists only a few years ago: this is the 'Quark', taken from the seagulls' mocking cry at the beginning of Book II, chapter iv (383.01): '— *Three quarks for Muster Mark!*' True, that is only a physicist's whimsical choice of a meaningless word, without connotations, for an entirely new concept; but it is appropriate that it should be drawn from the verbal universe, which Joyce tried to make as mysterious and complex as the physical universe. Joyce evidently studied such popularisation of the latest physics as he could find, and makes allusions to Einstein and Relativity, and to Eddington's 'expanding universe'. Joyce's world, with its continuous series of transformations, resembles the world of Lewis Carroll (one of his favourite authors) and both seem to be analogous to the post-Newtonian cosmos. On the level of biology, too, *Finnegans Wake* seems to be appropriate to the twentieth century, with its emphasis on the cycles of nature: the nitrogen cycle ('dust unto dust') and above all the water cycle. The book begins with the river ('riverrun'); in the course of the eighth chapter the Liffey's progress from source to Dublin is traced; in the last chapter the dying river merges with the sea, while her successor, the young river, will start again in the form of cloud and rain. Joyce's peculiar form of optimism seems to be based on a scientific view of nature. In nature, provided that it is undisturbed by man, 'whatever is, is right'. All ecological systems are self-cleansing and death is a biological advantage. The great cycles of death and decay, rebirth and growth are perfect. Everything in the biosphere is beautifully balanced: that which has evolved over millions of years is almost exactly what is necessary to the continuance of life on this planet. Nothing can be called evil in nature, in the long run: this can only be the best of possible worlds.

It is almost certainly wrong to transfer this optimistic view of the cyclical universe to the world of man. Human societies, unlike ecological systems, are not self-regulating; and, as far as we know, there is no reason to believe that everything is going to work for the best. Yet Joyce takes this step, probably as illegitimately as Pope does in his *Essay on Man*. He borrowed, as he made clear, from the eighteenth-century philosopher Giambattista Vico, the Neapolitan critic of Homer and philosopher of history. Vico argues that all societies pass through the same distinct stages, a theocratic followed by a feudal followed by a democratic age. Each age has its own language, symbols, forms of government and so on. After the democratic age society breaks up from its own internal contradictions; and after an attempt to stabilise it by authoritarian rule it collapses in chaos. But out of the primitive chaos society is reborn again and the cycle recommences. There does not seem to be any objective evidence for the correctness of this view. Historians, in fact, think it to be highly unlikely that any cyclic patterns can be traced in the story of mankind, despite claims to the contrary by Spengler and Toynbee. I suspect that Joyce did not very much care if Vico's theory was true or not, for he found it to be a most useful framework on which to build his fantastic tale. The whole work is divided into sets of four, each representing Vico's three ages and the 'ricorso' or return to the beginning. There are four books, the first with twice four chapters, the second and third with four chapters each; the last book is undivided into chapters, but like the other chapters, and even some paragraphs and sentences, it is subdivided into fours. The reader soon begins to recognise these patterns, like the recurrent multilettered thunder-word, representing the thunderclap which terrified the savage cavemen into religious belief and started off the cycle of civilisation.

*Finnegans Wake* is supposed to be a novel, with a plot and characters in the traditional sense. The chief character is one H. C. Earwicker, supposedly a publican of Chapelizod, a village near Dublin; and the book on one level is Earwicker's dream. He has committed some kind of misdemeanour in the Phoenix Park involving two girls and three soldiers; it is never clear just what he has done, but it seems to be exhibitionism, a common offence in parks. All night long his unconscious mind broods on this action, guiltily and obsessively: it is transformed, like everything else in the book, into a hundred different shapes. Earwicker dreams of the other characters: his wife Anna, his daughter Isabel, his twin sons Shem and Shaun, the servants and the customers of the public house, and so on. Again, the reader soon begins to recognise these personages, each of whom speaks in a different voice. Joyce uses the modulation of style for narrative purposes even more subtly than he does in *Ulysses*: there is no mistaking the dactylic, tumbling rhythms of Anna, the sleepy repetitive gossip of the four old men, or the unctuous sermonising of Shaun. The two sons are twins and rivals, Shem being a Bohemian artist, Shaun a successful man of the world, combining the roles of tenor, politician, and priest. But as the story is told with an infinite number of evasions and ambiguities, it becomes clear, if clear is the word, that the basis of the Earwicker and associated plots is simply James Joyce's autobiography in a disguised form: the book is a confession, like those of St Augustine and Rousseau, in which the author accuses himself of various crimes or shortcomings — in Joyce's case mainly sexual malpractices which are more probably fantasised than real.

These basic sexual themes are, of course, heavily disguised, just as they are in actual dreams, by the mechanism of the 'censor', according to Freudian theory. It is impossible to say with confidence whether Joyce really believed in Freud's ideas or not; but he makes considerable use of Freud, as he does with Vico or with the Christian religion (in which Joyce did not believe). The book can be regarded as an extended piece of self-analysis, in which the meaning of every part of the dream is interpreted by exploring ever-darker regions of the unconscious. Not only the symbolism but the language is Freudian; Joyce used not only Freud's *Interpretation of Dreams* but also his *Psychopathology of Everyday Life*, which discusses meaningful slips of the tongue. Every kind of speech disorder, like the Spoonerism, is imitated in *Finnegans Wake*. The basic type of pathological speech is of course Jabberwocky, the punning language of 'portmanteau' words, which is expounded by Humpty Dumpty in *Alice through the Looking Glass*. The basic device is the pun, by which multiple meanings can be packed into a newly-coined word. The trouble about this is that every pun is supposed to be a joke, as the words in *Alice* like 'galumphing' and 'chortled' are; but although Joyce makes some good jokes, like the girl who was 'yung and easily freudened', it is impossible for him to keep up the humour through a book of such length. Most of Joyce's puns provide not a sudden revelation of meaning causing laughter, but a code for laborious decipherment. The puns are vehicles for carrying an enormous mass of allusion; and the pleasure of reading *Finnegans Wake* lies largely in recognising these allusions and enjoying the wonderful ingenuity with which they are used.

The reading of *Finnegans Wake* is a huge process of self-education. There is nothing wrong with that, provided that this education could be a valuable one; and with *Finnegans Wake* that can be claimed with some justice. The allusions in the book can be grouped into various families, beginning with the literary. There are a large number of concealed quotations, chiefly of Shakespeare and the Bible; there are several well-known Latin tags hidden away but curiously enough not very many of the standard quotations of English literature other than Shakespeare. Many years ago Mabel Worthington and I showed that the titles and words of many popular songs are used, beginning with the title, which is from a comic Irish ballad 'Finnegan's Wake' (the apostrophe is correct there but not in the title of the book). At that time I did not know much about opera, but I have since found hundreds of allusions to Joyce's favourite art; the process of discovering this was wholly valuable to me, since it led me deeper into the pleasures of operatic music.

Next in importance to the literary and musical allusions are those to comparative mythology and to the religions of the world. Joyce's procedure is to pile myth on myth, at times almost parodying Sir James Frazer's *Golden Bough*, which is itself a much-used source. The author can be followed relatively easily into classical and Norse mythology, but that is not enough: there is much taken from Egyptian religion, especially *The Book of the Dead*, which I have found laborious to learn about; and I am not yet ready to understand, let alone expound, much of what he has to say about the Hindu and other Oriental myths. Yet they are important at the end of the last book. Akin to mythology is liturgy: not having been brought up as a Catholic, I found I had to learn a great deal about the Tridentine Latin Mass of the Catholic Church, which doubtless did me no harm. Ecclesiastical Latin is often of great beauty, but this is now useless knowledge except for the purpose of following Gregorian plainsong or the masses of the great composers, since it is now banned by the Church.

The next family of allusions is legendary and historical, and because of the Viconian framework these are very important. The reader has to know something of the histories of the classical, Judaic and modern Western European civilisations: there seems to be only a smattering of archaeology and oriental history, and not much about America, north or south. I think it is legitimate to ask this amount of historical knowledge of the reader, but what of Irish history? This is a subject which delights all Irishmen and bores nearly all non-Irishmen: even the small amount of the history of this small island that I have put in an earlier chapter will seem excessive to some. It is not just the general political history of Ireland that Joyce uses so vastly, but the local history of Dublin, its citizens, architecture and institutions. The conscientious reader needs to be equipped with guide-book, map, even street directory, and, as many have already done, will take a trip to the site. Joyce fortunately forgot something or never cared to learn everything about the rest of Ireland, but no detail of Dublin's past, however apparently trivial, seems to have escaped him. When it comes to the advertisements in ancient Dublin tramways, historiography yields to what is now called 'nostalgia', and this is hard to justify on educational or literary grounds. I can only say that I love the microcosm of Dublin and am ready to share Joyce's prime obsession to a considerable degree, though perhaps not as far as better readers.

These are the principal but not the only fields of knowledge necessary for an understanding of *Finnegans Wake*. They will be considered justifiable according to readers' tastes, but there is one field which I am sure is unjustifiable. This is the vexatious amount of foreign language, or more strictly of foreign *words*, scattered throughout the book. Joyce spoke French, German and Italian fluently and had a smattering of Norwegian and of classical Latin; he really did not know more about the languages of the world than that, yet he included many thousands of words from Hebrew, Arabic, and Chinese (admittedly great cultural languages) and even from Armenian and Albanian. He drew up lists of key words in several dozen languages, and at a very late stage in the revision of the text he threw them in, in a casual and even random manner, as if using a pepper-pot. Since he did not know these languages he often made mistakes, or so the experts tell us. The result is a wilful obscuring of that which was already highly obscure, while the passages most heavily loaded with obscure languages are neither very witty nor very melodious. These languages were added at a late stage of revision. The puns in the languages that Joyce earwigs in a flower-pot — a typical piece of false etymology. Names, of course, are of the utmost importance in the universe of *Finnegans Wake*: to every *numen* (sacred, essence) there corresponds a *nomen*. I have ascertained that Joyce uses almost every Christian name listed in Eric Partridge's *Name this Child* (1936), which is yet another basic text for readers, whether Joyce used it or another dictionary. He often gives the real or supposed etymology of the name: e.g. Bartholemew Vanhomrigh, Lord Mayor of Dublin, is called 'Soesown of Furrows' (535.02), which is not intelligible until one discovers that Bartholemew in Hebrew means 'son of *Talmai* (abounding in furrows)'. As with primitive man a first name is magical, conveying on its possessor the qualities it signifies.

The story of how Earwicker got his name is paralleled by other stories, like that of God naming Adam, and Adam naming the beasts. An outrageous sentence is drawn from Dickens's story of how the Chuzzlewits got their name:

> To such a suggestion the one selfrespecting answer is to affirm that there are certain statements which ought not to be, and one should like to hope to be able to add, ought not to be allowed to be made. (033)

From H. C. Earwicker's name to his early history: there are many rumours going around, about an encounter with a tramp in Phoenix Park, behaving as an exhibitionist or voyeur with two girls, a possibly homosexual episode with three soldiers; variants of these appear throughout the book but we are never to learn the exact truth. All this gossip is elaborated into a folk song by many Dubliners in collaboration, and this is finally published as a broadside ballad, like many others in the eighteenth and nineteenth centuries. The musical references begin to thicken from page 41 onwards, until there is a group concerning Wagner's *Parsifal* (Perceval, Persse, 043,35 purseyful): '"Ductor" Hitchcock hoisted his fezzy fuzz at bludgeon's height signum to his companions of the chalice . . . and *silentium in curia*' (044.02-3). The last words take up 'plaudits' of a few lines earlier, and refer to the prohibition against applause at performances of *Parsifal*; cf. 'silentium wach auf!' in the *Meistersinger*. The rest concerns the elevation of the Host and the company of knights of the Grail in *Parsifal*. The Ballad of Persse O'Reilly is too well known to need comment; it is obviously about Humpty Dumpty, Oscar Wilde and Cromwell.

knew well are a different matter: some are almost as good as the English ones. Among the languages he did not speak is of course Irish (also called Gaelic, Celtic or Erse) which is one of the official languages of his native land: his attitude to this tongue is disrespectful and mocking, but fortunately rather few native Irish speak Gaelic well enough to understand Joyce's jokes.

Every reader must make his own way into *Finnegans Wake*, led on by humour and beauty. Some parts of the book are very funny, as for example Shaun's sermon in Book III, chapter 2; other parts are linguistically and poetically beautiful, such as 'Anna Livia Plurabelle'. In the following pages I have tried to indicate the passages that are outstanding and to warn of the tedious ones; and to point out the marked degrees of difficulty and obscurity. To the reading of *Finnegans Wake* every reader must bring his own special knowledge. Irish readers, who know from childhood a thousand topographical and historical details that Joyce takes for granted, are at an advantage, but other readers need not despair. No single reader has ever deciphered the whole of the book, and perhaps no one ever will; but the delights and rewards of the chase are many.

## I.i (001-29). 'The Giant's Grave'

In the beginning, before God said 'Let there be light', there was only chaos, a confused heap of matter without form. So the first two paragraphs of *Finnegans Wake* are chaotic, but they contain many of the main themes and characters of the book. Since Joyce's creation is like the cosmological continuous creation, there is no real beginning but merely endless repetitions of Vico's cycle; the book begins and ends in the middle of a sentence: 'A way a lone a last a loved a long the / riverrun, past Eve and Adam's, from swerve of shore to bend of bay, brings us by a commodius vicus of recirculation back to Howth Castle and Environs.' Literally, the River Liffey has run out into Dublin Bay and vanished, but in the water cycle it is precipitated in the Wicklow Mountains and begins its nearly circular course again. There are many Wagnerian echoes on the last page: 'Away' is 'Weia!' the cry of the Rhinemaidens: it seems likely that 'riverrun' points to the first motif of the *Ring*, the arpeggios based on the common chord, symbolising the River Rhine, heard in the first bars of *Rheingold*. A few lines later we come across the rainbow, not only Noah's but the bridge to Wotan's Valhalla, hence 'ringsome'. The second paragraph knew well are a different matter: some are almost as good as the English ones. Among the languages he did not speak is of course Irish (also called Gaelic, Celtic or Erse) which is one of the official languages of his native land: his attitude to this tongue is disrespectful and mocking, but fortunately rather few native Irish speak Gaelic well enough to understand Joyce's jokes.

Every reader must make his own way into *Finnegans Wake*, led on by humour and beauty. Some parts of the book are very funny, as for example Shaun's sermon in Book III, chapter 2; other parts are linguistically and poetically beautiful, such as 'Anna Livia Plurabelle'. In the following pages I have tried to indicate the passages that are outstanding and to warn of the tedious ones; and to point out the marked degrees of difficulty and obscurity. To the reading of *Finnegans Wake* every reader must bring his own special knowledge. Irish readers, who know from childhood a thousand topographical and historical details that Joyce takes for granted, are at an advantage, but other readers need not despair. No single reader has ever deciphered the whole of the book, and perhaps no one ever will; but the delights and rewards of the chase are many.

## I.i (001–29). 'The Giant's Grave'

In the beginning, before God said 'Let there be light', there was only chaos, a confused heap of matter without form. So the first two paragraphs of *Finnegans Wake* are chaotic, but they contain many of the main themes and characters of the book. Since Joyce's creation is like the cosmological continuous creation, there is no real beginning but merely endless repetitions of Vico's cycle; the book begins and ends in the middle of a sentence: 'A way a lone a last a loved a long the / riverrun, past Eve and Adam's, from swerve of shore to bend of bay, brings us by a commodius vicus of recirculation back to Howth Castle and Environs.' Literally, the River Liffey has run out into Dublin Bay and vanished, but in the water cycle it is precipitated in the Wicklow Mountains and begins its nearly circular course again. There are many Wagnerian echoes on the last page: 'Away' is 'Weia!' the cry of the Rhinemaidens: it seems likely that 'riverrun' points to the first motif of the *Ring*, the arpeggios based on the common chord, symbolising the River Rhine, heard in the first bars of *Rheingold*. A few lines later we come across the rainbow, not only Noah's but the bridge to Wotan's Valhalla, hence 'ringsome'. The second paragraph presents the *leitmotifs* of Tristan and Isolde, St Patrick, Jonathan Swift, and others, which are to recur many times.

The story proper begins in the third paragraph, with the thunderclap that initiates Vico's first age, that of religion. It is also the Fall, of Satan, of Adam, of Humpty Dumpty and of Tim Finnegan, the building labourer of the Victorian comic song, who in death becomes a sleeping giant with his head at Howth and his upturned feet miles away in Phoenix Park. The rest of the chapter is about Finnegan and the wake held over his corpse, and about other giants. 'Giant's grave' is the Irish folk-name for a megalithic monument, cromlech, menhir and the like; many examples are mentioned in this chapter, besides 'stonengens' (005.31). There is a convenient list of legendary and historical giants in Brewer's *Dictionary of Phrase and Fable*, which Joyce seems to have used. Among them are Fafner and Fasolt, who built Valhalla or the 'Riesengeborg' (giant's castle, 005). At the end of the book we shall find the last words of various operatic characters, and here we have some of their first words: 'Waz iz? Iseut?' (004.14) will be recognised as Tristan's 'Was ist? Isolde?'

The dead giant is eaten cannibalistically, an act which is the equivalent of the eucharist. The first set piece is the 'Museyroom', in which we are taken on a guided tour of a museum on the battlefield of Waterloo, during which a strange encounter between Wellington and Napoleon is told. The next scene depicts a hen scratching about on a dunghill, unearthing the artefacts and records of the past like an archaeologist; the chief relic will turn out to be a letter from some exiled Irishwoman in Boston, Massachusetts; apparently trivial and fragmentary, it carries thematic material to be developed throughout the book. The primeval story is continued in parodies of the old Irish chronicles, and there follows one of the finest inventions in the book (015–17), the dialogue between Mutt and Jute, the dimwitted prehistoric natives and the first of many invaders of Ireland: 'Forshapen his pigmaid hoagshead, shroonk his plodsfoot. He hath locktoes, this shortshins, and, Obeold that's pectoral, his mammamuscles most mousterious. It is slaking nuncheon out of some thing's brain pan. Me seemeth a dragon man.' The invader gives the Neanderthal man a wooden nickel, asking for fortune telling. 'Let me fore all your hasitancy cross your qualm with trink gilt. Here you have sylvan coyne, a piece of oak. Ghinees hies good for you.'

Mutt describes the primeval scene of the coast at Clontarf, the many clashes between two races in Ireland, and in incomparable Homeric language, the deaths of many generations to come:

> Mearmerge two races, swete and brack. Morthering rue.
> Hither, craching eastwards, they are in surgence: hence cool
> at ebb, they requiesce. Countlessness of livestories have
> netherfallen by this plage, flicks flowflakes, litters from aloft,
> like a waast wizzard all of whirlworlds. Now are all tombed to
> the mound, isges to isges, erde from merde. Pride, O pride,
> thy prize!

Ashes to ashes, earth reborn from merde, is one of the most beautiful statements of the compost-cycle theme. The subject of archaeology is pursued with an account of the beginnings of writing. Another set piece, by no means as poetic as Mutt and Jute, introduces the Tristan theme: the Prankquean (21–3) is Brangwen or Brangäne who is responsible for mixing up the love-potion (021.27 lovespots) and the death-potion in the opera: they both look like a pint of Guinness; hence the thematic riddle 'Mark the Wans, why do I am alook alike a poss of porterpease?' (19–20). But in this story she mixes not only the drinks but two children, as in *H.M.S. Pinafore* (021.33 pinafrond) and in *Il Trovatore*, the opposing brothers of which are a major theme. The chapter ends with the giant Finnegan lying in his grave, while his worshippers tell him what is happening in the world. Of course, 'Everything's going on the same or so it appeals to all of us, in the old holmsted here.' All the characters are eternally present, eternally reborn; as, for example, the Two Girls, Hetty and Essie, 'Your remember Essie in our Luna's Convent? They called her Holly Merry her lips were so ruddyberry.' There is an echo of 'O ruddier than the cherry' sung by the *giant* Polyphemus in Handel's *Acis and Galatea*. But the dead primeval giant is to be superseded by the heroic-medieval figure of H. C. Earwicker, 'who will be ultimendly respunchable for the hubbub caused in Edenborough'.

## I.ii. (030–47). 'H. C. Earwicker'

Chapter II tells how Earwicker came by his extraordinary name. In fact, Joyce on a holiday in Bognor, Sussex, in 1923 must have found the name in the nearby village of Sidlesham (pronounced Siddles-ham) in the hundred of Manhood; it is hardly to be found anywhere else. A medieval king so named the hero when he found him catching earwigs in a flower-pot — a typical piece of false etymology. Names, of course, are of the utmost importance in the universe of *Finnegans Wake*: to every *numen* (sacred, essence) there corresponds a *nomen*. I have ascertained that Joyce uses almost every Christian name listed in Eric Partridge's *Name this Child* (1936), which is yet another basic text for readers, whether Joyce used it or another dictionary. He often gives the real or supposed etymology of the name: e.g. Bartholemew Vanhomrigh, Lord Mayor of Dublin, is called 'Soesown of Furrows' (535.02), which is not intelligible until one discovers that Bartholemew in Hebrew means 'son of *Talmai* (abounding in furrows)'. As with primitive man a first name is magical, conveying on its possessor the qualities it signifies.

The story of how Earwicker got his name is paralleled by other stories, like that of God naming Adam, and Adam naming the beasts. An outrageous sentence is drawn from Dickens's story of how the Chuzzlewits got their name:

> To such a suggestion the one selfrespecting answer is to affirm that there are certain statements which ought not to be, and one should like to hope to be able to add, ought not to be allowed to be made. (033)

From H. C. Earwicker's name to his early history: there are many rumours going around, about an encounter with a tramp in Phoenix Park, behaving as an exhibitionist or voyeur with two girls, a possibly homosexual episode with three soldiers; variants of these appear throughout the book but we are never to learn the exact truth. All this gossip is elaborated into a folk song by many Dubliners in collaboration, and this is finally published as a broadside ballad, like many others in the eighteenth and nineteenth centuries. The musical references begin to thicken from page 41 onwards, until there is a group concerning Wagner's *Parsifal* (Perceval, Persse, 043,35 purseyful): '"Ductor" Hitchcock hoisted his fezzy fuzz at bludgeon's height signum to his companions of the chalice . . . and *silentium in curia*' (044.02–3). The last words take up 'plaudits' of a few lines earlier, and refer to the prohibition against applause at performances of *Parsifal*; cf. 'silentium wach auf!' in the *Meistersinger*. The rest concerns the elevation of the Host and the company of knights of the Grail in *Parsifal*. The Ballad of Persse O'Reilly is too well known to need comment; it is obviously about Humpty Dumpty, Oscar Wilde and Cromwell.

I.iii (048–74). 'The Epic of Earwicker'

Chapter iii begins by describing the disappearance of the ballad's composers and singers. We are left contemplating the Dublin landscape, empty but full of signs of Earwicker if we can look with an archaeologist's eyes:

> It scenes like a landescape from Wildu Picturescu or some seem
> on some dimb Arras, dumb as Mum's mutyness, this mimage of
> the seventyseventh kusin of kristansen is odable to os across the
> wineless Ere no oedor nor mere eerie nor liss potent of suggestion
> than an in the tales of the tingmount (053.01–6)

parodying a beautiful sentence by Joyce in the *Portrait*:

> Like a scene on some vague arras, old as man's weariness, the
> image of the seventh city of christendom was visible to him
> across the timeless air, no older nor more weary nor less patient
> of subjection than in the days of the thingmote.

Earwicker has indeed fallen like the house of Atreus but like one of Frazer's dying gods he will be resurrected:

> As hollyday in his house so was he priest and king to that: ulvy
> came, envy saw, ivy conquered. Lou! Lou! They have waved
> his green boughs over him as they have torn him limb from
> lamb. (058)

That makes him also Caesar and Charles Stewart Parnell, the Uncrowned King of Ireland, torn to pieces by his own party, his memory kept alive by the ivy leaf. The rest of the chapter, which mostly does not show Joyce at his best, is concerned with rumours about the hero's death and resurrection; at the end, where he is at his best, Earwicker is back in the tomb again:

> Yed he med leave to many a door beside of Oxmanwold for so
> witness his chambered cairns a cloudletlitter silent that are at
> browse up hill and down coombe and on eolithostroton, at
> Howth or at Coolock or even at Enniskerry, a theory non too
> rectiline of the evoluation of human society and a testament of
> the rocks from all the dead unto some of the living. Olivers
> lambs we do call them, skaterlings of a stone, and they shall be
> gathered unto him, their herd and paladin, as nubilettes to cumule,

in that day hwen, same the lightning lancer of Azava
Arthur-honoured (some Finn, some Finn avant!), he skall wake
from earthsleep, haught crested elmer, in his valle of briers of
Greenman's Rise O, (lost leaders live! the heroes return!) and
so o'er dun and dale the Wuiverulverlord (protect us!) his
mighty horn skall roll, orland, roll. (073-4)

I shall not try to explain this exquisite paragraph in detail beyond
saying that it is about archaeology ('Chambered cairn', eolith), clouds
passing over the sky like sheep, the cloud-chamber of 1930s physics
which permits protons to be seen (-stroton), geology, Darwinian
evolution, King Arthur coming again, Roland's horn sounding again,
and the sleeping beauty (Brunnhilde) coming to life.

### I.iv (075-103). 'Lion'

Chapter iv, 'Lion', begins with a long description of Earwicker in
his tomb, or pyramid. There are more stories about fraternal conflict,
mainly between Irish Protestants and Catholics, over Partition, a
history which Joyce rightly saw would never end: 'the boarder incident
prerepeated itself' (081.32). The middle section is based on the remarkable evidence' (086.33) given to the Parnell Commission, which was
held to determine whether Parnell was implicated in the Fenian
terrorist movement and the Phoenix Park Murders. A *Diary* of the
Commission was published by John MacDonald, M.A. (087, Hyacinth
O'Donnell, B.A.) in which the rambling remarks of a variety of
Irish peasants on all kinds of irrelevant topics reads very much like
*Finnegans Wake*. Towards the end of the chapter Earwicker undergoes
binary fission into his two sons Shem and Shaun, the former shunned,
the latter made a fuss of by a group of girls. The archetypal hero Parnell
again is resurrected, this time as a fox (Mr Fox was one of his aliases),
who is hunted on pp. 097-9. The chapter is the last of a group of four
which centre on the Father-Hero: at its end we are introduced to the
Mother-Heroine, Anna Livia, who is to dominate the rest of Book I.
After a parody of the music-hall song 'At Trinity Church I met my
Doom', which provides the principal theme of marriage, there is a
delicate coda anticipating the washerwomen of chapter viii:

Nomad may roam with Nabuch but let naaman laugh at Jordan!
For we, we have taken our sheet upon her stones where we have

hanged our hearts in her trees, and we list, as she bibs us, by the waters of babalong. (103)

'The earth' in Norwegian is 'jorden'; Naaman the leper went down and dipped himself seven times in the Jordan — and his flesh came again like unto the flesh of a little child — but the little children have soiled themselves and need washing (2 Kings 5): 'we have hanged our harps upon the willow'. 'By the waters of Babylon we sat down and wept' (Psalm 137). This is a song of exile: Joyce-Ulysses-Noman wanders abroad, but his heart remains with the Liffey.

## I.v (104–25). 'Hen'

Chapter v contains two passages of Albanian words (111, 114) and some Armenian (107), but most of it is comparatively easy to read. It is a description and critique of the book itself, partly based on a description of the Book of Kells, the most famous early Irish manuscript, by Sir Edward Sullivan (*The Studio*, 1914, 1920). The elaborate patterns of this manuscript are the model for Joyce's own verbal elaborations, as he claimed. The chapter begins with three pages of alternative titles, one of which pays tribute to Wagner — 'Intimier Minnelisp of an Extoreor Monolothe' (105.11) — and states that the 'interior monologue' was anticipated by Mime in the *Ring*, when he reveals his unspoken thoughts to Siegfried.

On page 109 Joyce discusses the meaning of the book in terms of clothing: is there a real core or body, as distinct from the words that envelop the central meaning? His argument in terms of women's underclothes is only another version of Carlyle's *Sartor Resartus*, and Swift's *Tale of a Tub*, both of which are frequently referred to in the *Wake*. As for the aesthetics of the book, he admits that it does not conform to Aristotle's *Poetics*, where it is said that a probable impossible is better than an improbable possible: but in Ireland, as Sir John Mahaffy, Provost of Trinity College, Dublin (Mayhappy Mayhapnot) noted, 'the possible was the improbable and the improbable the inevitable' (110). The document to be interpreted is the Letter discovered in a dungheap by a Hen: like a Greek papyrus, it is legible only in places, and seems to have been written by an Irish exile in Boston, Massachusetts, to one Maggy back home, and mentioning a certain Father Michael, with other phrases which become *leitmotifs*, such as 'born gentleman' and 'grand funeral'. The message is distorted as

well as incomplete, and Aristotelian logic applies no more than
Aristotelian poetics. 'Horseness is the whatness of allhorse' in *Ulysses*
becomes:

> Well, almost any photoist worth his chemicots will tip anyone
> asking him the teaser that if a negative of a horse happens to
> melt enough while drying, well, what you get is, well, a
> positively grotesquely distorted macromass of all sorts of
> horsehappy values and masses of meltwhile horse. (111)

The Letter and *Finnegans Wake* itself can be interpreted in a number
of different ways. The first is psychoanalytical; any work of literature,
even one as apparently innocent as *Alice in Wonderland*, can be made
to yield all kinds of hidden meanings: 'But we grisly old Sykos who
have done our unsmiling bit on 'alices, when they were yung and
easily freudened' (115.22–4, the most famous pun in the book). But
the book can also be read as a political document, in a Marxist or in a
nationalist sense:

> for we also know, what we have perused from the pages of *I was*
> *a Gemral*, that Showting up of Bulsklivism by 'Schottenboum',
> that Father Michael about this red time of the white terror
> equals the old régime and Margaret is the social revolution while
> cakes mean the party funds and dear thank you signifies national
> gratitude. (116.5–10)

That refers to *The Shewing up of Blanco Posnett*, by G. B. Shaw, a
political writer of another kind, to a Bolshevik interpretation of 'How
Buckley Shot the Russian General' (a story told in Book III, Chapter
iii), and from a nationalist viewpoint it means that General Michael
Collins, one of the fathers of the Irish Free State, was shot down by
the Republicans, the Irish thus showing their gratitude.

The subject of authorship and forgery is discussed at length, to
cover the fake 'Mahatma Letters' of Madame Blavatsky and Shakespeare's spelling. From 119 to 123 there is a long paragraph parodying
Sullivan on *The Book of Kells* and simultaneously introducing every
chapter of *Ulysses* more or less in order. In the first line (119.10) the
'farmfrow' is the old milk-woman who appears in the first chapter,
'those so prudently bolted or blocked rounds' refers to the Martello
tower, and so on. 'A word as cunningly hidden in its maze of confused
drapery as a fieldmouse in a nest of coloured ribbons' (120.05–6)
corresponds to Mr Bloom contemplating the draper's window, while

the draper is Jonathan Swift of the *Drapier's Letters* (pseudonymous writing and other mystifications are part of the discussion); it is also a wonderful description of the linguistic procedure of *Finnegans Wake*. The learning takes in all kinds of palaeography from Egyptian hieroglyphics to Irish ogham (pronounced o-am) letters. 'The gipsy mating of a grand stylish gravedigging with secondbest buns' combines the 'Hades' chapter of *Ulysses*; 'the funeral bakedmeats shall furnish forth the marriage table' and the gravediggers in *Hamlet*; Shakespeare's second-best bed; the mixture of high and low styles in Shakespeare to which the neo-classical critics objected; the themes 'grand funeral' and 'cakes' of the Letter. In the coda the search for the author finally converges on one suspect. The theory that the book was composed by an ape hitting a typewriter at random has been dropped, but the author is a forger of Victorian melodrama, Jim the Penman:

> To all's much relief one's half hypothesis of that jabberjaw ape
> amok the showering jestnuts of Bruisanose was hotly dropped
> and his room taken up by that odious and still today
> insufficiently malestimated notesnatcher . . . Shem the Penman.

## I.vi (126–68). 'Questions and Answers'

Before we come to the new Portrait of the Shem-Artist, a chapter is interpolated consisting of Twelve Questions and Answers. It is not on such a high level as Chapters v, vii, or viii, but it does contain the delightful 'Fable of the Mookse and the Gripes'.

The first question begins '1. What secondtonone myther rector and maximost bridgesmaker was the first to rise taller through his beanstale than the bluegum buaboababbaun or the giganteous Wellingtonia Sequoiaa.' The biggest tree is the Sequoiadendron giganteum or Wellingtonia gigantea, while the tallest tree is the eucalyptus or blue gum and the widest is the baobab; this takes us back to the giants of Chapter i, and Finnegan as master-builder and pontifex maximus: Jack climbed up the giant beanstalk which is his own erection. This set of questions is like the clues of a crossword puzzle, or like the folk-genre of the riddle: with patience and a dictionary of quotations and proverbs most can be worked out. Some references are more erudite: 'as far as wind dries and rain eats and sun turns and water bounds' (136) is adapted from an ancient document called the 'Babylonian Job'; while Joyce in a piece of journalism explains that a medieval traveller in Galway City 'could see at one blick a saumon taken with a lance, hunters pursuing a doe, a swallowship in full sail, a whyterobe lifting a host' (139.2–3). A recurrent theme is that of Richard III ('Dook Hookback-crook'), representing Earwicker and his hump, but many other kings and heroes are mentioned. The answer is one who contains all men in himself, the ancestor, 'Finn MacCool' (139).

The second question concerns Anna Livia, the Mother, whose symbol is a triangle or delta: it is answered briefly to the tune of Prout's 'Bells of Shandon'. The third (139–40) asks what is the motto of the Inn or House, and this turns out to be the motto of Dublin itself: Obedientia civium urbis felicitas. The fourth is a fantasy on the number four: it weaves together the Four Old Men; the four cities of Eire, Belfast, Cork, Dublin, Galway, each speaking in regional dialect; four metals and ages, gold, silver, copper and iron; four stages of life, birth, marriage, death and rebirth, corresponding to Vico's ages; the four voices of a quartet, finally harmonised in a chime of the Bells of Shandon.

Question five begins a second cycle: the Father becomes the curate or manservant of the pub, who is described in Scandinavian terms; about a hundred Norwegian words are used in twenty lines, ending with a quotation from Ibsen's *Peer Gynt*. Similarly, the Mother is transformed into the old maidservant Kate in question six. The seventh question (142) is about the twelve (customers, disciples, notes of the chromatic scale, Dublin suburbs). The eighth (143) is about the book itself, and rehearses in a few lines the main themes: dreams, the watches of the night, the opposition of rival brothers, rainbow, Viconian cycle. Question ten begins with a quotation from one of Joyce's favourite Elizabethan airs, Rosseter's 'What then is love but mourning, What Desire but a self-burning, Till she that hates doth love return' which becomes 'What bitter's love but yurning, what'sour lovemutch but a bref burning till shee that drawes dothe smoake retourne'. The subject of love-hate is developed at length in a monologue by Isabelle (yet another transformation of the female). Words associated by Joyce with his wife Nora are woven into the text, as are soprano arias ('chasta dieva', 147.24); this Isolde is a rather nastier version of Gerty MacDowell.

The eleventh is a very long (148–68) monologue spoken by Shaun, mainly concerning his rival brother Shem; it is the third part of the third group of four, and therefore corresponds to Book III, 'The Four Watches of Shaun'. Shaun is polemical and holds forth in the style of George Bernard Shaw's prefaces to the plays; he also parodies another vigorous polemical writer, P. Wyndham Lewis, who attacked Joyce at great length in *Time and Western Man* and *The Apes of God*. Joyce's satire is somewhat dated, since very few people now read Wyndham Lewis; contemporaries are apt to mistake vigour for genius, but later ages demand more sustenance. Joyce, however, refers to a polemical writer of real genius, Richard Wagner, whose prose writings ramble obsessively but contain insights of great originality. This accounts for the Jewish references on page 150; Lewis becomes 'Professor Loewy-Brueller', the anthropologist Lévy-Bruhl and Wagner's Jewish conductor friend Levi; 'Levi Brullo' includes another Wagnerian conductor, von Bülow. Wagner's attacks on semitic music and defence of his own work are echoed on page 151.01. Then follow 'Cosm' (Wagner's wife Cosima, formerly wife of von Bülow); '*parcequeue*' (*Parsifal*); 'Nuremberg eggs' (*Meistersinger*, a kind of watch); 'watches cunldron' (the witch Kundry in *Parsifal*; also the cauldron into which Rachel is thrown in the Jewish Halévy's *La Juive*); .17 'Cupolar' (the dome of the Grail castle, celebrated by Verlaine); .19 'Mitleid', 124 'toray' (Durch Mitleid wissend, der reine Thor, Becoming wise through compassion, the pure fool, which is the chief theme of *Parsifal*); 152.01 'soar', .02 'cling' (Klingsor). The Wagnerian references continue in the 'Fable of the Mookse and the Gripes', which is immediately followed by 'No applause, please!' which is the Master's command to the audience after the first act of *Parsifal*. The chief subject of controversy is space versus time, following Lewis's opposition of the space-centred or classical artist (himself) to the time-centred or Romantic (Joyce). This entails philosophical principles which Joyce knew that Lewis did not understand very well, however many names he dropped; so Joyce drops the names of many philosophers, especially in 'The Mookse and the Gripes', and theorists of time, like Bergson and Einstein. Bergson influenced Proust, a writer on time with whom Joyce was often compared but whom he did not find time to read, hence 'who the lost time we had the pleasure we have had our little recherché brush with, what, Schott?' (149.23–4).

'The Mookse and the Gripes' (152–9) is very funny and quite accessible, even if it demands some knowledge of liturgical and ecclesiastical history, since it is about the struggle between the Eastern (Orthodox) and Western (Roman Catholic) churches, the former calling for Greek and Russian, the latter for Latin words: 155.27 'gresk, letton and russicruxian'. With the exception of the Russian element, the fable has been well annotated. It ends lyrically and almost transparently when Nuvoletta (little cloud, the beginning of the river) smiles down at the exhausted combatants. She is also Iseult or Isolde with her various titles, Princess of Brittany, wife of Mark of Cornwall, 'daughter of the queen of the Emperor of Ireland' and lover of Tristan (157–8). In anticipation of the end of 'Anna Livia Plurabelle' the Mookse and the Gripes (Fox and Grapes, Mock Turtle and Gryphon) are picked up by two washerwomen and end as an elm and a stone:

> Then Nuvoletta reflected for the last time in her little long life
> and she made up all her myriads of drifting minds in one. She
> cancelled all her engauzements. She climbed over the bannistars;
> she gave a childly cloudy cry: *Nuée! Nuée!* A lightdress fluttered.
> She was gone.

The eleventh answer continues with another fable, this time about Brutus and Cassius; although there are some more good jokes at the expense of Wyndham Lewis, these seem to be some of the thinnest pages in *Finnegans Wake*; the first draft was not much revised by Joyce.

The twelfth question-and-answer is the briefest: '12. *Sacer esto?* Answer: *Semus sumus!*' Shem is the author of the book, at once a sacred priest of the imagination and an accursed figure: the term 'sacer' in the primitive Roman Twelve Tables means a sacrificial victim. The portrait of the artist as an ambiguous angel-devil figure is explored in the next chapter.

## I. vii (169–95). 'Shem'

This is the most amusing chapter and, next to 'Anna Livia Plurabelle' and parts of 'Shaun', the easiest to read. It is obviously Joyce's auto-biography taken a stage further, since it mentions many of the events of his life after 1904. Though much of the details are historically true, it is nevertheless a fantastic self-portrait: Joyce presents himself as if he were another Rimbaud, bisexual, deranged and dirty, which hardly fits the facts; he rightly accuses himself of alcoholism, but apparently wrongly of being a drug-taker. After Rimbaud, Swift seems to be Joyce's more important avatar in this chapter, again with an emphasis on dirt and madness. There is much in the chapter about the Devil, minor devils in hell: for example, Shemus is the peasant in Yeats's play *The Countess Cathleen* who sells his soul to the devil. The geography, sins, punishments and characters of Dante's *Inferno* provide a general framework. Milton is the great authority on Satan, and *Paradise Lost* is quoted in 194.15: 'clothed upon with the metuor and shimmering like the horescens' (1.86 Clothed with transcendent brightness, 537 Shone like a meteor streaming to the wind), while Milton's blindness is paralleled with Joyce's on page 182. Rather a large number of foreign languages are used, the most esoteric of which are Lithuanian and Romany; and there is a fair amount of operatic material, mainly tenor arias.

'Shem is as short for Shemus as Jem is joky for Jacob' (169.01) states the equation between Jim Joyce and the deceitful rival brother Jacob. A short prelude implies that the Riddle of the Sphinx does not apply to Shem; for the answer to Haeckel's Riddle of the Universe 'when is a man not a man' is 'when he is a . . . Sham' (170). 'Shem was a sham and a low sham and his lowness creeped out first via foodstuffs', for he preferred tinned salmon to fresh: 'many was the time he repeated in his botulism that no junglegrown pineapple ever smacked like the whoppers who shook out of Ananias's cans, Findlater and Gladstone's, Corner House, England' (170. Salmon and Gluckstein are the owners of Lyons Corner Houses, Ananas means pineapples). 'He would far sooner muddle through the hash of lentils in Europe than meddle with Irrland's split little pea' (Jacob's mess of pottage, Joyce in exile). He is a drunkard, but won't touch honest gin or beer. 'O dear no! Instead the tragic jester [Rigoletto, Pagliacci] sobbed himself whey-whingingly sick of life on some sort of rhubarbarous maudarin yellagreen funkleblue windigut diodying applejack squeezed from sour grapefruice', which was a Swiss white wine that Joyce and Budgen called archduchess's urine. In exile, he cables for help 'from his Nearapoblican asylum to his jonathan for a brother' (172.23-4), as James did to Stanislaus; Neapolitan Vico and Jonathan Swift both died of senile dementia; the 'asylum' takes up 'hereditary' of line 13, and introduces one of Joyce's favourite arias 'Asile hereditaire' from Rossini's *Guillaume Tell*. Shem is a coward and would not fight in the First World War or in the Irish Troubles:

> Now it is notoriously known how on that surprisingly bludgeony Unity Sunday when the grand germogall allstar bout was harrily the rage between our weltingtoms extraordinary and our pettythicks the marshallaisy and Irish eyes of welcome were smiling daggers down their backs . . . categorically unimperatived by the maxims, a rank funk getting the better of him, the scut

in a bad fit of pyjamas fled lie a leveret for his bare lives [to Switzerland, where he hid under the bed] hemiparalysed by the tong warfare and all the shemozzle . . . his cheeks and trousers changing colour every time a gat croaked. (176–7)

Shem lives in a fantasy world, dreaming of women's underwear and success as a tenor:

an entire operahouse (there was to be stamping room only in the prompter's box and everthemore his queque kept swelling) or enthusiastic noblewomen flinging every coronetcrimsoned stitch they had off at his probscenium . . . when . . . he squealed the topsquall in *Deal Lil Shemlockup Yellin*. (179–80)

But in fact he can hardly write more than a word a week; and has to steal others' ideas and styles 'so as one day to utter an epical forged cheque on the public' (cf. the end of the *Portrait* and Siegfried forging Nothung). He would 'stipple endlessly inartistic portraits of himself in the act of reciting old Nichiabelli's monolook interyerear' (182.18–20, old Nick, the Devil, Nicholas Nickleby, Machiavelli; in the next lines we have Vanno Fucci and Paolo from the *Inferno*).

Shem's house is Shaw's *Heartbreak House* and Joyce's head, with a black patch over one eye, 'in which the soulcontracted son of the secret cell groped through life at the expense of the taxpayers, dejected into day and night with jesuit bark and bitter bite.' (Jesuit bark is quinine, his bark was worse than his bite.) There is a splendid description of the litter covering the walls and floor of his house, in terms of distorted clichés and Biblical texts; 'once current, puns, quashed quotatoes, messes of mottage . . . unloosed shoe latchets, crooked strait waistcoats' (183). When he runs out of paper and ink, Shem makes the latter out of his own excreta and 'wrote over every square inch of the only foolscap available, his own body' a universal 'cyclewheeling history' based on his personal experience: 'a dividual chaos, perilous, potent, common to allflesh, human only, mortal'; it is a philosophical principle of *Finnegans Wake* that individual experience is universal, unchanging humanity is mortal (186). Joyce identifies himself again with Parnell, the uncrowned and sacrificial king, with a reference to 'Ivy Day in the Committee Room', and then lists the other stories of *Dubliners* on pages 186–7.

Shem now encounters his enemy and opposite in the form of his good brother, a policeman called JUSTIUS, who lectures him on his failings (187–93):

You were bred, fed, fostered and fattened from holy childhood
up in this two easter island [the Celtic Church in Ireland once had
a different way of calculating Easter] on the piejaw of hilarious
heaven . . . and now, forsooth, a nogger among the blankards
of this dastard century, you have become of twosome twiminds
forenenst gods, hidden and discovered, nay, condemned fool,
anarch, egoarch, hiresiarch, you have reared your disunited
kingdom on the vacuum of your own most intensely doubtful
soul.

The denunciation warms up to a fine apocalyptic passage on pages
189–90; a prophet is not without honour save in his own country;
Romany 'porengro' means 'penman', and there are references to skin
diseases, auguries, birds, and the destruction of the public buildings
of Dublin between the Rising and the Civil War, 1916–22, such as
the Record Office and the Customs House. Out of destruction and
chaos came a new creation — though if you sup with a devil like
Shem you need a long spoon:

Sniffer of carrion, premature gravedigger . . . you with your
dislocated reason, have curely foretold, a jophet in your own
absence, by blind poring upon your many scalds and burns and
blisters, impetiginous sores and pustules, by the auspices of that
raven cloud, your shade, and by the auguries of rocks in
parliament, death with every disaster, the dynamitisation of
colleagues, and reducing of records to ashes, the levelling of all
customs by blazes, the return of a lot of sweetempered
gunpowdered didst unto dudst . . . the fiercer the fire and the
longer your spoon and the harder you gruel with more grease
to your elbow the merrier fumes your new Irish stew.

As Justinus inveighs against Shem he slowly changes into his unwitting
apologist, painting him as a Christ-like figure and describing the
events of the Passion: 'O, you were excruciated, in honour bound to
the cross of your own cruelfiction!' At the end he denounces him in
the name of Faith, Hope and Charity, putting a magic charm on him
like an Australian aborigine: 'He points the deathbone and the quick
are still' (193.29). Shem, now changed into Mercius, confesses his
sins and admits to being Richard III and Cain, and sterile to boot
(Luke 23:29 'Blessed are the barren, and the wombs that never bare,
and the breasts that never gave suck.') 'My fault, his fault, a kingship
through a fault! Pariah, cannibal Cain, I who oathily forswore the

womb that bore you and the paps I sometimes sucked' (193.31-4). In the confused grammar of this final passage the two brothers become one; they are reconciled in the presence of their mother the river, the Muse of the Wake, to whom the rest of Book I belongs. The frogs sing the chorus: what is it?

> as happy as the day is wet, babbling, bubbling, chattering to herself, deloothering the fields on their elbows leaning with the sloothering slide of her, giddygaddy, grannyma, gossipaceous Anna Livia.
> He lifts the lifeward and the dumb speak.
> — Quoiquoiquoiquoiquoiquoiquoiq!

## I. viii (196-216). 'Anna Livia Plurabelle'

This is the best-known chapter in the book, and the best loved. The rhythms of this river have been heard in much English poetry since the chapter was published as a pamphlet in 1930: without them, for example, Dylan Thomas's finest effects would have been impossible. Everyone knows that it is a dialogue between two washerwomen on opposite banks of the Liffey who tell the story of the river from Dublin Bay back to her source in the Wicklow Mountains, and that the names of hundreds of rivers have been woven into the text. Each of the women is a Grey Washer by the Ford, an Irish wraith; when a doomed man approaches, she holds up his phantom self with his death wounds. Earwicker is the doomed man, a condemned prisoner in his cell, 'hungerstriking all alone and holding doomsdag over hunselv' (199.04-5). (It was Ibsen who said that the artist must hold doomsday over himself.) After his death his widow distributes the fragments of his body as presents to the Dubliners, her thousand and one sons and daughters (210-12). This is the obverse of Isis collecting the fragments of Osiris.

The story is told in terms of Greek epic and mythology. It begins 'O tell me all about Anna Livia!', echoing the beginning of the *Odyssey*, 'Tell me, Muse!' This is followed by 'I want to hear all' (Hera), 'you know' (Juno), 'I know' (Ino). The climax of Homeric imitation is reached on pages 206-7 in a long and beautiful parody of Hera preparing to seduce her husband Zeus:

> With ambrosia first did she cleanse every stain from her winsome body and anointed her with olive oil, ambrosial, soft, and of a

sweet savour. . . . Therewith she anointed her fair body and combed her hair, and with her hands *plaited* her shining tresses, fair and ambrosial, flowing from her immortal head. Then she clad her in her fragrant robe. . . .

This becomes:

First she let her hair fal and down it flussed to her feet its teviots winding coils. Then, mothernaked, she sampood herself with galawater and fraguant pistania mud, wupper and lavar, from crown to sole. . . . Peeled gold of waxwork her jellybelly and her grains of incense anguille bronze. And after that she wove a garland for her hair. She pleated it. She plaited it. Of meadowgrass and river glags, the bulrush and waterweed, and of fallen griefs of weeping willow.

(206–7; Hera's veil appears on 208; the willow also suggests Desdemona, who is hinted at elsewhere in the chapter.) When her toilet is completed she dresses in grotesque and rustic clothes (208), and then goes out to give birthday presents to all her children, who are the entire poor population of Dublin, 'from the slime of their slums and artesaned welling, rickets and riots' (209.32–3). The old washerwomen are themselves of the slums, and one of them evokes the culture of poverty poignantly in a few words:

Amn't I up since the damp dawn, marthared mary allacook, with Corrigan's pulse and varicoarse veins, my pramaxle smashed, Alive Jane in decline and my oneeyed mongrel twice run over, soaking and bleaching boiler rags, a widow like me, for to deck my tennis champion son, the laundryman with the lavender flannels?

(214.22–8; Christ washes away the sins of the world, laundry and lavender come from the same root; the speaker is Martha, Mary and the Blessed Margaret Mary Alacoque.) The presents are the fragments of her husband's body, distributed as Holy Communion. Lastly, to the twenty-nine February-rainbow girls she gives his blood to drink as wine, that they may grow into maturity. 'She gave them ilcka madre's daughter a moonflower and a bloodvein; but the grapes that ripe before reason to them that devide the vinedress' (212.15–16).

The chapter ends with the great Night-piece which Joyce chose for eight minutes of recording, 'Well you know or don't you kennet or haven't I told you every telling has a taling and that's the he and she of it' (213.11–12). In the dusk one washerwoman gradually turns into a tree, the other into a stone. They lament the passing of the Irish overseas 'in Markland's Vineland beyond Brendan's herring pool': Martha's Vineyard, America, which the Viking discoverers called Vine-land, and which was discovered by the Irish Saint Brendan long before. They are such rough washers that there's nothing left of the clothes but 'one kneebuckle and two hooks in the front'. They see all the characters of the story looming up briefly out of the dusk, H. C. Earwicker, the Four Old Men and their Donkey, and Anna Livia: 'Ah, but she was the queer old skeowsha anyhow, Anna Livia, trinkettoes. And sure he was the quare old buntz too. Dear Dirty Dumpling, foostherfather of fingalls and dotthergills' (215.15).

The One becomes the Many, the Many becomes the One again, like white light in a prism; the answer to the nursery riddle 'How many were going to Saint Ives?' is 'Just one'. Arthur Rimbaud-Rainbow married a harem of Africans each speaking a different language, for trading purposes: 'He married his markets . . . in their pinky limony creamy birnies and their turkiss indienne mauves.' It is like the mystery of the Trinity, three-in-one, commemorated in a Dublin College; Sanskrit is an Aryan language, the Arian heresy denied the Trinity: 'Latin me that, my trinity scholard, out of eure sanscreed into our eryan!' At the end the washerwomen 'Can't hear with the waters of. The chittering waters of. . . .' It is all a tale told by an idiot, signifying nothing. 'Beside the rivering waters of, hitherandthithering waters of. Night!'

II. i (219–59). 'The Mime of Mick, Nick and the Maggies'

> The scheme of the piece I sent you is the game we used to call Angels and Devils or colours. The Angels, girls, are grouped behind the Angel, Shawn, and the Devil has to come over three times and ask for a colour. If the colour he asks for has been chosen by any girl she has to run and he tries to catch her. As far as I have written he has come twice and been twice baffled. The piece is full of rhythms taken from English singing games. When first baffled vindictively he thinks of publishing blackmail stuff about his father, mother, etc. etc. etc. The second time he wanders off into sentimental poetry of what [*sic*] I actually wrote at the age of nine: 'My cot alas that dear old shady home where

oft in youthful sport I played, upon they verdant grassy fields all
day or lingered for a moment in they bosom shade etc. etc. etc.
etc.' This is interpreted by a violent pang of toothache after
which he throws a fit. When he is baffled a second time the girl
angels sing a hymn of liberation around Shawn. . . . Note
specially the treatment of the double rainbow in which the
iritic colours are first normal and then reversed. (Joyce, letter to
Harriet Shaw Weaver, 22 November 1930)

In *Finnegans Wake* it is always difficult to see the wood for the trees.
For this chapter Joyce has fortunately given us a fair amount of
information about the wood or macrostructure; and it is not too
difficult to complete the outline from page 236 to the end of the
chapter, with the help of the *First Draft Version* (ed. David Hayman,
1963). The praise of Shaun-Chuff by the girls turns into an apocalyptic
vision of feminism. The Devil, Shem-Glugg, apparently dies (239)
but makes a comeback (240) and writes, as he has threatened, rude
stories about his parents (241). There is a beautiful interlude as night
falls on the animals of the Phoenix Park Zoo (244-5). The Devil
makes a third set of three guesses about the colour of the girls' drawers,
but fails as feebly as before (252); again he is mocked by the girls,
but now the parents appear to stop the games and send all the children
to bed (255) — the question remains unanswered. The Age of Play
is over, too soon will come the tasks of school (256). The father's
rectal thunder ends the cycle (257), the curtain falls on the play-
within-the-play; after prayers soon all is mum (259).

Joyce also gave some information about the trees or macrostructure
when he mentioned in another letter to Miss Weaver (4 March 1931)
some of 'the books I am using for the present fragment which include
Marie Corelli, Swedenborg, St Thomas, the Sudanese war, Indian
outcasts, Flammarion's *The End of the World*, scores of children's
singing games 'from Germany, France, England and Italy and so on....'
I cannot claim to have identified all this material, but the children's
games are not too hard to find. For example, 'Withasly glints in.
Andecoy glants out. They romp it a little, a lessle, a lissle. Then
rompride round in rout' (226) is based on 'Lubin Loo': 'put your
right foot in, put your right foot out; shake it a little; and turn right
round about.' If you have a memory of infants singing that, as I have,
you will be readier to appreciate the eerie charm of the chapter.

Children's games are a primitive kind of musical drama, and so opera, as we shall see, is a major constituent of the chapter; they are also a kind of ballet, employing the language of gesture, of which there are several mentions, bringing in the theories of Sir Richard Paget and the Abbé Jousse. Swedenborg was presumably drawn on for angelology, Marie Corelli's *The Sorrows of Satan* for demonology. Since the latter, with its attendant topics of witchcraft and black magic, is so prevalent in the 'Mime', I propose to deal with it in a little detail.

The Devil is traditionally worshipped by a coven of twelve witches. A major poetic source for this worship is Robert Burns's *Tam O' Shanter* 229.21, 'tomashunders', 255.04 'Tamor', 241.25 'tammy', 240.30 'shantungs'. The Scots names for the Devil, quoted by Burns are 'Clootie' (239.18 'Klitty'), 'Hangie' and 'Hornie' (several references to the last two, especially 'horneypipe', 231.31). The worship consists largely in kissing the devil's arse, hence 251.11 'Blackarss', also 'Black arts' with witches, devil and sorcerers in the context. The witches in Shakespeare's *Macbeth* appear several times. For a list of the traditional demons one need look no further than Milton's *Nativity Ode* and *Paradise Lost* I and II. All or nearly all of them appear in the 'Mime' or in I.vii which deals with Shem as devil: Beelzebub, Moloch, Chemos (177.05 'shemozzle'), Baalim, Ashtaroth, Thammauz, Dagon, Belial, Mammon, Azazel (258.07 'Azrael'). More elaborate lists can be found in *Lemegeton* and other grimoires, conveniently summarised by Richard Cavendish in *The Black Arts* (London, Routledge & Kegan Paul, 1967), including Astaroth (Astarte, 232.12 'astarted'), Nergel (234.31 'nargleygargley'), Behemoth (244.36), Lilith and so on. The *Grand Grimoire* (243.09 'grime') tells how one may make a pact not with the Devil but with one of his subordinates, Lucifuge Rofocale: Joyce mentioned the latter to Jolas for a note in *transition*, glossing 250.27 'Rosocale' (cf. 354.32 'lucifug lancifer').

Black magic and sorcery play an important part in this chapter, as they did in the intellectual life of nineteenth-century Europe, and again do so in the mid-twentieth century. (I do not intend here to go into the question of whether Joyce believed in magic, white or black, or astrology or the occult or ESP.) The most important author and practitioner of the nineteenth century was Eliphas Levi (244.35 'Eliphas', 230.34 'levirs'), and of the twentieth Aleister Crowley, who believed that he was a reincarnation of Eliphas Levi and called himself the 'Great Beast' of the Apocalypse: hence 232.28 'crowy', 129.12 'Cro-whore', and I think 231.05 *'alas, that dear'*. He is named more clearly outside the chapter as Crowalley (105.27), but he is very clearly called the Great Beast and associated with Levi in the Phoenix Park Zoo episode: 244.35 '*Great is Eliphas Magistrodontos*'. Crowley was associated with McGregor Mathers, the founder of the occultist Order of the Golden Dawn, of which W. B. Yeats was an active member. I cannot find Mathers in this chapter, though he is named several times elsewhere in the *Wake*, but the Order appears 222.18 'Radium Wedding of Neid and Moorning and the Dawn of Peace', while 220.21 'perdunamento' is based on *Perdurabo*, the magic motto-name that Crowley assumed on joining the Order. W. B. Yeats assumed the more interesting motto-name of *Daemon est Deus inversus*, which, if not quoted, is beautifully Joycean.

Less spectacular than the calling up of evil spirits are the various species of fortune-telling; the most notorious, again in vogue today, is the Tarot pack. Space forbids a full treatment of this subject, but if the reader will inspect a standard Marseilles tarot pack while consulting Hart's *Concordance* he will be able to judge whether the following is correct or not. The four suits are Épée (Swords, 'spades' 222.22, 250.35), Coupe (Cups, 'hearts', 242.04 'coupoll'), Denier (Coins or Pentacles, 'diamonds' 256.29), Baton or Baston (Wands, 'staffs', 'clubs', 254.14 'Bastienne'). The following are the twenty-two 'Major Trumps': I think I have found nearly all of them but shall give the references only to the more interesting.

o Le Mat, Fool. 245.29 'matt'; 238.24 'fools'; 222.23 'Fools'.
1 Le Bateleur, Juggler.
2 Papesse, Female Pope.
3 L'Emperatrice.
4 L'empereur.
5 Pape, Pope. 223.10 'pop'. 227.16 'papavere's'.
6 L'amoureux, lover. 231.08 'amourmeant'.
7 Chariot. 22.31 'jarrety'.
8 Justice.
9 Hermite.
10 La Roue de Fortune, wheel of fortune. 221.12, 231.21; 227.10.
11 Justice.
12 Le Pendu, the Hanged Man. 243.26, 248.15.
13 (No French name) Death.
14 Temperance.
15 Diable, devil (passim).
16 La Maison Dieu, usually 'Falling Tower' as in the picture

244.21 'maize'; 224.12 'towerable'.
17 L'Etoile, Stars.
18 Lune, Moon.
19 Soleil, Sun.
20 Le Jugement, the Day of Judgment. 257–8 passim.
21 Le Monde, the World.

The Tarot itself appears in various *tar -s*, of which at least six can be found in the *Concordance*. Other methods of divination are mentioned at 221.13: Telling fortunes, 14 card, palm, tea (leaves), and doubtless much more could be gleaned from the 'Mime'.

I turn to a more congenial topic, namely operas that have to do with the Devil or devils. The very first is 219.23 'robot', which points to Meyerbeer's *Robert le diable*. The most striking is Weber's *Der Freischutz* (1821). Act I: Max (tenor, 248.34), in love with Agathe (soprano, 250.27 'Aghatharept'), is eager to win a shooting competition to decide who is to be the next head ranger, but loses in a trial. Kaspar (bass, 256.35 'Caspi'), who has sold his soul to the evil spirit Zamiel (spoken part, 242.20 'Samhar', 253.12 'sammarc', 222.36 'Sammy') advises Max to get magic bullets from Zamiel. Act II: Agathe is nervous, though calmed by her friend Aennchen (one of A.L.P.'s names) when Max tells her he must fetch a stag he has shot in the haunted Wolf's Glen (223.03 'Woolf' (who's afraid of?), 221.08 'Glen'); the music of the Wolf's Glen scene that follows is one of the most famous in Romantic music. I shall not describe the rest of the plot, which has a happy ending with a chorus of bridesmaids (220.03 'Bride's', 237,06 'bridawl', 222.05 'chorale', 234.36 'chor'). This bridal chorus is associated in the 'Mime' with the chorus of flower-maidens in *Parsifal*, of which one of the chief characters is the wicked magician Klingsor, creator of the magic garden. There are many references to *Parsifal* and the flower-maidens, but, as we shall see, in the context of the angelic rather than the demonic. On the latter theme, one of the best-known operas is Gounod's *Faust*: Mephistopheles appears as 'muffinstuffinaches' (225.11); Marguerite and her Jewel Song 'Faiteslui mes aveux' as 'uniomargrits . . . avowals' (249.12). Mozart's *Magic Flute* also deals with the conflict of good and evil magic: 220.26 'magical helmet cap-a-pipe' (also referring to the magic helmet of the *Ring*); 222.10–11 'Rasche . . . Mitscht' (the Queen of Night's aria II.14 'Der Holle Rache'); 222.18 'Neid and Moorning' (night and morning, the Moor); 223.19–21 'Arrest thee, scaldbrother . . . ill s'arrested' (the magician Sarastro, plus 'Arretez, mes frères' from Saint-Saëns's *Samson et Dalila*); 241.22 'the benighted queendom'; 254.12 'Sara's drawhead' (Sarastro).

The plot of the 'Mime' centres on the asking and answering or failing to answer three questions or riddles, and this is also given extended treatment in operatic terms. Question-master in television feature: 'In what two well-known operas do Questions and Answers figure prominently?' Experts on panel: '*Turandot* by Puccini and *Siegfried*, the third part of Richard Wagner's *Ring*.' 'Full marks.'

At the risk of spelling out the obvious, here is the plot of *Turandot*. In a fairy-tale in China it is decreed that Princess Turandot will only marry a suitor if he can solve three riddles that she sets; failure means instant death. ('Gli enigme sono tre — la morte è una!') In Peking arrive an Unknown Prince (whose real name is Calaf), his father Timur, a deposed king of Tartary, and attendant slavegirl Liú. Calaf falls in love with Turandot and decides to attempt the riddles, although he is advised against this by Ping, Pang and Pong, the three ministers, Timur and finally Liú. Calaf remains resolute ('Non piangere, Liú'). In Act II Turandot explains why she has made such a cruel decree: a thousand thousand years ago a princess was abducted and raped by a barbarian, and she is the reincarnation and avenger of this princess ('In questa reggia'). The Prince answers the first two riddles correctly with 'la speranza' (hope) and 'il sangue' (blood). When the third is set, 'What is the ice that gives you fire?' he hesitates but gets it right as 'Turandot herself'. He has now won the princess, but to save her from humiliation he generously allows her to answer a question: if she can find out what his name is, she will be free and he will die. In Act III heralds proclaim that no one in the city must sleep until the Prince's name is discovered ('Nessun dorma'). Liú is arrested and tortured but does not reveal Calaf's name: she reproaches Turandot, predicts that she will capitulate to the Prince, and then commits suicide. In the very last part (completed by Alfano after Puccini's death) the Princess does melt, and Calaf tells her his name, which she announces to the people is 'love'. Turandot's and Calaf's names are half hidden and half revealed throughout the 'Mime': e.g. 235.08 'turquewashed'; 230.13 'tourments of tosend years' (which also introduces the thousand thousand years of 'In questa reggia'); 227.35 [t. . .t. . .t. . .t. . .t. . .t. . .] tour-noun'; 232.27, 238.01 'dot'. Cf. 236.20 'taeorns' (also bringing in the theme of past aeons and epochs), and she is hidden in the thunderword on page 257 and elsewhere. As for Calaf, 'Only the caul knows his thousandfirst name' 254.19; cf. 240.24 'calaboosh', .25 'calico', .26 'what name', 255.14 'Calavera', 254.35 'prince', 255.01 'the hero, Capellisato'. His father Timur appears at 231.10 'Timor' and 255.14 'Tamor', which also means that his true name is 'Amore'. After a three-question sequence we have the three ministers: 233.28 'Ping an ping nwan ping pwan pong'. Little Liú is hidden away in 236.17 'Anne-liuia!' (426.16 Shaun sings 'Non piangere, Liú' in pidgin Chinese: 'no belong sollow mole . . . Fu Li's'). Fragments of the questions and answers appear in both English and Italian.

In *Siegfried* the young hero has been brought up by the evil Nibelung dwarf Mime. A Wanderer enters who is Wotan in disguise; he asks Mime to set him three questions, offering his own head as forfeit. He answers all three of them correctly, naming the Nibelungs, the giants, and the gods; and then sets three questions to Mime, on the same conditions. In fear Mime agrees, correctly answers the first and second (the Walsungs, and Nothung, the famous sword), but when the Wanderer asks the third question 'Who will reforge the sword?' he cannot answer. The Wanderer tells him the correct answer, which is that the sword can be reforged only by one who has never known fear — and that turns out to be Siegfried. The Wanderer does not take Mime's life but says that the fearless one will take it, as duly comes about. The 'Mime' of the title (219.18) appears with Wagner's head god here and elsewhere (especially in II. iii, 313.23 'if you guess mimic miening'): 226.15 'Mimmy', 247.36 'mimosa', 245.24 'wenderer', 229.14 'wondering', 231.20 'forget', .22 'gnawthing' (forge Nothung). *Ring* is a common word in the 'Mime', describing also the girls' dance-game; the last words of the cycle, spoken not sung by Hagen, 'Zurück vom Ring!' 'Get back from the ring', are quoted on 249.20; 'Oh backed von dem zug!' Siegfried and Sigmund are named in 243.16 'signur's'. *Die Walküre* in 220.05 'valkyrienne'; Brünnhilde in 246.32 'healing and Brune'; Freia in 231.13 'freytherem'. Siegfried's horn, as he journeys down the Rhine, is heard in 245.01 'Rhinohorn'. At the end there is an extended apocalypse, mentioning *Götterdämmerung* ('Twilight of the Gods'), 258.02 'gttdmmrng', followed by 'Hlls vlls', which means Valhalla, Wallhall, the palace of the gods, destroyed at the end of the cycle. To go from last to first, as one often does in *Finnegans Wake*, we hear Wotan's first words in the *Ring* (*Rheingold*) which are addressed to Walhall, 'Du wonnige selige Saal', 246.13–15 'ing . . . joyous guard . . . palashe . . . wonner', 245.01 'Rhinohorn'; 245.10 'toran' introduces not only Siegfried's

horn, but 'Der reine Thor', 'the pure fool', *Hauptmotiv* of *Parsifal*.
Parsifal is an analogue of Chuff, and the Blumenmädchen, flower-
maidens of Klingsor's enchanted garden, of the girls who worship
Chuff like so many teenyboppers. Flowers are, of course, a basic part
of the 'Mime', the most important being the heliotrope, the answer
to one of the riddles. There are many echoes of his name in 'Percy'
and 'Persse' throughout the *Wake*; the girls dance round him in a
ring, singing *come*, and these are commonly repeated words in the
chapter.

Parsifal is sexually pure and resists temptation (cf. 'innocent', pages
235, 240) and in this and other respects he is like the heroes of *Patience*
by Gilbert and Sullivan (who are especial favourites of Joyce). Reginald
Bunthorne (a Fleshly Poet) and Archibald Grosvenor (an Idyllic Poet)
are pursued by a chorus of 'Rapturous Maidens', of 'greenery-yallery',
cf. 226.31 'greenerin'; 254.35-6 'Bunnicombe . . . the herblord the
gillyflowerets so fain fan to flatter about'. The Ladies Angela, Saphir,
Ella and Jane all put in an appearance. Among the many other Gilbert
and Sullivan references in a pleasant one to *The Mikado*, 244.18ff,
'Where is our highly honourworthy salutable spousefoundress? The
foolish one of the family is within. Haha! Huzoor, where's he? At
house, to's pitty. With Nancy Hands.' A parody of Japanese polite
constructions is followed by Pitty-Sing and Nanki-Pooh; on 236.4-5
the Lord High Executioner Koko appears in 'Cococream . . . stick-
word'. The most elaborate allusion is on 243.35, 'Luiz-Marios Josephs'.
It is well known that this is one of the many allusions to Napoleon's
Josephine and Marie-Louise, and also to three tenors, Ludwig, Mario
and Joseph Maas, who appear elsewhere. It is not so obvious that it
contains also the three 'kings' of *The Gondoliers*, Luiz, Marco and
Giuseppe; and also a minor opera by Montemezzi, *L'Amore dei Tre Re*.
On the previous page *Trial by Jury* is used, as Mabel Worthington has
shown, to bring in the theme of an old man in love with a young girl.

It is impossible to do justice to the dense clusters of operatic references
in the 'Mime' except by producing long and cumbersome lists. I can
only suggest that the reader uses his own 'Do-it-yourself kit'; let him
look for operatic allusion to maidens, flowers and fairy-tale-like plots
(like Rossini's *Cenerentola*, Cinderella) and he should be able to improve
on my own findings. I confess that I have not yet found much about
ballet in the *Wake*, and perhaps Joyce was not so interested in this
art form; but the traditional British pantomime, which like *Parsifal*
usually contains a transformation scene, is almost as important in the

'Mime' as in the last section of the *Wake*. One would expect to find names of heroines from many operas in so female a chapter (Carmen, Santa, Lola, Mimi, Lucia and so on), but Joyce also decorates his text, to a degree that will not be believed except by opera buffs and collectors of historical discs, with the names of singers: in 'Shaun' (III.i) of tenors, in the 'Mime' mainly of sopranos and contraltos. The repetitions of 'tur' and 'turn' conceal not only Turandot but the most famous singer of this role, Eva Turner. 'The flowers of the ancelles' garden' (227.17) refers not only to the Blumenmädchen but to the soprano Mary Garden, who also comes in on 252.33. Many others can be discovered by looking through the entries in the *Oxford Dictionary of Opera*. The importance of this topic is announced by the bold opposition of the tenors McCormack and Sullivan at the beginning of the chapter (222).

In this discussion I seem to have moved from the wood to the trees, from plot and structure to a web of allusions; but I begin to doubt whether there is really much distinction drawn between the two in *Finnegans Wake*. To put it in Wagnerian terms, one cannot say that the essence of *Tristan und Isolde* is in the plot concerning the love-potion rather than in the sequence of chromatic harmonies that spell out 'Liebestod'.

The essence of the 'Mime' is the evocation of childhood, innocent and gay, but with sinister undertones of black magic and death. The shadow of death falls over a beautiful passage near the end, which concerns legitimate drama rather than opera: 'Home all go. Halome. Blare no more ramsblares, oddmund barkes! And cease your fumings, kindalled bushies! And sherriegoldies, yeassymgnays; your wildeshaweshowe moves swiftly sterneward! For here the holy language. Soons to come. To pausse' (256.11–15).

The basic quotation is the dirge from *Cymbeline*: 'Fear no more the heat o' the sun ... Golden lads and girls all must, As chimney-sweepers, come to dust.' 'Cease your funnings', from *The Beggar's Opera*, implies that the children's play is over: Moses's bush is a burned-out case. The Anglo-Irish dramatists, Sheridan, Goldsmith, Yeats, Synge, Wilde (*Salome*) and Shaw, take their final bows before 'The curtain drops by deep request' (257.31–2), from the hymn, 'The day thou gavest, Lord, has ended, The darkness falls at thy behest'. The chapter moves to its end in religious and specifically Old Testament terms: the awe-inspiring effects of the Viconian thunderclap is worked out in terms of the *Shema* ('Hear O Israel',

Deuteronomy 6) and a dense combination of quotations from Sisera's Song (Judges 5), Genesis and the Psalms (258). At the very end there is a shift to the Anglican Prayer Book, with its grave and soothing cadences. Joyce wrote the chapter in a year of great affliction, partly caused by his daughter's and his own health. He must have seen himself as Job, on whom the Lord heaped miseries; and yet as he wrote to Miss Weaver, 'I think the piece I sent you is the gayest and lightest thing I have done in spite of the circumstances'. Stoicism and humour finally prevailed. Lord have mercy on us, indeed, but 'incline our hearts to keep thy law': the mummers' show must go on.

Loud, heap miseries upon us yet entwine our arts with laughters low!

He he hi ho hu.

Mummum.

## II.ii (260–308). 'The Studies'

This is a far less attractive section than the 'Mime', mostly rather difficult, although the plot is simple enough. Joyce wrote to Miss Weaver that 'Shem is coaching Shaun how to do Euclid Book I.1.1.'. In fact, he makes his innocent brother draw a geometrical diagram of their mother's private parts: when Shaun finds out he hits his brother and gives him a black eye. The chapter is written in the form of a school text; to begin with there are solemn headings in the right margin and irreverent graffiti in the left; later, after an episode of day-dreaming by Dolph (Shem), 287–92, left and right are reversed. According to Mr J. S. Atherton, this is partly based on Lewis Carroll's *A Tangled Tale*; also Carrollian is the mathematical lore, to which is added the mathematical speculation of the Kabbala and other occultist material, including Yeats's *A Vision*. The opposition of angels and devils, heaven and hell, is continued from the last chapter; but now it is expressed in terms of Dante's *Divina Commedia*: there are a few quotations concerning Paolo and Francesca who live in the *Inferno*, but most are from the *Paradiso*. The framework of Dante's heavenly economy is the Ptolemaic system of nested planetary spheres, each planet corresponding to a particular virtue and inhabited by one or more characters who represent that virtue: for example, 'Pickardstown' (262.22) is Piccarda; 'Zeus, the O'Meghisthest of all' (269.18–19) gives the planets Jupiter and Mercury = Hermes Trismegistus, thrice-great, alpha to omega, and the other planets and virtues can soon be found. Not only are many of Dante's blessed mentioned, but the chapter is full of other saints' names, as a look at the *Penguin Dictionary of Saints* will soon show: Felicity (277), Christine (280), Canute and Zita (285.03) are only a few of them; 'Ignotus Loquor' (263.03) combines Saints Ignatius Loyola and Alphonsus Liguori.

An introductory passage asks who is God the Father — is he a myth or an allegory? 'To see in his horrorscup he is mehrkurios than saltz of sulphur. Terror of the noonstruck by day, cryptogram of each nightly bridable' (261). The sequence runs: horoscope; planet Mercury; the three substances of alchemy, mercury, salt and sulphur; Psalm 91 'Thou shalt not be afraid of the terror by night'; mushroom; Ignatius Donnelly, who began the nonsense about Bacon and Shakespeare with his book *The Great Cryptogram* — the Baconian heresy is pursued at intervals throughout this chapter, as is the subject of cyphers and codes.

If the heavenly paradise is Dante's 'eternal Rome', the Earthly Paradise is the suburb, once separate village, of Chapelizod on the Liffey. Mr McHugh has recently discovered that much of pages 264–5 is taken from the names of houses in the Chapelizod section of Thom's *Dublin Dictionary*. Upstairs in a Chapelizod public house the two boys are beginning their studies, it would seem, rather than at school. One of the subjects is history: 'Storiella as she is syung' (267.07–8), which was Joyce's original title for part of this chapter when published separately; this is partly based on *English as she is spoke*, a ridiculously inaccurate Portuguese grammar which Joyce had in his library. Grammar begins with the sounds of the language, and so on page 267 there is a play on Arthur Rimbaud-Rainbow's sonnet 'Voyelles', in which each vowel is assigned a colour and other occult qualities. Grammar is further discussed on pages 268–9 with sexual overtones; the topic shifts to Lewis Carroll: 'Though Wonderlawn's lost us for ever, Alis, alas, she broke the glass. Liddell' (270.19–21). The other episodes and chapters of the *Wake* are scrambled into the school textbook (e.g. the Letter on page 280). Suddenly there appears a long quotation in straight French (page 281), by the historian Quinet, who says beautifully if not very profoundly that the same wild flowers bloom every year as during the Roman Empire; and though civilisations may break up, 'leurs paisibles générations ont traversé les âges et sont arrivées jusqu'à nous, fraîches et riantes comme aux jours de bataille' ('their peaceful generations have crossed the ages and arrived in our own time, fresh and joyful as on the day of battle'). Since

Joyce repeats this passage with variations, it may be taken as his ecological philosophy: the rise and fall of civilisations are only minor episodes in the epic of nature.

The darker side of the dream is usually expressed by Shakespearean references, to the knives of *Julius Caesar*, the blood and darkness of *Macbeth*, and the violent jealousy (an emotion that Joyce felt powerfully) of *Othello*. All appear on page 281, with Verdi's *Otello* (*il fazzoletto*, the handkerchief), Desdemona, the Moor, Ancient Iago, and 'Not that I loved Caesar less but that I loved Rome more'; together with Ruhm (reputation), and Sieger (victor), also Siegfried; the reader may object with Plato that this is not real jealousy and murder, just the shadow of a shadow, but that would make little difference.

> But Bruto and Cassio are ware only of trifid tongues the
> whispered wilfulness, ('tis demonal!) and shadows shadows
> multiplicating (il folsoletto nel falsoletto con fazzolotto dal
> fuzzolezzo), totients quotients, they tackle their quarrel.
> Sickamoor's so woful sally. Ancient's aerger. And eachway
> bothwise glory signs. What if she love Sieger less though she
> leave Ruhm moan? (281.15–23)

On page 282 the topic changes from grammar to arithmetic, with many ingenious parodies of school problems; and then on page 286 to geometry, where the basic problem is the construction of an equilateral triangle, using ruler and compasses. After some pages of day-dreaming (which are very hard to understand) this is done on page 293: the triangle is the delta-symbol of A.L.P. but the drawing is clearly sexual. Shem laughs at his ingenuity: 'Fantastic! Early clever, surely doomed, to Swift's, alas, the galehus! Match of a matchness' (Berlioz's *Symphonie fantastique*, 'the march to the gallows'). After making more sexual and scatological jokes at the expense of their mother, the good boy Kev-Shaun becomes wroth with his brother, like Cain (303.15) and hits him: Shem sees stars, but seems to accept the reproof in a spirit of reconciliation. A short coda (306.8) presents the main themes of the book in the form of essay-topics.

## II.iii (309–82). 'The Stories'

This very long chapter consists of three stories joined with short narrative links. The first two were favourites of Joyce's father. A hunch-backed Norwegian captain orders a suit of clothes from a tailor and accuses him of producing a bad fit; the tailor retorts that it would be impossible to fit a figure like the captain — there was apparently a lot of invective and cross-talk in the story, but unfortunately we never get it in clear language, so that some of the point has been lost. Whether Joyce added this or not to his father's story, the sailor woos and marries the tailor's daughter.

On the other hand, it is possible to reconstruct the story of 'How Buckley shot the Russian General' almost completely: an Irish soldier in the Crimea finds he has a Russian general in the sights of his rifle; he is about to fire when the general lets down his trousers in order to defecate and he is restrained by common humanity. But when he see the general pick up a sod of green turf to wipe himself ('Another insult to Ireland' commented Samuel Beckett) he becomes furious and squeezes the trigger. This is told in the form of a dialogue between two comedians called Butt and Taff, broadcast on the primitive television of the 1930s. This section (338-55) is very densely packed and is now quite well understood, thanks to a great deal of co-operative work by European scholars, mainly at seminars in Amsterdam 1970 and Brighton 1971; the fruits of their labours were presented to the Joyce Symposium at Trieste 1971.

These two stories are supposed to be told in Earwicker's public house, or shown on TV to the customers. The publican then gets drunk himself and after closing-time he drinks up all the dregs and passes out on the floor. This becomes the third story, 'Roderick O'Connor', which combines the death of the last paramount King of Ireland, who bore that name, with the death of Rory O'Connor, the Republican leader defeated and killed by the Free-Staters in the Civil War. This was the very first section of *Finnegans Wake* that Joyce drafted, not long after O'Connor's death. The chapter is full of references to modern Irish history, from Easter 1916 to the Treaty and the Civil War: this is set in the framework of a wider European history, involving Russia, Scandinavia and the early voyagers.

The first section is Scandinavian and between pages 311 and 331 incorporates hundreds of Norwegian words. The prelude (309-10) reminds us that the Scandinavians founded the early kingdoms of Russia, just as they did that of Dublin: hence 'ruric' (309.10), 'birth of an otion' (.12 nation), 'Askold' (320.16 Hoskuld). Several Irish words suggest the Viking conquest of the Gaels, the most significant being 'serostaatarean' (310.08) or Saorstát Éireann, Irish Free State, whose origin is described. The prelude is full of technical terms of 1930s radio, and what follows is partly a sound broadcast programme. The narrative proper begins on 311.05: 'It was long after there was a lealand in the luffing.' That suggests Daland, the captain in *The Flying Dutchman* (cf. 327.23 'the flyend of a touchman'). The tailor's daughter is paralleled with Senta, and there are other echoes of Wagnerian opera in this section. Since the Portuguese and the Finns are great sailors, their languages are added to the mix. The captain keeps setting out and putting into port again; the suit of clothes is never finished but he pursues his suit of the tailor's daughter successfully: she is identified with Ireland herself, and the wedding with victory celebrations after the Treaty in 1921, and simultaneously the beginning of the Civil War between Free-Staters and Republicans: Joyce saw the Irish as eternally divided and aggressive, with hands on their swords: 'It was joobileejeu that All Sorts' Jour. Freestouters and public-ranks, hafts on glaives. You could hear them swearing threaties on the Cymylaya Mountains, man' (329).

On the next page the peaceful Norwegian national anthem ('Ja, vi elsker dette landet . . . med de tusen hjem', 'Yes, we love this land with its thousand homes') is combined with the violent Irish anthem ('Mid cannons' roar and rifles' peal, We'll chant a Soldier's Song'): 'Twere yeg will elsecare doatty lanv meet they dowscent hyemn to cannons' roar and rifles' peal will shantey soloweys sang!' (330.07–8).

A short bridge passage is obscure to me (332–7). Apparently the woman servant Kate comes down to the publican with a message from his wife, but what it is or why there is a mass of Polish on page 333 and Maori on page 335 I do not know. But the television sketch 'How Buckley shot the Russian General' (338–55) is highly readable. The comedians are called Butt and Taff; the first being connected with Melville's Billy Budd, and with the often repeated Irish word for penis, bod. Taff, the Shaun of the pair, is a Welshman, probably Wyndham Lewis again. They are the rivals of Verdi's *Il Trovatore*: 'Humme to our mounthings' (338.16–17); 'Say mangraphique, may say nay por daguerre' (339.23, Manrico and the Graf or Count); 'The balacleivka! Trovatarovitch! I trumble!' (341.09; this is the moment when the Count hears a lute and exclaims 'Il trovatore! Io fremo!' — the lute has been translated into a balalaika, the troubadour into a tovaritch). There is a great deal of Russian throughout, with the places and people of the Crimean War; and appropriately Russian and other Slavonic languages — it is hard to see why other languages including Malay are also used. The shooting of the general has a basically

Freudian meaning: 'And may he be too an intrepidation of our dreams' (338.29–30); it means not just the Oedipal killing of the father, but the primal killing of the father by his sons banded together, a romance that Freud tells brilliantly in *Totem and Taboo*. There is of course a dense tangle of sexual meanings, which can be separated if you have patience and a low enough mind; many of them are homosexual. Apart from the Crimea there are many military references, to guerrilla warfare, the American Civil War, accompanied by martial songs. Half way through there is a commentary on a race meeting: Joyce is fond of using technical terms about horses and bookies. The imagery becomes more and more apocalyptic as the death of the Russian general grows nearer. On 349–50 the general confesses his sins and prepares to receive Extreme Unction. The shooting is equated to the Death of Cock Robin ('I, said the Sparrow, with my little arrow') and at once causes an atomic explosion, about which there was some speculation when Joyce wrote this in the 1930s; this is Ragnarok, or Doomsday:

> With my how on armer and hits leg an arrow cockshock rockrogn. Sparro!
>
> *The abnihilisation of the etym by the grisning of the grosning of the grinder of the grunder of the first lord of Hurtreford expolodotonates through Parsuralia with an ivanmorinthorrorumble fragoromboassity amidwhiches general uttermosts confussion are perceivable moletons skaping with mulicules.* (353.20–6)

That takes in the thunderclap at the beginning of the Viconian cycle; Joyce's language and use of etymology; Tsar Ivan the Terrible; nihilists; and a little-known play by Oscar Wilde about Russia, *Vera, or the Nihilists*, in which a father Tsar is murdered by the nihilist friends of the Tsarevitch (there are references to Wilde throughout, and to Vera on page 348.23). At the end the two comedians Butt and Taff are reunited, and the great crime atoned for.

The rest of the chapter (355–82) is not nearly so well understood, at least by me. Earwicker, the publican, seems to have ceased playing the part of the Norwegian captain and the Russian general, and to be confessing his sins more openly. There is a fairly lucid interval on page 359 and page 360 which describes a BBC broadcast of the nightingale's song, as was done live in the 1930s. This passage, which is full of composers' names, was moderately well explained by me in the *Cambridge Journal* over twenty years ago and the explication repeated in *Song in the Work of James Joyce*; but I missed a good deal, such as the bird in *Siegfried* and the Queen of Night in Mozart's *Magic Flute*. A fairly explicit confession begins on page 363: 'Guilty but fellows culpows' — all his readers are fellow-culprits and it was after all a *felix culpa* or Fortunate Fall.

The key sentence is 'While I reveal thus my deepseep daughter which was bourne up pridely out of medsdreams undoubted' (366.13–15). Next there is an episode of punishment; a voice whose identity is uncertain takes the hero to task and urges on a lynching party (373–80). He is used as a ball by a rugger team, and then hanged and burned by an Irish nationalist mob. In the coda (380–2) he is defeated and killed, like the last King of Ireland, or Rory O'Connor in the Four Courts in 1922. This was the first episode of *Finnegans Wake* that Joyce drafted, in the following year. At the end he reverts to the condition of a great ape, an ourang-outan or Wild Man from Borneo: 'our wineman from Barleyhome he just slumped to throne.'

## II.iv (383–99). 'The Four Old Men'

This short chapter was rapidly given its final form by combining two early drafts with a minimum of revision. The first is a vulgar and funny account of the cuckolding of King Mark by Tristan and Isolde on board ship; the second consists of the rambling monologues of the Four Old Men, dying in an old persons' home. They are also birds of the sea and voyeurs at the famous adultery: 'they trolled out rightbold when they smacked the big kuss of Tristan with Usolde', and they speak the first chorus, mocking the old king: '— *Three quarks for Muster Mark!*' The old men, by now androgynous, reminisce about the good old days in Dublin, thinking of 'auld luke syne, and she haihaihail her kobbok kohinor sehehet on the praze savohole shanghai' (398). The Tristan story is told partly in the idiom of a rugger club member, probably half-drunk. Iseult is described as 'a strapping modern old ancient Irish princess, so and so hands high, such and such paddock weight . . . nothing under her hat but red hair and solid ivory' (396). Tristan is identified with Parnell, escaping down the fire-escape in his night-shirt: 'fariescapading in his natsirt. . . . And mild aunt Liza is as loose as her neese' (388.03–4). He is a Byronic hero, exhorting the deep and dark blue ocean to roll, and thinking of Macpherson's *Ossian* and Roland's horn: 'listening to Rolando's deependarbluns Ossian roll' (388) . . . 'while his deepseepeepers gazed and sazed and dazecrazemazed into her dullokbloom rodolling olosheen eyenbowls' (389).

The chapter ends with Tristan's song of praise and triumph; its four stanzas give the four provinces of Ireland, gospels, the gold, silver, copper, iron ages, and Vico's four epochs.

### III.i (403–28). 'The First Watch of Shaun'

Book III is the Book of the Sons and of the Third Viconian Age. It is both a celebration of and a satire on modern civilisation and political democracy. The protagonist is Shaun, a popular Irish political boss and tenor, whom Joyce in a letter identified as Count John McCormack, possessor of a beautiful voice but with a penchant for sentimental lyrics. There are many references to McCormack and to other operatic tenors, and even to many other male and female singers and composers. The first two chapters are perhaps the most musical sections of the *Wake*. Joyce wrote to Miss Weaver in 1924 that 'Shaun' (he also called Book III 'The Four Watches of Shaun') is

> a description of a postman travelling backwards in the night
> through the events already narrated. It is written in the form of a
> *via crucis* of fourteen stations but in reality it is only a barrel
> rolling down the river Liffey.

This barrel turns out to be one of Guinness, and also the coffin of the dead and dismembered god Osiris floating down the Nile. Shaun the the Post is a character in Dion Boucicault's play *Arrah-na-Pogue* from which Joyce drew a great deal (as Mr J. S. Atherton pointed out long ago), including incidental songs, costumes and stage directions. It is a nationalistic play, in which the patriotic song 'The Wearing of the Green' appears prominently; Shaun's interrogation by an English major is the basis of the dialogue in the third chapter of Book III. Shaun is also a popular trendy Christ, who sings a sentimental version of his own passion: the Stations of the Cross are not too easy to find, since they seem to run both forwards and backwards throughout the first two chapters. The following is a suggested reverse order:

1 Jesus is condemned to death. 472.29 'unclaimed by the death angel'; 472.33 'depart this earth'.
2 Jesus is made to bear the cross. 471.12 'with the sign of the southern cross'; 470.35 'waved instead a handacross the sea'.

3  First fall. 469.13 'We felt the fall.'

4  Jesus meets his mother. 469.13 'was not my olty mutther'.

5  The Cross is laid on Simon of Cyrene. 464.03 'David R. Crozier'; 463.05 'Bearer may leave the church'; 462.19 'in the fraction of a crust'; 462.16 'my darling proxy'.

6  Veronica wipes the face of Jesus. 458.14 'veronique'; 458.02 'a linenhall valentino' (draft: 'a proper handkerchief'); 457.34 'nosepaper'; and see Izzy's speech, 457–61 passim.

7  Second fall. 455.33 'I fill twice'.

8  Jesus speaks to the daughters of Jerusalem ('Weep not for me'). 453.34 'So cut out the lonesome stuff', .27 'let ye not be getting grief out of it'; 453.02 'let he create no scenes in my poor primmafore's wake'.

9  Third fall. 442.15 'pebbles spinning from beneath our footslips'; 432.04 'I rise'.

10  Jesus is stripped of his garments. 430.17 'doffed a hat'; 429.03 'to loosen (let God's son now be looking down on the poor preambler!) both of his bruised brogues'.

11  Jesus is nailed to the Cross. 427.05 'before he was really uprighted'; .04 'the crucet-house'.

12  Jesus dies. 427.18 'thou art passing hence'; 426.33 'collapsed'; .30 'over he careened'.

13  Jesus is taken down from the cross. 426.13 'as the freshfallen calef'; .07 'he virtually broke down'.

14  Jesus is placed in the sepulchre. 422.35 'after laying out his litterery bed, for two days she kept squealing'; 410.13 'or bury myself'; 409.17 'My heaviest crux and dairy lot it is, with a bed as hard'; 408.03 'he sank his hunk, dowanouet to resk at once, exhaust'; 407.35 'a houseful of deadheads'.

It is rather easier to find other references to the crucifixion and to the Seven Last Words from the Cross, e.g. 'I thirst' (405.33), 'My God, why hast thou forsaken me?' (405.35 'forsoaken'). 'Mother, behold thy son' (408.24–5, 'Be old! that other of mine)', 'Eloi' (405.26 'Elieu'), 'Father, forgive them, for they know not what they do' (409.33–4 'Forgive . . . not what I wants to do'), etc. Shaun is also Saint John and there are references to various saints of that name, especially to the author of Revelation. Thornton Wilder pointed out another important religious theme, the trial, torture and death of Joyce's hero Giordano Bruno at the hands of the Inquisition on

17 February 1600. But the main subjects of III.i, 'The First Watch of Shaun', are music and food (McCormack was a famous eater). The beginning with its set of numbers recalls three operas:

Hark!
Tolv two elf kater ten (it can't be) sax.
Hork!
Pedwar pemp foify tray (it must be) twelve. (403)

Mozart's *Le Nozze di Figaro* begins with counting 'Cinque — dieci — venti — trenta — trenta sei — quaranta tre' (measuring the furniture). We are also to think of the night watchman in Wagner's *Meistersinger* II.v: 'Hort, ihr Leut' und lass uns sagen/Die Glöck' hat zehn geschlagen', and again to Isolde's 'horch' at the beginning of *Tristan* Act II. A little further on 'midnight's chimes from out the belfry' (403.21-2) suggests Tannhäuser in Venusberg hearing the church bells above. Next to appear is Verdi's famous chorus of exiled slaves, dreaming of their homeland, in *Nabucco*, 'Va pensier sull' ali dorati': 'becco . . . pensee . . . veilch veilchen . . . aal in her dhoves.'

After this overture much of the chapter consists of a discussion between Shaun and the Old Man's Donkey: 'I, poor ass, am but as their fourpart tinckler's dunkey' (405.6-7); cf. the aria from Rossini's *Barbiere* 'Dunque io son'. A series of tenors is named, some obvious, others obscure. Mierswinki (404.19), Tamagno (404.26), Lauri-Volpi (406.06 'wolp'), Caruso (406.25), Nourrit (406.31), De Reszke (408.04), Bonci (408.26), Thill (409.30), Gigli (421.32 'Gilligan'), *et al*. Arias, mainly tenor, are drawn from 'the Anglo-Irish Ring', *The Bohemian Girl*, *The Lily of Killarney* and *Maritana*, but there are others from Italian and French opera: 'Ecco ridente' (409), 'A te, o caro' (409), 'En fermant les yeux' (424.04-5), 'Un bel di' (425.25-6 'one of these fine days'). *Turandot* is appropriately translated into pidgin English, so that 'Non piangere, Liú' becomes 'no belong sollow mole. . . . Fu Li's' (426). More transparently, five lines on page 427 are closely based on 'E lucevan le stelle' which leads up to the death of the hero in *Tosca*, in parallel with the death of Shaun. He is to be reborn in the next chapter as Don Juan, and there are anticipatory echoes of Mozart's *Don Giovanni*: Shaun's 'barbaro appetito' (412), 'il catologo' (409.11 'catlick'), 'Notte e giorno faticar' (409.16 'Fatiguing, very fatiguing'). The dialogue with the donkey explores topics like scandals in the Irish Post Office, Swift's relationship with Stella (there are many cruel quotations from Swift on page 413) and Shaun's relationship with his brother Shem. The last is illustrated by the philosophical fable of the Ondt and the Gracehoper (414–19) in which Shaun the Ant represents Space, and Shem the Grasshopper represents Time. These pages contain hundreds of entomological puns, in scientific Latin and other languages, and the names of philosophers; but tenors and music continue to appear. The Ondt says scornfully of his opponent (418.10ff), 'Let him be Artalone the Weeps, with his parisites peeling off him.' ('Yours is my heart alone', as sung by Tauber and 'O Paradis' from *L'Africaine*); 'I'll be Highfee the Crackasider' (Tenor's high C and fees); 'Conte Carme makes the melody that mints the money' (McCormack making a fortune by singing in *Carmen*). In the philosophical debate Wyndham Lewis the painter (Space) appears to have the upper hand over Shaun–Joyce (Time), as he did in his book *Time and Western Man*; but in the end music, which rather than literature is the supreme art of time, is victorious:

> *Your genius its worldwide, your spacest sublime!*
> *But, Holy Saltmartin, why can't you beat time?* (419)

Shaun goes on with the attack on his brother's literary and linguistic inventions, insinuating that like Tchaikovsky and Proust, he is homosexual: 'Asbestopoulos! Inkpot! He has encaust in the blood. Shim! I have the utmost contempt for. Prost bitten! Conshy! Tiberia is waiting for you, arestocrank! Chaka a seagull ticket' (424: Sebastopol, Inkerman, Crimean War, Proust, frostbitten, labour camp for conscientious objectors and aristocrats; Konchak in *Prince Igor*; not only Siberia but Beria, head of the secret police, formerly the Cheka; Tchaikovsky; Chekhov's *The Seagull* — a densely Russian passage).

Finally Shaun collapses like a radio mast (426) and there is a brief lament over his grave; but he will be back again one day, escaping from a sack like Houdini, canonised as a saint; he won't let the grass grow under his feet; one day he will be Prime Minister (Taoiseach) of Ireland: 'you will ... round up in your own escapology some canonisator's day or other, sack a back, alack! ... may the tussocks grow quickly under your trampthickets and the daisies trip lightly over your battercops.' (429)

## III.ii (429–73). 'The Second Watch of Shaun'

In the 'Second Watch' Shaun turns up in his incarnation as Don Juan. The legend of the great libertine who is dragged off to hell by the

stone statue has had many literary treatments between Molière and
Shaw; doubtless many of them are quoted somewhere in this chapter,
but the most important are Da Ponte's libretto for Mozart's *Don
Giovanni* and Byron's satirical romance. Both have been prepared
for by allusions in the last chapter: Mozart as noted, Byron by the
'pillgrimace of Childe Horrid' (423), 'Beppy's' (Beppo, 415), 'gam-
bills' (414, the Gambas, family of Teresa Guiccioli), 'allergrossest'
(425, his daughter Allegra). These are multiplied in the present
chapter: the poor condition of Shaun's legs as he walks through the
night (414 'lamely') is based on Byron's deformity; Byron's half-sister
Augusta Leigh (468.04 'augustan') with whom he is supposed to have
committed incest is one of the originals of Izzy, who has ambiguous
relations with her brother Shaun. Byron was supposed to be the
father of Augusta's daughter Medora (459.27 'myodorers'). Shaun
preaches against 'the valses of lewd Buylan' (435). Joyce typically
mixes up life and literature, historical persons with characters from
poems, like Gulbeyas (462.15 'gullaby') in *Don Juan* and the *Corsair*
(444.27 'coresehairs'). Byronic references extend beyond this chapter,
and most of the best-known quotations from his works appear somewhere in the book, e.g. 389.27 'dullokbloon rodolling olosheen'.

In III.ii Juan is a priest and much of the chapter is given to a sermon
he delivers to the twenty-nine daughters of February Filldyke. This
is perhaps the funniest and the easiest part of the *Wake* to read. There
is no better example of Joyce's poetic wit than: 'There's many the
icepolled globetopper is haunted by the hottest spot under his equator
like Ramrod, the meaty hunter, always jaeger for a thrust' (435.12–14).
That needs no explanation, except perhaps a reminder of the Biblical
text about Nimrod, the mighty hunter, for which the German is
'Jaeger'.

This chapter is more feminine than the last: there are many sopranos'
names among the tenors (contraltos and basses are rarer), and there
are also quite a few female saints, like St Teresa of Lisieux (432). The
Apocalypse of St John of Patmos is a basic text, and there are references
to the Wagnerian apocalypse or *Götterdämmerung*: 'nor could he forget
her so tarnelly easy as all that since he was brother besides to her
benedict godfather.' On page 431 Siegfried wears the magic Tarnhelm,
and later forgets Brünnhilde; the brother–sister incest theme is suggested by references not only to Byron but also to Siegmund and
Sieglinde. On page 432 Shaun begins his long sermon to the girls,
which includes the precepts of the Church: 433.10 'Never miss your

lostsomewhere mass' (the first precept is to hear Mass on Sunday; also 'The Last Rose of Summer', one of the many sentimental ballads sounding in this chapter). The letters of St Jerome, containing moral advice to the early Christian community, are drawn on frequently. Shaun gives practical advice on clothes, forbidding the girls to wear Limerick lace: 'Sure, what is it on the whole only holes tied together, the merest and transparent washingtones to make Languid Lola's lingery longer? Scenta Clauthes stiffstuffs your hose and hearties full of temptiness' (434). That introduces Santa Claus, the two rival girls, Senta and Lola, from *Cavalleria Rusticana*, and from the *Flying Dutchman*. Shaun recommends Charles Dickens as suitable reading:

> Whalebones and buskbutts may hurt you (thwackawatythwuck!) but never lay bare your breast secret (dickette's place!) to Joy a Jonas in the Dolphin's Barncar until your meetual fan, Doveyed Covetfilles, comepulsing paynattention spasms between the averthisment for Ulikah's wine and a pair of pulldoors of the old cupiosity chape (434)

Apart from the Dickensian characters, David Copperfield, Uriah Heep and Jonas Chuzzlewit, there are the corset and the 'pandybat' of the *Portrait*, both made of whalebone, hence dolphin and Jonah, and King David composing psalms in penitence for what he did to Uriah's wife. Mr Pickwick appears on the next page in association with Ulysses and the Sirens: 'Stick wicks in your earshells when you hear the prompter's voice.' Juan's double-entendres are fairly easy to follow, as he lectures on keeping fit in mind and body. He quotes Wagner on diet: vegetarianism is best, but Nordic peoples may be allowed to eat meat because of the climate: 'You can down all the dripping you can dumple to . . . in these lassitudes!' (441). This is followed by *Rheingold* and Gounod's *Faust*: 'Guard that gem . . . the jewel . . . stoles . . . Sing him a ring.' Wagner gives way to Mozart on page 442: 'a Constantineal namesuch' is explained by the fact that Mozart's wife Constanza is the namesake of a character in the *Seraglio*; in the next few pages we find 'tammany', 'Blonderboss', 'Dora's', 'fluther's', 'Wolf and Ganger', and 'papapardon' (445), which will not cause any difficulty to Mozart-lovers.

Juan's discourse turns to topics of contemporary interest: to birth-control (with advice on sexual techniques from Dr Marie Stopes, 444), and to the Dublin environment (with pollution and litter, 447–8). From 448.34 to 452.07 there is a passage which Joyce partially explained

to Stuart Gilbert for publication in *Our Exagmination*. The overtones
are of music, Christ's miracles and Dickens, as before, but now with
the names of many birds and fishes. Shaun is now courting his 'Sis
dearest' in ever more lyrical terms, and evoking a lyrical moonlight
scene in the woods. The arias include 'Una voce poco fa' (448.34–5
'with voise somewhit murky, what though still fa luting'), 'Voi che
sapete' (450, 12–24) and 'shake a place of sparkling eyes' (451.24–5
Gilbert and Sullivan, 'Take a pair of sparkling eyes'). There are also
many technical terms of music: 450.25 'bemolly and jiesis', is not only
Mary and Jesus, but *bémol* (flat) and *dièse* (sharp). The *Liebestod* motif
shows an interesting variation on page 450 where the death potion of
*Tristan und Isolde* is compounded of natural poisons, as befits the
woodland setting: 'Lethals lurk heimlocked in logans. Loath laburnums.
Dash the gaudy death-cup! Bryony O'Briony, they name is Belladama'
(450.30–2, hemlock, laburnum, deathcap toadstool, bryony and
deadly nightshade, etc.). At the end of his speech to Izzy and the
Rainbow girls Shaun says he is dying; but they must cheer up, since
they will meet again in the Elysian Fields or the New Jerusalem:
'Johanniburg's a revelation! Deck the diamonds that never die' (415.33–
34), bringing in the Revelation of St John, South African diamonds,
and 'Johannistag!' in the *Meistersinger*. Shaun preaches about death
and the apocalypse at 454–5: 'Seekit headup!' (454.35) means Sekhet
Hetep, the Elysian Fields of Ancient Egypt. In heaven they neither
marry nor are given in marriage (455) but on earth it is better to marry
than burn, as St Paul tells us: 'with the Byrns which is far better'
(Byron again). 'You will hardly reconnoitre the old wife in the new
bustles' (old wine in new bottles), 'and the former shinner in his
latterday paint' (the former Sinn Feiner terrorist in evening dress,
the former sinner transformed into a latterday saint or Mormon). He
returns to the subject of food and his rival brother before Izzy inter-
rupts him (457–61). She too talks in musical language, but her favourite
opera seems to be Gounod's *Faust*: 458.01 'Valentino', .10 'Maggy',
460.26 'Margrite', and finally the Jewel Song 'Ah, je ris': 461.10 'me
laughing'; and she ends with 'ah ah ah ah . . .' which is also the Bell
Song from Delibes's *Lakmé* and the laughing song from the *Merry
Widow*.

Juan replies with a splendid set of quotations from *Il Trovatore*, an
opera about two rival brothers, one of whom is a troubadour, the
other a Count di Luna, who when he hears a lute exclaims: 'Il trovatore!
Io fremo!' This becomes (462.26) 'Lumtum lumtum! Now! The

froubadour! I fremble.' Other quotations include 'O'Looniys' (464), 'County de Loona' (465), 'light your pyre' (466.07). Juan describes at length his brother in the guise of 'Dave the Dancekerl', that is, King David dancing before the Ark. Dickensian and Biblical quotations continue: 'jubalharp . . . Jingle joys' (466) includes Jubal's harp, Mr Jingle, and 'Vesti la Giubba' sung by Joyce's *bête noire* Gigli. The motto 'How are you today, my dear sir?' which occurs in many languages, is here in German and includes 'Gott! welch Dunkel hier!' from *Fidelio*: 'mind Uncle Hare' (466.30). 'Behind the curtain . . . worrid' is Turiddu singing behind the curtain in the prologue to *Cavalleria Rusticana*. A cluster of sinister death-motifs introduces Jack the Ripper (466): Chapman the poisoner was suspected of being Jack the Ripper and one of the witnesses was Annie Chapman (467.26 'chaplan'). Like many an operatic character Juan takes a long time to say goodbye, or 'Addio', but finally does so on page 468: 'Gulp a bulper at parting and the moore the melodies. Farewell but whenever . . .' contains two of Moore's *Irish Melodies*, 'One bumper at parting' and 'Farewell but whenever' and the aria of Othello 'Ora e per sempre, addio'. When he has done, the girls bewail him chorally in the Maronite liturgy for Good Friday, as Joyce explained in a letter to Miss Weaver: 'dosiriosly it paslmodied . . . tomaronite's wail' (470) means that Juan is not only the dead Christ but the dead Osiris and the doomed Mario Cavaradossi in *Tosca*, whose last aria is quoted. The liturgical Latin on page 470 is taken from the Vulgate translation of Ecclesiasticus 24, 'Quasi cedrus exaltata sum in Libanon'. The 'Pax' is part of the Maronite liturgy, and twenty-nine other words for 'peace' in different languages are pronounced by the girls (471). Shaun turns into a letter, is stamped and posted, and then into a barrel of Guinness floating down the Liffey; but he is still a postman walking on a final journey. The last tenor to be mentioned is the youngest to achieve fame before 1939, the boy wonder Jussi Björling (now thought by many to be one of the greatest ever recorded): 'that borne of bjoerne' (471), 'our Joss-el-Jovan' (472).

As Patrick heard the voices of the Irish calling him in a dream, 'Come and walk among us once more', so in such words the girls implore him to return (472). The saint, whose biography is further explored in the next chapter, was called 'Victoricus'; the chorus in *Aïda* sing 'Ritorni vincitor': hence 472.20 'victorihoarse', (34) 'retourneys'. There is much about walking on the last page: e.g. Handel's 'Where 'er you walk'. 'Walker . . . Walzer . . . comes marching ahome on the summer crust of the flagway' involves Johnny Walker whisky, Walther von Stolzing, the victorious hero of the *Meistersinger*, 'When Johnny comes marching home', and Flagstad, the latest Wagnerian soprano to come to the top before 1939. Siegfried's pyre is combined with 'De quella pira' and 'Stride le vampa' from *Il Trovatore*, and the chapter ends (page 473) with two quotations from the Gospel of St John: 'Yet a little while is the light with you, Walk while ye have the light, lest darkness come upon you'; 'I must work the work of him that sent me, while it is day: the night cometh, when no man can work.' 'Walk while ye have the night for morn, lightbreakfast-bringer, morroweth whereon every past shall full fost asleep. Amain.'

III.iii (474–554). 'The Third Watch of Shaun' 'Haveth Childers Everywhere'

Shaun has now become Yawn, and is lying fast asleep, or in suspended animation, in a burial mound at the centre of Ireland. The Four Old Men hold a coroner's inquest over his body: this turns into an inter-rogation of a political suspect and then into a spiritualist séance. It is hard to find living witnesses, so the dead have to be asked to give evidence, which turns out to be inconclusive until the last spirit speaks. This is H. C. Earwicker himself, who gives a wonderful survey of the City in all its aspects and a triumphant vindication of his marriage: this section (532–54), first published separately as 'Haveth Childers Everywhere', contains the clearest and most masculine and smooth writing in the book. The rest of the chapter is not up to the same high level, though there are three or four fine passages. Spiritualism provides not only the frame but also many of the allusions; another set of allusions is to explorers, continuing from those of Book II.iii. Saint Patrick's life is used a good deal, but much is still very obscure, perhaps because Joyce is using occultist sources.

The nightmare of history is represented by the words for 'fear' in various languages on page 475: 'Feefee' (Giant theme, 'Fee fi fo fum'), 'phopho' (Greek, phobia), 'foorchtha' (German, *Furcht*), 'aggala' (Irish *eagla*), 'jeeshee' (?Japanese), 'paloola' (Italian, *paura*) and 'ooridominy' (Assyrian, according to Joyce, *Letters*, i, 225). Yawn is deeply asleep, 'laying too amengst the poppies' (476) like Otello in his fit (447 'Ecco il leone', as Iago sings). But he soon begins to speak, identifying himself with Saint Patrick and with Parnell, who asked his colleagues, 'Do not fling me to the wolves.'

Among the exploration motifs is 'The *Pourquoi Pas*, bound for Weissduwasland...Webster says... our ship that ne're returned' (479). A French polar research ship of that name went down off Iceland in 1936; Joyce added this piece of news to an earlier draft, as is typical of his method. He also alludes to Goethe's 'Kennst du das Land' and there is something about Goethe on the next page; what Webster said was 'My soul is a ship in a black storm, Driven I know not whither.' The voice of Tristan joins that of St Patrick on page 486; while on 492–3 Anna Livia herself begins to speak, coming to the defence of her maligned husband; the density of references to East India points to an underlying history of the British Empire. The first great passage is on pages 497–8, giving yet another description of the Wake, with crowds of worshippers coming to pay their respects to the dead king and to eat his corpse eucharistically. This communion begins in the Holy Grail of King Arthur's Court (498.24 'arthurious clayroses', the king is dead of arterio-sclerosis, 498.24 'on the table round') and of *Parsifal*, the Arthurian legend and Wagnerian music-drama. Persse O'Reilly is Perceval or Parsifal, who will succeed to 'the vacant fhroneroom' (also the Peacock Throne-Room) at the Castle of Montsalvat (498.22); the wounded king (familiar from Eliot's *Waste Land*) is Amfortas, finally to be healed by Parsifal: 'in ringcampf, circumassembled by his daughters in the foregiftness of his sons . . . fluorescent of his swathings, round him . . . healed cured and embalsamate' (498.26–499.01).

There are several references to hell, and the Devil who lives in the 'lowest basement' of Dante's *Inferno*, on page 535. The voice is that of Swift, who was cared for by one Martha Whiteway in his last year, and referred to himself as a 'poor old man'; and this is combined with the voice of Oscar Wilde, who once reported in a séance that he thought very little of Joyce's *Ulysses*, and who wrote *De Profundis*:

— Old Whitehowth he is speaking again. Ope Eustace tube! Pity poor whiteoath! Dear gone mummeries, goby! Tell the woyld I have lived true thousand hells. Pity, please, lady, for the poor O.W. in this profundust snobbing I have caught.

Another disguise of H.C.E. is Odin or Wotan, and in this character he speaks in praise of his wife and denies allegations against himself: 'I have been told I own Stolemines or something of that sorth in the sooth of Spainien. Hohohoho!' (539.14–15, the mines of the Nibelung Alberich and the forging song of Siegfried, who are both named a few lines later). Then Earwicker begins his history of the City on page 540:

— Things are not as they were. Let me briefly survey. . . .
Ubipop jay piped, ibipep goes the whistle [Ubi bene, ibi patria].
Here Tyeburn throttled, massed murmars march [Hyde Park,
where there were once public hangings, now demonstrations]:
where the bus stops there shop I; here which ye see, yea reste.
On me, your sleeping giant.

The names of the cities of the world are as thick on the page as the rivers in 'Anna Livia Plurabelle', and so are the parts of cities, like the Seven Hills of Rome and of Edinburgh (541.02–4), Unter den Linden, the Akropolis and so on; he also surveys the institutions of the great cities, such as public health and prostitution: 'in my bethel of Solyman's I accouched their rotundaties and I turnkeyed most insultantly over raped lutetias in the lock' (542, involving Dr Bethel Solomons, a leading Dublin midwife, the Rotunda maternity hospital, Dublin, Lutetia or Paris, the Rape of Lucretia, the Rape of the Lock). Pages 541–2 are based on the seven corporal works of mercy: to feed the hungry, give drink to the thirsty, clothe the naked, harbour the homeless, visit the sick, visit the imprisoned and bury the dead; giving drink to the thirsty is combined with the municipal water-supply and the temperance movement, the appeal from Philip drunk to Philip sober, chained cups in public fountains and Cowper's cup that cheers: 'I made sprouts fantaneously from Philuppe Sobriety in the coupe that's cheyned for noon inebriates' (542.09–10). The only difficulty of the section arises from the minutiae of Dublin topography and history, which must be learned from one of the books mentioned in the text. Pages 543–5 consist of the plainest English in the whole of *Finnegans Wake*, being nothing but slightly edited quotations from a pioneer sociological work, Rowntree's *Poverty*; Joyce's collage presents urban blight with visionary dreariness. This is immediately followed by the chapter of Henry II, granting Dublin to the citizens of Bristol; other medieval documents concern the miracle plays put on by the guilds, while the bourgeoisie of the Middle Ages is represented by the characters from Chaucer's General Prologue to the *Canterbury Tales*, who are not hard to find. The City explains that he has built all these places and institutions for the sake of his dear Wife the River.

The musical elements of this passage have been prepared for by earlier references. The riotous scene of the Wake is described in some detail on pages 510-11; one of the celebrants is the dancing Shem, or 'Jambs' — a cluster of balletic and operatic references on page 513 gives the name of the Russian General as Polkan from Rimsky-Korsakov's *Golden Cockerel* (the sun is said to dance on Easter morning): '— Dawncing the kniejinsky choreopiscopally like an easter sun round the colander, the vice! Taranta boontoday! You should pree him prance the polcat.' The events discussed run backwards in sequence through the chapters of Book I, to the giants and Wagnerian Fafner of Chapter i. The allusions become more and more Wagnerian from 530 onwards, in preparation for H. C. Earwicker's great panegyric of the City, which is the heavenly 'Burg' of Wotan or Valhalla: '— Wallpurgies! And it's this your defied city? . . . Bigmesser's' (the last being not only Ibsen's Masterbuilder, but Beckmesser of the *Meistersinger*). The episode of 'Haveth Childers Everywhere' begins on page 532 with the motif of Brünnhilde's awakening: 'Heil dir, Sonne!': 'Amstadam, sir, to you! Eternest cittas, heil! Here we are again!' If it is the Heavenly City of Nordic paganism, it is also the earthly city of men, of which Dublin is the archetype, and the infernal city of Christianity, as described by Dante. Once this pattern is seen, the twenty-two pages are not difficult to grasp and they are immensely entertaining.

Wagnerian references become more pronounced than ever, the two most poetic being to the rainbow bridge from earth to Valhalla. To understand the first, one need only play the last minutes of *Rheingold* in which Donner the Thunder God shouts 'Heda, hedo!' and builds the bridge; it is obviously combined with the mating of Galatea and the marriage rites of the Anglican Prayerbook:

> and knew her flshly when with all my bawdy did I her whorship. min bryllupwwibe: Heaven, he hallthundered; Heydays, he flung blissforhers. And I cast my tenspan joys on her, arsched overtupped, from bank of call to echobank, by dint of strongbow (Galata! Galata!) (547.26-31)

The second ingeniously combines the notions of the City as heaven and hell, with a tribute to the Salvation Army and the mysteries of Swedenborg: 'oathiose infernals to Booth Salvation, arcane celestials to Sweatenburgs Welhell.' At the end of this miniature history of civilisation the human characters all turn into horses, Swift's Houyhnhnms, and take part in a great victory parade:

the mule and the hinny and the jennet and the mustard nag and
and piebald shjelties and skewbald awkness steppit lively . . . for
her pleashadure and she lalaughed in her diddydid domino to the
switcheries of the whip. . . . Mattahah! Marahah! Luahah!
Joahanahanahana!

There sound the voices of the Rhinemaidens, with which the *Ring*
begins and ends.

III.iv (555–90). 'The Fourth Watch of Shaun'

This is still one of the most obscure parts of the book. It appears to be
dealing on the literal level with the publican of Chapelizod, his wife
and children, in a naturalist setting. The parents wake up, comfort a
child who is having a nightmare, go back to bed and make love,
unsatisfactorily it would seem, just before dawn. But this is probably
an illusion; the husband and wife may not have woken up at all, but
merely have dreamed of normal events naturalistically, as everyone
does sometimes: while the Dreamer of the whole book, whoever he
may be, remains asleep until the last page. The structure is musical:
the four Viconian ages and the Four Old Men correspond to the
positions of the triad or common chord (in sol-fa notation, do-mi-sol,
mi-sol-do, sol-do-mi). Thus at page 559.21, 'first position of harmony'
is followed by a number of words beginning with *do*. Page 465.01
'second position of discordance', (04) 'It is so called for its discord the
meseedo'. Mi-so-do in sol-fa gives E, B natural, C in the key of C,
which is a discord: in German notation it reads ECH, another variation
of Earwicker's initials. This is analogous to the themes based on
B.A.C.H. (B flat, A, C, D natural), used by many composers. There
are terms of harmony on the next pages, e.g. 565.02 'wolvertones'
means 'Harmonic overtones', .22 'thoroughbass', .23 'bottomside'
(i.e. fundamental). After 570 there are several words beginning 'sol-',
anticipating 582.29 'Third position of concord'. With 590.22 'Fourth
position of solution', i.e. resolution of the dissonance, we return to
the original C major triad.

To each position there is assigned one of the Four Old Men, or
Evangelists, who are standing round the bed ('Matthew, Mark, Luke
and John, Guard the bed that I lie on'). The bedroom scene is described
realistically in the style of a film script. Then the members of the family
are presented in turn, Izzy most lyrically on page 561 in terms of
flowers and of the Virgin Mary. In the 'second position', page 564,

H.C.E.'s backside is described as if it were the Phoenix Park, in guide-book language: 'How tannoboom held tonobloom. How roodinor-landes. The black and blue marks acorss the weald, which now barely is so stripped, indicated the presence of sylvious beltings. Therewithal shady rides lend themselves out to rustic cavalry' (564. Tonio and Sylvio are characters in *Pagliacci*, which is usually staged with *Cavalleria Rusticana*; 'rood' means cross: Christ is stripped of his garments and flogged by the soldiers); 'a depression called Holl Hollow. It is often quite gutterglooming in our duol and gives wankyrious thoughts to the head but the banders of the pentapolitan poleetsfurcers bassoons into it on windy Woodensdays their wellbooming wolvertones' (565. Valhalla, Götterdämmerung, Valkyries, Wotan, harmonic overtones, German *Furz*, fart).

The soldiers are always associated with homosexuality, which is the subject of deep anxiety in this chapter, on page 565 and again on pages 587–8. There are a series of abrupt transitions, like a film: to a medieval scene (536) and to Verdi's *Falstaff* (567 'Nanetta . . . mellems the third and fourth of the clock', *mentre le due e le tre*, Ford, knechts, widows, Quick, and 569.01–2 shows Falstaff in the buckbasket). Earwicker's phallus is described at great length from all angles, and leads to the erotic theme of Tristan: 'how it is triste to death, all his dark ivytod' (571.14, *Liebestod*). There is another abrupt shift to a plain-language passage drawn from a Jesuit book of casuistry (Matha-ran, *Casus de matrimonio*) in which various kinds of sexual relationships and practices are discussed with technical frankness: under Latin pseudonyms, the Earwicker family are imagined as having every kind of incestuous relationship. This is followed by an account of the marital affairs of Henry VIII, the Reformation, and the Baconian controversy. I do not find these pages very amusing, and prefer the beautiful prayer for the safe journey through life of the married couple on pages 576–7:

> Prospector projector and boomooster, giant builder of all
> causeways woesoever . . . guide them through the labyrinths of
> their samilikes and the alteregos of their pseudoselves, hedge
> them bothways from all the roamers whose names are ligious,
> from loss of bearings deliver them.

(Let them bet on the chances of life 'each way', hedging the bet; protect them from the devils whose name is legion, and from the Roman legions marching.) From this point onwards the husband and

wife are travelling on a journey to an unknown destination, like Shaun
in the previous chapters. This journey is also the history of mankind,
told in the style of Swift's *A Tale of a Tub* (579–80). 'The third
position of concord' (582) shows them voyaging through the solar
system: page 583 lists the planets and their satellites (Ganymede,
Titan, Rhea, Iapetus, Phobos, Phoebe). The next paragraph describes
with the technical terms of cricket and with the names of famous
cricketers a bedroom sport which, as has been said, is hardly cricket.
Although the marital act has been unsatisfactory, the couple are asked
to 'Retire to rest without first misturbing your nighboor, mankind
of baffling descriptions' (585). The three soldiers give their version
of the story (587), and there is a final account of the scandalous adven-
ture of H.C.E. with the two girls. We are taken back to the early
chapters of Book I, to Genesis and universal history: despite a series of
awful disasters mankind just manages to survive (589–90). In 'the
fourth position of solution' all discords are resolved, the fourth age
offers a new start: at the end Earwicker dreams that he has achieved
successful coition, to the accompaniment of the world's applause:
'Tiers, tiers and tiers. Rounds.'

## IV (593–628). 'Dawn: Return to the Beginning'

The fourth book is the book of the dawn. With the exception of the
final monologue, which is a masterpiece, it is not one of Joyce's
greatest successes. It was drafted late, when he was perhaps weary
and summoning his resources for the final monologue; the texture is
very dense in places, although it is supposed to be showing the
disappearance of darkness and nightmare.

> The smog is lofting. (593) The spearspid of dawnfire tötouches
> ain the tablestoane ath the centre of the great circle of the
> macroliths of Helusbelus, in the boshiman brush on this our
> peneplain by Fangaluvu Bight whence the horned cairns erge,
> stanserstanded, to floran frohn, idols of isthmians. (594)

This refers to the midsummer sun rising over the Heel (or Hele)
Stone of Stonehenge; a 'horned cairn' is a technical term for one kind
of megalithic tomb. So we are back in the prehistoric and primitive
world (the Bushmen are about the most primitive people living today).
Stonehenge and other megalithic monuments were once supposed to
have been associated with the Druids, who play an important part in

this chapter. They are taken as the priests of the ancient pagan religion of Ireland, and were in legend defeated by St Patrick before High King Leary, who was then converted along with his subjects. The Druids are associated with the Irish philosopher Bishop Berkeley: his extreme form of idealism is taken as a sign of Irish mysticism and obscurantism: he represents the seven colours of the rainbow and is conquered by St Patrick, who represents the single white light of day (611–12).

Another short piece, which has considerable charm, describes St Kevin (a Shaun type) in his portable bath-tub-cum-altar, in a pool in the middle of an island in the middle of the loch at Glendalough, meditating 'with seraphic ardour the primal sacrament of baptism or the regeneration of all men by affusion of water'. The rest of the chapter, however, is made too difficult by the addition of many Sanskrit words and references to Indian religion; and by the heavily altered version of every theme or *leitmotif* of the book, as it appears for the last time.

## IV (619–28). 'The Final Monologue'

'The Final Monologue' is the most beautiful episode that Joyce ever wrote, and contains the last pages that he drafted. Once again it concerns the River; but now the River speaks in the voice of an old and dying woman. It is based on a realistic and touching treatment of the subject, comparable to the pathos in some of the *Dubliners* stories, in particular 'The Dead'. The old woman recalls the happy days of her married life, the delights of children, her pride in her strong husband, with whom she imagines she is taking a walk to Howth. She sees herself and him as one of the married couples who have appeared in the *Wake*, such as the tailor's daughter who married the Norwegian captain, after he had courted her on the telephone:

> When that hark from the air said it was Captain Finsen makes cumhulments and was mayit pressing for his suit I said are you there here's nobody here only me. But I near fell off the pile of samples. (624)

Gradually she turns away from memories of her adult life, and begins to despise the people she has known after her childhood: 'all my life I have lived among them but now they are becoming lothed to me' (627). She accepts the fact that her daughter has taken her place: 'Yes, you're changing, sonhusband, and you're turning, I can feel you, for a daughterwife from the hills again.' She will come down from the clouds to begin as the endlessly renewed river: 'and let her rain [reign] now if she likes.' She is now ready to disappear: 'O bitter ending! I'll slip away before they're up. They'll never see. Nor know. Nor miss me.' On the last page she thinks only of her father, the sea-god Manannan Mac Lir or King Lear, and, like many dying persons, she becomes a child again: 'Carry me along, taddy, like you done through the toy fair!'

The 'Final Monologue' is remarkable for the quantity of operatic references it contains, and for the highly appropriate way they are used. Joyce has taken the final situations and in some cases the very last words of several tragic operas, and woven them into the text. One can recognise *Götterdämmerung*, which is the end of the endless *Ring*; *Tristan und Isolde*; *Don Giovanni*; *Aïda*; *Rigoletto*; Gounod's *Faust* (as well as Marlowe's *Doctor Faustus*); Purcell's *Dido and Aeneas*; and there are probably others. There are also allusions to the endings of Shakespearean tragedies: it is difficult to say whether Shakespeare or Verdi's *Otello* and *Macbeth* are being quoted — probably both; but there are clear allusions to *Antony and Cleopatra* and *King Lear*. These references are especially thickly clustered on the last half a dozen pages, when the river mingles with the sea and disappears and the old woman draws her last breath.

624.10–20 'one fine day' is the famous aria in *Madame Butterfly*, whose last word occurs on the next page, 625.03 'play', a translation of 'gioca': but being Japanese she would have pronounced it 'pray', which occurs a little later. 625.12 'morrow': Italian 'morro', 'I shall die', cf. *Madame Butterfly* 'con onore muore'.

626.26 'pray' not only Cio-Cio San's 'play', but Gilda's dying 'preghera', her last word in *Rigoletto*. Two lines below, 'joy' is Violetta's last word in *Traviata*, 'gioia'. 627.27ff after a description of the Valkyries, we have Brünnhilde's last word in *Götterdämmerung*: 'Heiaho!' and 'Siegfried sieh!': 'sea' continued on 628.04 'sea-silt . . . see'. 628.05 'Onetwo'; .06 'moremens more. So. Avelaval.' This combines Shakespeare's Desdemona: ('Kill me tomorrow; let me live tonight. . . . But half an hour. . . . But while I say my *prayers*') with Verdi's Desdemona, who sings the *Ave Maria*; 'more' is the Moor.

628.05–6 'Save me from these therrble prongs. . . . Onetwo moremens more.' This is obviously the Faust story, as in Gounod; 'therrble' refers to Marguerite's last word 'horreur'. A little further on 'toy fair' — 'Arkangels' mean the Teufel or Devil and the angels, who rescue Marguerite at the last moment and carry her up to heaven. 'Terror' is the last word of *Don Giovanni*, as the Stone Statue carries *him* off, but to Hell. There are many allusions to Marguerite and the Don throughout the book, especially near the end.

621.20 'Give me your great bearspaw', (24) 'hand', (26) 'ice'. This combines 'la ci darem la mano', 'Che gelido manino' and Mimi's death with the Commendatore taking the Don's in his own icy hand. 623.06 'promnentory' is the Commendatore again; 'you invoiced him last Eatster' is obviously 'Don Giovanni! A cenar teco M'invitasti.'

628.11 'die down', (14) 'mememormee!': 'Remember me' is the Ghost in *Hamlet* but also Dido's lament 'When I am laid in earth'. On page 628 'Liebestod' from *Tristan und Isolde* is suggested by 'leaves . . . Lff . . . taddy'; but there is a clearer borrowing from this opera in ll. 10–11 'I sink I'd die down over his feet . . . only to washup' ('O sink hernieder' of Act II). The basic idea is 'versinken/wach auf', i.e. death and resurrection. The last appearance of this great motif is a variant of Isolde's last words:

'In dem wogendem Schwall,
in dem tonenden Schall,
in des Welt-Atems
wehenden All —
ertrinken,
*versinken* —
unbewusst —
höchste Lust!'

This is not quite the last operatic quotation in the book: the very last seems to be in the last unfinished sentence 'A way a lone a last a loved a long the' which contains the cry of the Rhinemaidens at the beginning of the *Ring*: 'Weia!'

In the background there are several strands of non-operatic drama. Mr J. S. Atherton discovered the text of an unpublished play by W. G. Wills called *A Royal Divorce*, which is referred to throughout the *Wake*, and it is used at length. It seems to be a faintly ridiculous melodrama about Napoleon and Josephine, which ends with Josephine's dying soliloquy: 'O save me. . . .' Combined with *Faust*, it becomes 'I see them rising. Save me from those therrble prongs.' Joyce has once more transformed rubbish into literature, as he has done with pantomime and other bits of popular culture in this episode. The references to pantomime, which suit the idea of reversion to childhood, occur from the beginning to the end: 'As were we their babes in. And robins in crews so' (619); 'I thought you were all glittering with the noblest of carriage. You're only a bumpkin' (627) [Babes in the Wood, Robinson Crusoe, Cinderella].

Everything that is good and bad about Joyce appears in the final pages. On the debit side is the excessive ingenuity, which makes him continue to pun in obscure languages; his self-centred obsession with his autobiography; his fondness for trivialities. On the credit side, there is first of all his sense of form. All the motifs and themes of the book are sounded for the last time in a manner that gives the illusion of a completed musical coda. Joyce is more successful than any other writer, with the exception of T. S. Eliot, at imitating musical structure in words. Second, there is his sense of history. As the characters of the book make their final appearance there is a strong feeling that we are coming to the end of a cycle of history. Finally Joyce has attained the epic sweep at which he had been aiming from his earliest days as a writer. The cycle of history is also a cycle of nature: there is a beautiful sense of movement in the passage, an invocation of the river running out to sea, 'dying' as it loses its individuality as a river and coming to life again as rain. As Joyce tells this he is not only using myth but he is *creating* a myth, with the enduring poetic force of the greatest myths. Anna Liffey, river-goddess, mother-principle, is a truly convincing divine figure. Yet at the same time she is equally convincing as a dying old woman of the Dublin lower middle class. Joyce has solved the problem of combining myth and reality, and has shown how the humblest human being can possess universal significance. Anna is a more sympathetic and more powerful creature of the imagination than Gabriel Conroy, Stephen Dedalus or even Molly Bloom whose monologues and figurative deaths end Joyce's previous three books. Her simplicity is suggested by the folktales and pantomimes scattered throughout her monologue; it is easy to accompany her on her journey back into childhood; and yet she epitomises the whole of *Finnegans Wake*. The pathos of the end is intense, but the humour, as always in Joyce at his best, is equally marked. It may be true that Joyce failed in his attempt to write a universal epic, and that he thought he had failed; and *Finnegans Wake* may have collapsed under the weight of its symbolism. But it is a glorious failure.

# Bibliography

## 1  Joyce's Works (first editions and a selection of other editions)

*Chamber Music*, London, Elkin Matthews, 1907.

*Dubliners*, London, Grant Richards, 1914.

*A Portrait of the Artist as a Young Man*, London, Egoist Press, 1917; New York,
B. W. Huebsch, 1917.

*Ulysses*, Paris, Shakespeare and Co., 1922; Hamburg, The Odyssey Press, 1933;
London, John Lane, the Bodley Head, 1934; New York, Random House,
1934.

*Pomes Penyeach*, Paris, Shakespeare and Co., 1927.

*Finnegans Wake*, London, Faber and Faber, 1939; New York, Viking, 1939.

*Collected Poems*, New York, Viking, 1946.

*Exiles*, ed. Padraic Colum, New York, Viking, 1951.

*Stephen Hero*, ed. Theodore Spencer, New York, New Directions, 1963.

*The Critical Writings of James Joyce*, ed. Ellsworth Mason and Richard Ellmann,
New York, Viking, 1959.

*Letters*, vol. 1, ed. Stuart Gilbert, London, Faber and Faber, 1957; New York,
Viking, 1957; vols. 2 and 3, ed. Richard Ellmann, London, Faber and Faber.
1966; New York, Viking, 1966.


## 2  Bibliography

Beebe, Maurice and Litz, A. Walton, 'Criticism of James Joyce', in *Modern
Fiction Studies*, IV, Spring, 1958.

Slocum, John J. and Cahoon, Herbert, *A Bibliography of James Joyce*, New
Haven, Yale University Press, 1953.

## 3 Biography

Ellmann, Richard, *James Joyce*, London, Oxford University Press, 1959.
Joyce, Stanislaus, *My Brother's Keeper*, London, Faber and Faber, 1958.


## 4 Criticism

### A On *Dubliners* and *A Portrait of the Artist as a Young Man*

Connolly, Thomas, ed., *Joyce's Portrait, Criticisms and Critiques*, New York, Appleton-Century-Crofts, 1952.
Gifford, Don Creighton, and Seidman, Robert J., *Notes for Joyce: Dubliners and A Portrait*, New York, Dutton, 1960.
Hart, Clive, ed., *James Joyce's Dubliners, Critical Essays*, London, Faber and Faber, 1969; New York, Viking Press, 1970.


### B On *Ulysses*

Adams, Robert M., *Surface and Symbol, The Consistency of James Joyce's Ulysses*, New York, Oxford University Press, 1962.
Budgen, Frank, *James Joyce and the Making of Ulysses*, London, Grayson, 1934. New edition with other writings by Budgen and introduction by Clive Hart, London, Oxford University Press, 1972.
Ellmann, Richard, *Ulysses on the Liffey*, London, Faber and Faber, 1972.
Gifford, Don Creighton, with Seidman, Robert J., *Notes for Joyce: an Annotation of James Joyce's Ulysses*, New York, Dutton, 1974.
Gilbert, Stuart, *James Joyce's Ulysses*, London, Faber and Faber, 1930.
Hart, Clive and Hayman, David, eds, *James Joyce's Ulysses, Critical Essays*, Berkeley, University of California Press, 1974.
Kain, Richard M., *Fabulous Voyager*, New York, Viking Compass Books, 1959.
Noon, William T., *Joyce and Aquinas*, New Haven, Yale University Press, 1957.
Schutte, William, *Joyce and Shakespeare*, New Haven, Yale University Press, 1957.


### C On *Finnegans Wake*

Atherton, James S., *The Books at the Wake*, London, Faber and Faber, 1960.
Beckett, Samuel, ed., *Our Exagmination Round his Factification for Incamination of Work in Progress*, new edn, London, Faber and Faber, 1972.
Begnal, Michael H., and Senn, Fritz, eds, *A Conceptual Guide to Finnegans Wake*, Philadelphia, Pennsylvania State University Press, 1974.
Glasheen, Adaline, *Third Census of Finnegans Wake*, Berkeley, University of California Press, 1977.
O'Hehir, Brendan, *A Gaelic Lexicon for Finnegans Wake*, Berkeley, University of California Press, 1967.

O'Hehir, Brendan, and Dillon, John M., *A Classical Lexicon for Finnegans Wake*, Berkeley, University of California Press, 1977.

Tindall, W. Y., *Reader's Guide to Finnegans Wake*, London, Thames and Hudson, 1969.

## D  General

Adams, Robert M., *James Joyce: Common Sense and Beyond*, New York, Random House, 1971.

Cixous, Hélène, *L'Exil de James Joyce ou l'art du remplacement*, Paris, B. Grasset, 1968; translated as *The Exile of James Joyce*, by Sally A. J. Punell, New York, D. Lewis, 1972.

Deming, Robert H., *James Joyce: the Critical Heritage*, 2 vols, London, Routledge & Kegan Paul, 1970.

Goldman, Arnold, *The Joyce Paradox: Form and Freedom in his Fiction*, London, Routledge & Kegan Paul, 1966.

Hanley, Miles L., *Word Index to James Joyce's Ulysses*, Madison, University of Wisconsin Press, 1937, 1951.

Hart, Clive, *Concordance to Finnegans Wake*, Minneapolis, University of Minnesota Press, 1963.

Hodgart, Matthew J. C., and Worthington, Mabel, *Song in the Work of James Joyce*, New York, Columbia University Press, 1959.

Kenner, Hugh, *Dublin's Joyce*, London, Faber and Faber, 1956.

Levin, Harry, *James Joyce: A Critical Introduction*, New York, New Directions, 1941.

*The James Joyce Quarterly*, presently edited at the University of Tulsa.

*A Wake Newsletter*, presently edited at the University of Essex.

# Index